THE FIRST BOOK OF SAMUEL

A DEVOTIONAL COMMENTARY
Edited by the Rev. C. H. IRWIN, D.D.

THE FIRST BOOK OF SAMUEL

By the

Rev. W. H. RIGG, D.D.
Vicar of Beverley Minster, E. Yorkshire

LONDON
THE RELIGIOUS TRACT SOCIETY
BOUVERIE ST. and 65 ST. PAUL'S CHURCHYARD, E.C.4

Printed in Great Britain
by
William Clowes & Sons, Limited,
London and Beccles.

PREFACE

A DEVOTIONAL and practical commentary on a Book of the Bible can scarcely be expected to include in its scope discussions as to the historicity and composition of the narratives therein contained. I have therefore deemed it best to pass over these subjects in silence, not from any desire to minimise their importance, but rather in the spirit of the Wise Man who said, "To everything there is a season, and a time to every purpose under the heaven." For those who wish to exercise themselves in such high matters there are many valuable helps, such as *The Cambridge Bible for Schools and Colleges* (Dr. Kirkpatrick), *The Revised Version for Schools* (Dr. Oesterley), *The Century Bible* (Professor A. R. S. Kennedy), *The International Critical Commentary* (Professor H. P. Smith), *The Commentarg of the Bible,* edited by Professor Peake (Principal W. H. Bennett).

Of my debt to all these commentaries I should like to make full and ample acknowledgment here, but for reasons other than those just stated. Rather do I record my appreciation of them for the light they have thrown on the First Book of

5

Preface

Samuel as a whole, and also for their elucidation of the meaning of the text.

It is also impossible for me to review the various interpretations given to certain passages and verses which occur. Fortunately for my purpose, so far as the First Book of Samuel is concerned, the great spiritual and moral truths it enforces are almost entirely independent of them.

Mine is a very different task. Making use of other men's labours, I have tried to write a little book on the First Book of Samuel, which may prove a help to those who read it, in their devotional and practical life.

One golden thread runs through the whole of the Bible, and that is Christ. He is the explanation of the Old Testament, as He is the Revelation of the New. Hence for the Christian who reads the Scriptures, his primary aim and purpose must be that, in dependence upon the Holy Spirit, he, through them, may become more closely acquainted with the Mind and the Spirit of the Master, and that his devotion to Him may be kindled anew and deepened. Thus will he be helped to become more Christlike in his daily life and conduct.

I hope that some of those who read this little commentary may find their hearts burn within them, hearing the Voice of the Risen and Ascended Lord afresh, as He speaks to their hearts and consciences, and expounds to them the things concerning Himself in this First Book of Samuel.

Dr. Moffatt, in a speech made at Mürren in September, 1924, ventured "to suggest that Bible-

Preface

reading is a Sacrament. The more you think of it, the more you will find that Bible-reading has done, and is doing, for many people what a Sacrament does, bringing them, through a sensible sign, into direct touch with the living God."

He who will read quietly and thoughtfully through this First Book of Samuel, living for a time with those characters so simply and graphically drawn from the life will, I feel sure, experience for himself the truth of Dr. Moffatt's words, as I myself have done. No one can study this First Book of Samuel without being deeply impressed and stirred.

The Authorised Version has been used in the passages attached as headings to the chapters, but in the actual expositions themselves, unless otherwise stated, the Revised Version has been quoted, though the reader will see that Dr. Moffatt's New Translation of the Old Testament has been constantly by my side. I can only add my humble testimony to that of many others, to the obligations that his excellent work has laid upon all serious students of the Scriptures.

In conclusion, I desire to express to Miss A. E. Dawson, who has looked over the manuscript, my deep sense of gratitude for the ungrudging help she has given, and also for the many suggestions she has placed at my service.

CONTENTS

9

Contents

10

Contents

Contents

THE FIRST BOOK OF SAMUEL

I

SELF-SACRIFICE AND ITS GREAT REWARD

I

Now there was a certain man of Ramathaim-zophim, of
mount Ephraim, and his name *was* Elkanah, the son of Jeroham,
the son of Elihu, the son of Tohu, the son of Zuph, an Ephrathite : And he had two wives ; the name of the one *was* Hannah,
and the name of the other Peninnah : and Peninnah had
children, but Hannah had no children. And this man went up
out of his city yearly to worship and to sacrifice unto the LORD
of hosts in Shiloh. And the two sons of Eli, Hophni and
Phinehas, the priests of the LORD, *were* there.

And when the time was that Elkanah offered, he gave to
Peninnah his wife, and to all her sons and her daughters,
portions : But unto Hannah he gave a worthy portion ; for
he loved Hannah : but the LORD had shut up her womb. And
her adversary also provoked her sore, for to make her fret,
because the LORD had shut up her womb. And *as* he did so
year by year, when she went up to the house of the LORD, so
she provoked her ; therefore she wept, and did not eat.   Then
said Elkanah her husband to her, Hannah, why weepest thou ?
and why eatest thou not ? and why is thy heart grieved ? *am*
not I better to thee than ten sons ?

So Hannah rose up after they had eaten in Shiloh, and after

13

The First Book of Samuel

they had drunk. Now Eli the priest sat upon a seat by a post of the temple of the LORD. And she *was* in bitterness of soul, and prayed unto the LORD, and wept sore. And she vowed a vow, and said, O LORD of hosts, if thou wilt indeed look on the affliction of thine handmaid, and remember me, and not forget thine handmaid, but wilt give unto thine handmaid a man child, then I will give him unto the LORD all the days of his life, and there shall no razor come upon his head. And it came to pass, as she continued praying before the LORD, that Eli marked her mouth. Now Hannah, she spake in her heart ; only her lips moved, but her voice was not heard : therefore Eli thought she had been drunken. And Eli said unto her, How long wilt thou be drunken ? put away thy wine from thee. And Hannah answered and said, No, my lord, I *am* a woman of a sorrowful spirit : I have drunk neither wine nor strong drink, but have poured out my soul before the LORD. Count not thine handmaid for a daughter of Belial : for out of the abundance of my complaint and grief have I spoken hitherto. Then Eli answered and said, Go in peace : and the God of Israel grant *thee* thy petition that thou hast asked of him. And she said, Let thine handmaid find grace in thy sight. So the woman went her way, and did eat, and her countenance was no more *sad*.

And they rose up in the morning early, and worshipped before the LORD, and returned, and came to their house to Ramah : and Elkanah knew Hannah his wife ; and the LORD remembered her. Wherefore it came to pass, when the time was come about after Hannah had conceived, that she bare a son, and called his name Samuel, *saying*, Because I have asked him of the LORD. And the man Elkanah, and all his house, went up to offer unto the LORD the yearly sacrifice, and his vow. But Hannah went not up ; for she said unto her husband, *I will not go up* until the child be weaned, and *then* I will bring him, that he may appear before the LORD, and there abide for ever. And Elkanah her husband said unto her, Do what seemeth thee good ; tarry until thou have weaned him ; only the LORD establish his word. So the woman abode, and gave her son suck until she weaned him.

And when she had weaned him, she took him up with her, with three bullocks, and one ephah of flour, and a bottle of wine, and brought him unto the house of the LORD in Shiloh : and the child *was* young. And they slew a bullock, and brought the child to Eli. And she said, O my lord, *as* thy soul liveth,

14

Self-Sacrifice and its Great Reward

my lord, I *am* the woman that stood by thee here, praying unto the LORD. For this child I prayed : and the LORD hath given me my petition which I asked of him : Therefore also I have lent him to the LORD ; as long as he liveth he shall be lent to the LORD. And he worshipped the LORD there.

II

But Samuel ministered before the LORD, *being* a child, girded with a linen ephod. Moreover his mother made him a little coat, and brought *it* to him from year to year, when she came up with her husband to offer the yearly sacrifice.

And Eli blessed Elkanah and his wife, and said, The LORD give thee seed of this woman for the loan which is lent to the LORD. And they went unto their own home. And the LORD visited Hannah, so that she conceived, and bare three sons and two daughters. And the child Samuel grew before the LORD. —1 SAM. I. and II. 18–21.

THE two books of Samuel form one single book, and the probable reason for their being called by the name of Samuel is, that not only are the opening chapters mainly devoted to him, but that, like Moses, he was identified with one of the great crises in the history of Israel, namely, the establishment of the monarchy. Both Saul and David, who are the principal characters of the book, owed their kingship, under God, to Samuel, and long after the Prophet's removal from the scene of his earthly labours, " he, being dead," yet, in more senses than one, continued to speak.

1 Sam. i. and ii. 18–21. The reason of the name of the two books of Samuel.

In this first chapter, a description is given of the circumstances leading up to the birth of Samuel. Three figures are introduced to us, Elkanah and his two wives, Hannah and Peninnah, Peninnah the mother of a family, Hannah the childless wife. Their home was at Ramathaim-zophim, in the

Elkanah and his two wives.

15

1 Sam. i. and ii. 18–21. Their pilgrimage to Shiloh. highlands of Ephraim (verse 1 ; cf. ix. 5). The head of the household was a religious man. Once a year the ordinary routine of domestic life was interrupted by a pilgrimage to Shiloh, at the Feast of Ingathering, at the conclusion of the vintage and the olive harvest. Shiloh was the principal sanctuary of Israel during the time of the Judges, and continued to be so until the Ark was taken by the Philistines at the battle of Ebenezer (Joshua xviii. 1 and 1 Sam. iv.). It lay in the territory of Ephraim, about five miles north-east of Gilgal, and twelve miles south of Shechem.

Affords us a glimpse of their inner life. Whilst Elkanah and his family are at Shiloh, the writer draws the curtain aside and gives us a glimpse of their inner life. According to custom, Elkanah, as head of the family, brought his thank-offering. Certain portions of an ox or a sheep were given to God, another portion being reserved for the priests, in payment for their services, what was left being partaken of by the family.

Peninnah taunts Hannah with her childlessness. Unfortunately, in the case of Elkanah's family, this time of rejoicing was marred by the attitude of Peninnah towards Hannah, whom she regarded as her rival, and whom she taunted with unwomanly cruelty. At this feast Elkanah was in the habit of giving portions to Peninnah, to her sons and daughters, but one portion only did he bestow upon Hannah, for we must follow the rendering of the margin of the Revised Version, " *But unto Hannah he gave a single portion* " (" only a single share," Dr. Moffatt), and not that of the Authorised Version and the text of the Revised Version, " a worthy

16

Self-Sacrifice and its Great Reward

portion," "a double portion," as she had no child. **1 Sam. i.** In the East, for a wife to be childless was looked **and ii.** upon as a grave misfortune. Not that Elkanah **18–21.** loved Hannah any the less for this, "*howbeit he loved her*" (verse 5, R.V. marg.), nay, he went out of the way to assure her of his devotion, "*Why is thy heart grieved? am not I better to thee than ten sons?*" (verse 8). But Hannah could not be comforted, and the same ordeal awaited her each year at the hands of Peninnah.

On one occasion the childless wife was so deeply **Leaving the** wounded by her rival's bitter tongue that she rose **feast, she** from the table, and separating herself from the **goes to the** company, went to the Temple of the Lord. She **Temple of the Lord.** took up her position near to where Eli was sitting, and there she poured forth her soul to God. All the **Her bitter-** bitterness and longing of her soul welled up within **ness.** her, and were poured forth in earnest supplication to the Lord : "*she was in bitterness of soul, and prayed unto the Lord, and wept sore*" (verse 10). She afforded an apt illustration of the Jewish saying, "There are three kinds of prayers, each loftier than **Her prayer.** the preceding : prayer, crying, and tears. Prayer is made in silence ; crying with raised voice ; but tears overcome all things" (cf. Heb. v. 7). With fervent entreaty, Hannah besought the Lord that, of His great goodness and mercy, He would bestow upon her the gift of a son. In return for this favour **Her vow.** she vowed to dedicate the child to a lifelong service of devotion. "*I will give him unto the Lord all the days of his life.*" Besides this, he should be a Nazarite, that is, abstain from all intoxicants, and from the fruit of the vine in any form (Num. vi. 3, 4). *" No razor "* shall be allowed to *" come upon his head "* (1 Sam. i. 11), and further, though it is thought by many scholars that this would not apply to Samuel, he shall not come near a dead body (Num. vi. 6). As a rule these vows were of a temporary nature, but in Samuel's case they were made for life. Whatever their original significance, they evidently bore witness to an ideal of self-denial, purity of life, and the dedication of all a man's powers to the service of God.

Whilst Hannah was thus engaged, she attracted Eli's attention, he noticed that her lips moved but uttered no word. At once he formed the conclusion, confirmed by his past experience of other worshippers, that the woman by his side was under the influence of drink. Such instances were not rare in those days any more than in those of Isaiah, who had to rebuke the excesses prevailing at religious festivals (Isa. xxviii. 7 ff.). Eli therefore proceeded to upbraid her. Following Dr. Moffatt's translation, for it brings out more forcibly than does the Revised Version how disgraceful he believed her behaviour to be, *" How long will you go on, you drunken creature ? "* he sternly demanded, and forthwith bade her depart. *" Away with you, go and sleep off your drunkenness "* (verse 14).

Either Hannah was too sore at heart to feel resentful at this grave imputation upon her character, or else reverence for his high office caused her to return him a soft answer. Anyway, her self-restraint is worthy of commendation. When God

18

is in the heart, He takes control of the tongue. In defence of herself she laid bare her heart before Eli, and besought him not to take her for a daughter of Belial, or as we should say to-day a low and worthless character. Struck by her humility and gentleness, Eli was at once mollified, and dismissed her with his blessing, as well as with a prayer that God might grant to her the desire of her heart. Whereupon she went her way, much comforted. *1 Sam. i. and ii. 18-21.*

Twelve months passed by, and a little son was born to Hannah, " *and she called his name Samuel* " (verse 20). The derivation of the name is doubtful. It probably means " Name of God," for, as Dr. Oesterley says, " similarity of sound, not etymology, was the Hebrew writer's object in placing the words close together, namely, Shĕmuel (= ' Samuel '), and Shĕiltiv (= ' I have asked him ') ; this device occurs very often in the Hebrew Old Testament." *Her prayer is granted.*

The next time Elkanah and his family went up to Shiloh for their annual pilgrimage, Hannah remained at home, the child being too young to accompany them. Another year went by, and then, in fulfilment of her vow, she took her little two-year-old son to Shiloh (verse 24). *Hannah fulfils her vow.*

" *A bullock of three years old* " (verse 24, R.V. margin) was also taken as a dedication offering for the child, " an unusually valuable sacrifice " (Professor H. P. Smith), together with an ephah or bushel of flour, and a skin of wine. The latter would be used at the feast of rejoicing to take place after the sacrifices had been offered. Hannah reminded Eli that she was the same woman who had

1 Sam. i. and ii. 18–21. stood before him two years ago, and told him that the prayer she offered then had been answered, *" For this child I prayed ; and the Lord hath given me my petition which I asked of Him : Therefore I also have granted him to the Lord ; as long as he liveth he is granted to the Lord "* (verses 27, 28). Forthwith she sang her song of rejoicing, the Magnificat of the Old Testament (1 Sam. ii. 1–10), and then she committed her little son to the keeping of Eli.

The cost of her sacrifice only mothers can estimate. The cost of a sacrifice such as Hannah's none but a woman can estimate. To part with the little child, so longed and prayed for, and at that engaging age when each day the child would furnish some glad surprise to his mother—the broken words, the dawning mind struggling to express itself, the winsome ways, the soft caresses, the innocent play, and then the wonder of the growing intelligence, to forgo all these ! such a sacrifice the Mother-heart alone can fathom or imagine. To tear herself away from the clinging arms and tears of her child, as he would weep and inarticulately pray her not to leave him to another, a stranger and an aged man, this would be almost more than flesh and blood could bear.

Think, too, of the return home, with the room where she was wont to care for and tend him, so quiet and empty now. The little things he used must be put out of sight, she could not bear to see them. His little treasures, some of which had doubtless been left behind, would be tenderly laid away, to be gazed upon at times when Hannah knew herself secure from interruption and from prying eyes.

1 Sam. i. and ii. 18–21.

Yes, all this must have been an agony, long drawn out, and renewed each year as she went to see him at the feast. The parting would become more cruel every time, as the child opened out more and more into the fine and attractive boy, with this added bitterness—she could never be to him as other mothers to their sons.

The parting each year.

We almost feel the sympathy of the writer with her maternal love and longing, as with simple pathos he tells us of "*the little coat*" (A.V.) which his mother made and brought to him from year to year. We can visualise her bending over it, every stitch of that little garment representing a kiss and a prayer. Few mothers can have known the loneliness and the heartache experienced by Hannah. But the reward! God's personal revelation of Himself to this child, his future office and renown, his name immortal in the world's history. And to herself were other children given. God is King, He will not suffer Himself to be in the debt of any man or woman. "*I will repay, saith the Lord*" (cf. Ezek. xxix. 20). Sacrifice contains within itself its own reward, for "like a jewel it shines by its own light, as a thing which has its value in itself" (Kant).

The little coat

Hannah's reward.

Ezek. xxix. 20.

Let us look at the Cross, the supreme instance of self-sacrifice. It was an act of humiliation. "He humbled Himself, becoming obedient even unto death, yea, the death of the Cross" (Phil. ii. 8). He was "made to be sin,"—mysterious words—that we

The Cross the supreme instance of self-sacrifice.

21

The First Book of Samuel

might be made righteous (2 Cor. v. 21 ; cf. Gal. iii.
13). The Saviour shrank from bearing the load of
sin. " Now is My soul troubled ; and what shall I
say ? Father, save Me from this hour " (St. John
xii. 27). " Abba, Father, all things are possible
unto Thee ; remove this cup from Me " (St. Mark
xiv. 36). Our ransom was effected at terrible cost.

Its terrible cost.

God's love extended to the uttermost length.
Christ also knew the meaning of loneliness. To
Him the words of the Psalmist apply, " Be not far
from Me ; for trouble is near ; for there is none to
help " (Ps. xxii. 11). " Behold," the Master says
to His disciples on the eve of His Passion, " the hour
cometh, yea, is come, that ye shall be scattered
every man to his own, and shall leave Me alone " ;
but there still remained to Him the greatest consolation of all, " and yet I am not alone, because the
Father is with Me." But even this blessed and
holy companionship must be withdrawn from the
Son of His Love, in order that the Son might taste
the exceeding bitterness of sin, for us men and for

The cry of desolation.

our salvation, and so the cry of desolation was
wrung from the lips of the dying Saviour, " My God,
My God, why hast Thou forsaken Me ? " Hence
the fitness of the petition occurring in an ancient
liturgy, " By thine unknown sufferings, Good Lord
deliver us."

Christ's reward.

Great was that Sacrifice, and great was the reward.
As some Roman general, after a victorious campaign,
followed by a long train of captives and the spoils

His triumph.

of the enemy, made his triumphal entry into the
City, so did Jesus Christ enter the Heavens, followed

22

by a countless host of captives, men and women 1 Sam. i. and ii. redeemed from sin, bound to Him by chains of adoring love and gratitude (cf. 2 Cor. ii. 14 ; Col. ii. 18–21. 15). A Name has been given to Him above every 2 Cor. ii. 14. name, whether in Heaven or on earth. He has been crowned with glory and honour (Heb. ii. 9, 10). He has seen of the travail of His Soul and is satisfied. The Reward of His Sacrifice was, and is, great (Phil. ii. 9–11 ; Heb. xii. 2 ; cf. ii. 10).

Humiliating as was the Cross, there is another side to it, that which is presented to us in St. John's Gospel. There the Cross is regarded not as a The Cross is also a throne. scaffold, but as a throne. The procession to Calvary might almost represent a royal progress. The Cross is a revelation of glory. "The hour," our Lord says, "is come that the Son of Man should be glorified" (St. John xii. 23 ; xiii. 31 ; xvii. 4, 5).

Self-sacrifice is painful in relation to sin, but in The joy of self-sacrifice. itself it is a joy. Love must express itself, and only in giving does it find its completion and crown. The selfish life is cramped and confined, " imprisoned in the dungeon of itself " ; but when the self loses itself in the service of others, then only does it realise its own true freedom and end. This truth is writ large in nature. " Except a grain of wheat St. John xii. 24. fall into the earth and die, it abideth by itself alone ; but if it die, it beareth much fruit " (St. John xii. 24).

Hannah's self-sacrifice has a direct bearing on the Hannah's example, and its bearing on Church life of to-day. In our own land nearly every profession is overcrowded, there are more

The First Book of Samuel

1 Sam. i.
and ii.
18-21.

present-day
Church
life.

All pro-
fessions
crowded,
with one
exception.

The sacred
Ministry.

Its wages.

Well done !

applicants than posts to be filled, and most parents are much exercised in their minds as to how and where they may place their sons. One important exception there is to this. The ranks of the sacred Ministry are thin and depleted. Fewer men come forward to take Holy Orders than before the war. Often those who have received the Divine Call to become " ministers and stewards of the mysteries of God," receive no encouragement from those at home.

From a worldly point of view, this profession holds out little hope of wealth, or advancement in social position, and this being so, would-be candidates are discouraged by those who should know better. And yet there is no other profession to be compared with it. Those who embrace it serve the very best of all masters, Jesus Christ, and their wages are love, and that service which is perfect freedom.

England needs more mothers like Hannah, mothers who will dedicate their sons to Christ from their birth, and, when the time comes, allow them to go forth to the Mission Field with a smile, albeit their hearts are well-nigh breaking, whose constant prayer will be that they may be partakers of His Holiness, and that, counting all else but loss, they may receive at last the great " Well Done " from the lips of the Lord Himself.

Our true reward is expressed in the words found on the wall of a French convent, thus translated :

> " O Master, May I not seek so much—
> To be comforted—as to comfort,

Self-Sacrifice and its Great Reward

To be understood—as to understand,
To be loved—as to love ;

For

It is in giving that we receive,
It is in losing that we find,
It is in forgiving that we are forgiven,
It is in dying that we rise to the Life Eternal."

I Sam. i.
and ii.
18–21.

II

THE FIRST MAGNIFICAT

And Hannah prayed, and said, My heart rejoiceth in the LORD, mine horn is exalted in the LORD : my mouth is enlarged over mine enemies ; because I rejoice in thy salvation. *There is* none holy as the LORD : for *there is* none beside thee : neither *is there* any rock like our God. Talk no more so exceeding proudly ; let *not* arrogancy come out of your mouth : for the LORD *is* a God of knowledge, and by him actions are weighed. The bows of the mighty men *are* broken, and they that stumbled are girded with strength. *They that were* full have hired out themselves for bread ; and *they that were* hungry ceased ; so that the barren hath born seven ; and she that hath many children is waxed feeble. The LORD killeth, and maketh alive : he bringeth down to the grave, and bringeth up. The LORD maketh poor, and maketh rich : he bringeth low, and lifteth up. He raiseth up the poor out of the dust, *and* lifteth up the beggar from the dunghill, to set *them* among princes, and to make them inherit the throne of glory : for the pillars of the earth *are* the LORD'S, and he hath set the world upon them. He will keep the feet of his saints, and the wicked shall be silent in darkness ; for by strength shall no man prevail. The adversaries of the LORD shall be broken to pieces ; out of heaven shall he thunder upon them : the LORD shall judge the ends of the earth ; and he shall give strength unto his king, and exalt the horn of his anointed.—1 SAM. ii. 1–10.

1 Sam. ii. 1–10.

The first Magnificat recorded in the Bible.

THIS is the " first Magnificat " recorded in the Bible. Expressions of delight for joy that a man is born into the world, are mentioned quite early in the history of the human race. Sarah rejoiced when Isaac her son was born ; fain would she tell others of the wondrous gift God had bestowed upon her ;

26

The First Magnificat

she felt that all those who heard of it would be glad on her account (Gen. xxi. 6). But in her case no lyrical outburst of praise is handed down to us. With Hannah, a psalm of thanksgiving flows out of the abundance of her heart. 1 Sam. ii. 1—10.

1 Sam. ii. 1—10.

Hannah's Psalm of Thanksgiving.

Her thoughts centre upon God, what He is in Himself (verses 2 and 3), what He has done for her (verses 1 and 6), and what He will do for His people. From her own fortunes her mind turns to those of her nation. God's power is manifested in all the vicissitudes of life, and the reversals of human destinies (verses 4 and 8). This power is not the expression of an arbitrary will, but of One who pursues righteous ends, triumphing over wickedness, breaking in pieces those who withstand Him (verse 10), while His chosen ones, His beloved, He will keep in all their ways (verse 9). As she proceeds, her faith soars to loftier heights. God's judgements shall extend over all the earth, and in due time a Messiah King shall make His appearance, bringing order out of confusion, and executing righteousness and truth (verse 10).

Her thoughts centre upon God.

What He will do for His people.

His judgements are universal.

A Messiah King will appear.

"*There is none holy as the Lord*" (verse 2). Holiness, as we understand it to-day, is associated with goodness; but outside the Old Testament, it had originally no moral significance whatsoever. So far as it is capable of definition, the idea is that of separateness. God is wholly separate from man in the sense of majesty and power. Doubtless Hannah would be familiar with this conception of Holiness, and to a pious Jewess, separateness in the moral sphere also, absolute separation from the sin

The Holiness of God.

The First Book of Samuel

and weakness of man, would be included in it. *"For there is none beside Thee."* High and lifted up (Isa. vi. 1), clouds and thick darkness are round about Him (Ps. xcvii. 2). "The Wholly Other." None can by searching find Him out (Job xi. 7).

> "Him who dare name?
> And who proclaim?
> Him I believe." (GOETHE.)

His knowledge.

Yet He is not a God Who dwells in regions far apart, indifferent to human concerns. *"The Lord is a God of knowledge"* (verse 3), fully acquainted with all that goes on in men's hearts, "understanding their thoughts afar off"; that is, not merely the thought itself, but its remote spring, its concealed motive. Thus He estimates their actions at their true value (1 Sam. xvi. 7).

He tries the hearts of men.

"By Him actions are weighed." The solemn thought of the Divine trial of men, their hearts and actions, is often represented by "measuring" or by "weighing" (cf. Job xxxi. 6; Prov. xvi. 2; Dan. v. 27). We may deceive others, we may even deceive ourselves (1 St. John i. 8), but nothing that we can say, or think, or do, can conceal itself from the penetrating gaze of Him, Whose Eyes are as a flame of fire (Rev. i. 14). Would we have it otherwise? Perfect intercourse between two friends implies that there is no holding back of anything on either side. Like St. Peter, we can throw ourselves on Christ's all-knowing Love: "Lord, Thou knowest all things" (St. John xxi. 17). Only by so doing can we still our hearts before Him

Christ's knowledge of us.

The First Magnificat

(1 St. John iii. 19, 20). And would Heaven itself **1 Sam. ii.**
be Heaven, could we dwell there, our Saviour not **1—10.**
knowing our worst as well as our best?

His love
even greater
than His
knowledge.

"Thou know'st our bitterness—our joys are Thine,
No stranger Thou to all our wanderings wild.
Nor could we bear to think how every line
Of us, Thy darkened likeness and defiled,

Stands in full sunshine of Thy piercing Eye,
But that Thou call'st us Brethren; sweet repose
Is in that word! The Lord who dwells on high
Knows all, yet loves us better than He knows."

(KEBLE, *Christian Year*.)

Although Hannah understood by the words,
"*the Lord killeth, and maketh alive*" (verse 6), the **God, the**
cutting off of men in the prime of their life, and the **Lord of life**
restoration to health, life and gladness of those **and death.**
who had been brought nigh unto the gates of death,
yet in the fuller light of Divine Revelation, we may
read into these words the promise that those who
were "dead in trespasses and sins" (Eph. ii. 1, 5;
Col. ii. 13), may be made alive in Christ. The son
who was dead is alive; he that was lost is found.
The Light that burns, also heals. The hand that
wounds, binds up. He that bringeth us to the
depths of humiliation, also lifts us up, and bids us
stand upon our feet (Ezek. ii. 1, 2). "*He bringeth* **He daily**
low, He also lifteth up" (verse 7), and it is only the **preserves**
lowly, self-distrustful, who are kept on their feet. **us.**

"He that is down, need fear no fall;
He that is low, no pride.
He that is humble ever shall
Have God to be his Guide."

(The Shepherd Boy in BUNYAN'S *Pilgrim's Progress*.)

The First Book of Samuel

I Sam. ii. 1-10.

The changes and chances of this mortal life.

"*He will keep the feet of His holy ones*" (verse 9), Jude 24). "He that made all things for love," as Lady Julian writes, "by the same love keepeth them, and shall keep them without end"; and higher still shall we go, for we shall sit with Him in heavenly places (Eph. i. 3; Col. iii. 1–4).

And this God of ours is a Rock.

God endures for ever.

"*Neither is there any rock like our God*" (verse 2). In contrast to the eternal fastness, we come to know, as life goes on, the shifting nature, the ephemeral duration, of all earth's hopes and ambitions. This Rock alone can resist, unmoved, the wildest storms, the tumults of the people, and afford firm foothold when all else slips from us. Even now the world is passing away (1 St. John ii. 17). A faint glimmer of this truth we catch as we behold the ups and downs of human fortunes. Men who started life in the possession of great wealth have ended their days in poverty. "*They that were full have hired out themselves for bread*" (verse 5). Others, high up in the social scale, have descended lower and lower, till they ended their days amid surroundings of poverty, and it may be even of squalor. "*The bows of the mighty men are broken*" (verse 4).

No room for for boasting on man's part.

And although some, from positions of obscurity, have climbed the ladder of fame, and made their way to its highest step (verse 8), there is, nevertheless, no room for boasting: "*let not arrogancy come out of your mouth*" (verse 3).

The expression "self-made man" is a misnomer. Those who boast of what they have done, and of the way in which they have reached a certain position

30

entirely by their own exertions, betray a lack of the **1 Sam. ii.** sense of humour ; for their very blindness makes **1—10.** them ridiculous. " What hast thou that thou didst not receive ? " is a question that admits of only one answer (1 Cor. iv. 7 ; cf. Deut. viii. 17, 18). The ordinary phrase, " a talented man," or better still, " a gifted man," bears witness to the rich endowments wherewith he started in life. Genius has been defined as " an infinite capacity for taking pains " ; but apart from the capacity which must be implanted within a man from the outset, this definition is only a half-truth : " *for by strength shall no man prevail* " (verse 9).

Hannah's song closes on the prophetic note. God **The pro-** is the universal Judge : " *The Lord shall judge the* **phetic note** *ends of the earth*," and He will rule by His Messiah : **in Hannah's** " *And He shall give strength unto His King and exalt* **song.** *the horn of His anointed* " (verse 10). This points **The second** to the second and greater Magnificat, uttered many **and greater** centuries later by Mary, the Virgin. She had gone **Magnificat.** to visit her cousin, and on arriving at her house, had been greeted by Elizabeth with the salutation : " Blessed art thou among women " (St. Luke i. 42). Blessed indeed she was, seeing that she was about to become the mother, according to the flesh, of the Saviour and Redeemer of the world. Like all **The Virgin** Jewish maidens, Mary must have been familiar **Mary's** with the songs of her race, especially those uttered **use of** by the women of olden time ; and thus, under the **song.** stress of a deep and holy emotion, her thoughts and aspirations naturally clothed themselves in the garb of the sacred language of her people. And,

31

The First Book of Samuel

almost without being aware of it, the Lord's Mother made use of Hannah's song.

Their resemblances. Both in form and structure, the resemblances between the two Magnificats are very similar. Place 1 Sam. ii. 1, 2 side by side with St. Luke i. 46, 47 ; 1 Sam. ii. 4 with St. Luke i. 52 ; and 1 Sam. ii. 5, 7 with St. Luke i. 53 ; and the resemblances are seen to be striking. On the other hand, the **Their differences.** spirit which animated these two was by no means the same. Hannah had felt very keenly her position as a childless wife. Nor had Elkanah's other wife, Peninnah, been loth to remind her that the possession of children had been denied her, and she " provoked her sore, for to make her fret, because the Lord had shut up her womb " (1 Sam. i. 6). Little is said in her song about herself, but she cannot altogether restrain her feelings of exultation. " *Her heart rejoiceth,*" or rather, " *exulteth in the Lord* " (ii. 1), and whereas, on previous occasions, she could say nothing in answer to Peninnah's taunts, her *mouth* now " *is enlarged* " or " *opened wide.*"

With the Lord's Mother the sentiments of humility and restraint were uppermost. Her joy was deeper and more inward, she " delights in God her Saviour." Salvation, too, had for her a more spiritual significance. Not that, in Mary's sense, salvation can be stripped of all national associations, but whereas on Hannah's lips salvation would consist chiefly of deliverance from external enemies, whether national or personal, the Virgin would dwell upon the inward deliverance which should

32

come to her, and to all the silent ones in the land, **I Sam. ii.**
and not only to them, but to future generations, **I—10.**
by the birth of her Divine Son, Who was to be called
Jesus : " for it is He that shall save His people
from their sins " (St. Matt. i. 20, 21). Deeply **The honour**
conscious of the honour conferred upon her, a **conferred**
humble village maiden, by her elevation to the **upon Mary,**
position of Mother of the Messiah, no thought of **the Virgin.**
personal worthiness could ever cross her mind. In **A daughter,**
Bengel's words, she was and is "a daughter of **not a**
grace, not a mother of grace." Generations of men **mother of**
and women will not call on her to bless them, but **grace.**
will call her " blessed." Could she see to-day the
place she occupies in the affections and minds of
vast multitudes of people at the expense of her Son,
the sword (or Thracian pike) would pierce her soul,
and she would experience her eighth and longest
sorrow ! Only one command of hers is recorded
in the Bible, and that was at the Marriage of Cana
of Galilee : " Whatsoever He saith unto you, do
it " (St. John ii. 5). Her whole soul was wrapt
up in her Son.

How fitting that He Who invited all men to come **The**
and learn from Him, Who was meek and lowly in **humility of**
heart (St. Matt. xi. 29), should be brought up by **the Son of**
one of low degree, and above all by such a self- **God.**
effacing and humble-minded woman as was Mary !

The reversal, not of human destinies, but rather **The**
of the ideas which men entertain concerning position, **reversal of**
wealth and honour, was also the theme of her song, **human**
the triumph of humility, the glorification of meek- **values.**
ness, the enrichment of poverty. A " transvalua-

33 c

The First Book of Samuel

"tion of values" effected by the coming Messiah, was already foreshadowed, or, if that is too strong a word, hinted at in her song.

The first and second Magnificats contrasted once more.

The first Magnificat looked forward to the coming of a King, Who should be God's Ruler and Judge. The second Magnificat, "the most magnificent cry of joy that has ever issued from a human breast," anticipated the wonderful approach as Saviour, Ruler, of Him Who should fulfil the longing expectation of Israel for that "faithful Priest, that shall do according to that which is in Mine heart, and in My Mind" (1 Sam. ii. 35).

The Sursum Corda of both.

Thus these two, separated by long distances of time, expressed each her Sursum Corda,

> "Lift up your hearts!"
> "We lift them up unto the Lord.'

34

FAITHLESS PRIESTS AND THE FAITHFUL HIGH PRIEST

Now the sons of Eli *were* sons of Belial ; they knew not the
LORD. And the priest's custom with the people *was, that,*
when any man offered sacrifice, the priest's servant came, while
the flesh was in seething, with a fleshhook of three teeth in his
hand ; And he struck *it* into the pan, or kettle, or caldron, or
pot ; all that the fleshhook brought up the priest took for
himself. So they did in Shiloh unto all the Israelites that came
thither. Also before they burnt the fat, the priest's servant
came, and said to the man that sacrificed, Give flesh to roast
for the priest ; for he will not have sodden flesh of thee, but
raw. And *if* any man said unto him, Let them not fail to burn
the fat presently, and *then* take *as much* as thy soul desireth ;
then he would answer him, *Nay ;* but thou shalt give *it me*
now : and if not, I will take *it* by force. Wherefore the sin of
the young men was very great before the LORD : for men
abhorred the offering of the LORD.

Now Eli was very old, and heard all that his sons did unto
all Israel ; and how they lay with the women that assembled
at the door of the tabernacle of the congregation. And he
said unto them, Why do ye such things ? for I hear of your evil
dealings by all this people. Nay, my sons ; for *it is* no good
report that I hear : ye make the LORD'S people to transgress.
If one man sin against another, the judge shall judge him : but
if a man sin against the LORD, who shall intreat for him ?
Notwithstanding they hearkened not unto the voice of their
father, because the LORD would slay them. And the child
Samuel grew on, and was in favour both with the LORD, and
also with men.

And there came a man of God unto Eli, and said unto him,
Thus saith the LORD, Did I plainly appear unto the house of
thy father, when they were in Egypt in Pharaoh's house ?

And did I choose him out of all the tribes of Israel *to be* my priest, to offer upon mine altar, to burn incense, to wear an ephod before me ? and did I give unto the house of thy father all the offerings made by fire of the children of Israel ? Wherefore kick ye at my sacrifice and at mine offering, which I have commanded *in my* habitation ; and honourest thy sons above me, to make yourselves fat with the chiefest of all the offerings of Israel my people ? Wherefore the LORD God of Israel saith, I said indeed *that* thy house, and the house of thy father, should walk before me for ever : but now the LORD saith, Be it far from me ; for them that honour me I will honour, and they that despise me shall be lightly esteemed. Behold, the days come, that I will cut off thine arm, and the arm of thy father's house, that there shall not be an old man in thine house. And thou shalt see an enemy *in my* habitation, in all *the wealth* which *God* shall give Israel : and there shall not be an old man in thine house for ever. And the man of thine, *whom* I shall not cut off from mine altar, *shall be* to consume thine eyes, and to grieve thine heart : and all the increase of thine house shall die in the flower of their age. And this *shall be* a sign unto thee, that shall come upon thy two sons, on Hophni and Phinehas ; in one day they shall die both of them. And I will raise me up a faithful priest, *that* shall do according to *that* which *is* in mine heart and in my mind : and I will build him a sure house ; and he shall walk before mine anointed for ever. And it shall come to pass, *that* every one that is left in thine house shall come *and* crouch to him for a piece of silver and a morsel of bread, and shall say, Put me, I pray thee, into one of the priests' offices, that I may eat a piece of bread.—1 SAM. II. 12–17 ; 22–36.

1 Sam. ii. 12–17 ; 22–36.

Hophni and Phinehas, priests at Shiloh.

Their evil lives.

HOPHNI and Phinehas, the sons of Eli, were the priests who presided at the sacrifices at Shiloh. They were *" sons of Belial "* (ii. 12), thoroughly depraved men. *" They knew not the Lord."*

No attempt was made by them to keep up appearances, but their utter ungodliness, and disregard of the plainest commandments of Jehovah, were an open scandal in the city of Shiloh. They robbed the people of their share in the sacrifices they offered.

Faithless Priests

From Deuteronomy xviii. 3 (cf. Lev. vii. 29–34) we **I Sam. ii.**
learn that the priest was entitled to take as his **12–17 ;**
perquisites, the shoulder, the two cheeks, and the **22–36.**
maw, whether of an ox or a sheep, from those who
came to offer sacrifice.

Not content with these, Hophni and Phinehas
sent a servant, in the course of the preparation of
the sacrificial meal, with instructions to plunge his
three-pronged fork into the pot or pan, and to claim
for the priest whatever it brought up. But worse
than this, they were guilty of gross sacrilege, for
it was a Divine ordinance that, before any one could
partake of the sacrifice, the fat must be burned on
the altar to Jehovah. Instead of this, these two
priests demanded their portion first (Lev. iii. 3–5),
a direct and intentional affront to Him Whom by
their profession they were bound to serve. The
remonstrances of the worshippers were of no avail.
Rather than renounce their habits of extortion,
Hophni and Phinehas were prepared to resort to
violence. Thus was the service of God rendered Render the
contemptible in the eyes of the people (cf. Mal. ii. service of
7–9). God con-
temptible.

The cup of their iniquity was not yet full to the
brim. To these violations of God's law they added
the sin of immorality. Words fail to describe the
grievous harm to the cause of God and their country
brought about by their evil lives.

They were also without excuse. Reports of their Eli reproves
doings had reached their father's ears, until he felt them.
constrained to remonstrate with them. *" Nay, my
sons ; for it is no good report that I hear : ye make the*

The First Book of Samuel

Lord's people to transgress" (1 Sam. ii. 24). He quoted to them an ancient proverb, which may have sounded commonplace in their ears, so hardened were their hearts. *"If a man sin against a man, God will mediate. But if against Yahweh one sin, who shall act as mediator?"* (Professor H. P. Smith). But to no effect.

A prophet expostulates with Eli concerning them.

Later on, a prophet was commissioned by God to expostulate with Eli on the notoriously wicked lives of his sons. He reminded him of the noble tree from which they sprang, of their long line of descent, dating back to the times of the Egyptian bondage, from Levi, whom God chose out from all the tribes of Israel to be His priest (verse 28). Did they not remember the privileges which God had bestowed upon them and their forefathers, when in return for all His goodness, they treated His service with studied contempt ? The covenant which Jehovah had made with the house of Aaron, that the priesthood should remain in his family for ever, had been invalidated by their utter refusal to carry out their side of the agreement. *"But now the Lord saith, Be it far from Me ; for them that honour Me I will honour ; and they that despise Me shall*

Judgement is pronounced upon Eli's house.

be lightly esteemed" (verse 30). In consequence of this, judgement had been already pronounced upon Eli, his sons, and their descendants. Of Eli's family, with one exception, all should be cut off in the prime of life, *" There shall not be an old man in thine house"* (verse 31), and the greater part of them should die by the sword (verse 33, Dr. Moffatt). Of the one exception, following Dr. Moffatt's trans-

38

Faithless Priests

lation of verse 33 (and in this he is supported by Professors Kennedy, Smith, and Dr. Oesterley), it was said, "*I will spare him to consume his eyes with longing and to wear out his heart.*" Their sins had been due to covetousness, the punishment should be fitted to the offence. Their survivors should be reduced to extreme poverty (verse 36), their seed begging their bread.

1 Sam. ii. 12–17 ; 22–36.

> "These on whose heads no covering hair is found
>   Were clerks of Popes' and Cardinals' degrees,
>   In whom doth avarice in excess abound."

> "Now, son, thou may'st behold the short-lived sport
>   Of goods that are in Fortune's trust as prize
>   For which the human race has ever fought.
>   Since all the gold beneath the moon that lies,
>   Or e'er did lie, could not give one alone
>   Of these tired souls rest from its miseries."

> DANTE, *Inferno*, vii. 46–48, 61–66 (Haselfoot's
>   translation).

As a proof to Eli that these prophecies should be fulfilled, Hophni and Phinehas were both to meet their end on the same day (verse 34).

How the prophecies were fulfilled.

After Eli's death, the priests of Nob, at Saul's bidding, were put to death by Doeg (1 Sam. xxii. 18–23), and only one of their number, Abiathar, escaped, he doubtless being the exception referred to in verse 33 of this chapter. At the end of David's reign, Abiathar, with Joab, the son of Zeruiah, joined Adonijah in the latter's attempt to secure the throne destined by David for Solomon.

After Adonijah's death, Solomon refused to put Abiathar to death on account of his having borne

39

The First Book of Samuel

1 Sam. ii.
12–17 ;
22–36.

The announcement of the Divine purpose.

the Ark of the Lord before David his father, and having been afflicted in all wherein his father was afflicted (1 Kings ii. 26, 27), but he deposed him from the priesthood, and banished him to Anathoth.

Having foretold these judgements, the man of God proceeded to announce the Divine purpose. "*I will raise Me up a faithful priest, that shall do according to that which is in Mine heart and in My mind : and I will build him a sure house ; and he shall walk before Mine anointed for ever*" (verse 35). Who was this faithful priest ? Not Samuel, but Zadok, made priest in the place of Eli's great-grandson, Abiathar, "And Zadok the priest did the king put in the room of Abiathar" (1 Kings ii. 35).

It is fulfilled in our Lord.

For us, however, the words point beyond Zadok to another and greater High Priest, our Lord and Saviour Jesus Christ. Alone among the sons of men is He a faithful High Priest (Heb. ii. 17), faithful to Him that appointed Him (Heb. iii. 2), Who has never fallen short of the Divine ideal, but has perfectly performed all "which is in the heart and mind of God." In all points tempted as we are, yet without sin (Heb. iv. 15), in Him the words are fulfilled, "Lo, I am come . . . to do Thy will, O God" (Heb. x. 7, 9; cf. St. John iv. 34, v. 19, vi. 38, xvii. 4).

The contrast between Israel's faithless priests and our great High Priest.

There could be no greater contrast than that between Israel's faithless priests and our faithful High Priest. The Lord was ever regardless of His own needs, weary often, hungry, thirsty, "He had not where to lay His Head." There should be no lot of man in which He had not a share. Hophni and Phinehas, on the other hand, ever had their

40

eyes open to the acquisition of gain and were greedy **1 Sam. ii.** of filthy lucre, and lent a ready ear to the suggestions **12–17 ;** of evil, both from without and from their own **22–36.** wicked hearts. Our great High Priest, Victor over all solicitations to evil, ever waited upon His Father's Will : " I can of Myself do nothing : as I hear, I judge : and My judgement is righteous ; because I seek not Mine own will, but the Will of Him that sent Me " (St. John v. 30). Even His delays, as when He refused to go up to the Feast with His brethren (St. John vii. 8), and when He abode for two days after He had received news of Lazarus's sickness (St. John xi. 6), were owing to this cause, He waited for His Father's instructions. As regards Hophni and Phinehas, desecrators of the sacrifices to Jehovah, the words of Eli fell on heedless ears. Our great High Priest, during the whole of His Life, and when He laid it down, glorified His Father, and proved to all who have eyes to see, the supremacy of the Father's Will in that Life and Death—we would rather say, the absolute union of His Will with the Will of His Father.

No one before or since His coming has known the Father as He knew Him (St. Matt. xi. 27 ; St. Luke x. 22). With a right accorded to no other teacher in history, He could claim that " He that hath seen Me hath seen the Father " (St. John xiv. 9).

Hophni and Phinehas were guilty of robbery and even of violence to attain their ends. Our Lord, Who made His grave with the wicked and with the rich in His death, had done no violence (Isa. liii. 9). To accomplish His great purpose, He steadfastly

1 Sam. ii. 12–17 ; 22–36. refused to make use of force. The inhabitants of a Samaritan village refusing to receive Him and His disciples, James and John demand whether they shall call down fire from heaven to destroy them; He rebuked them (St. Luke ix. 51–55). When apprehended in the Garden of Gethsemane by Judas Iscariot, and those who were with him, one of His followers drew his sword to defend his Master. Our Lord at once ordered him to put up his sword into its place, adding that if He had so desired it, His Father would have sent Him at any moment twelve legions of angels (St. Matt. xxvi. 51–53 ; cf. St. John xviii. 36).

No Mediator in the Old Testament. We have seen how Eli remonstrated with his sons in that they made the Lord's people to transgress, expressing the truth that, in a case of man's sin against his fellow-man, God would judge between them, whereas in sinning against God, he possessed no intercessor (verse 25 ; cf. Job ix. 32–33). The teaching of the Old Testament, as well as the witness of the conscience, testify to this. The Psalmist wrote : "None of them can by any means redeem his brother, nor give to God a ransom for him **Ps. xlix. 7, 8.** (For the redemption of their soul is costly and must be let alone for ever) " (Ps. xlix. 7, 8). Not without reason did the Pharisees ask, after our Lord's words to the sick of the palsy, "Son, thy sins are forgiven," "Who can forgive sins but one, even God ? " (St. Mark ii. 7). But in Christ, because **Christ our Mediator.** He is both God and Man, we have the One Mediator, Intercessor, and Advocate, "The Man Christ Jesus." Hence He is our faithful High Priest.

42

Faithless Priests

Not only so, He is the Victim as well. Hence the perfection of the Sacrifice which He offered up, the sacrifice of a Life of complete surrender and utmost obedience on behalf of sin-stricken humanity, to the Father, culminating in the sacrifice on the Cross. The Jewish priests offered daily sacrifices, the high priest himself entered the Holy of Holies year by year, with the blood of reconciliation. Our High Priest offered the one Sacrifice for ever, once for all (Heb. ix. 7–12), even Himself, effectual to "the uttermost," never to be repeated. Truly, what an offering! The Son of God Himself tasting for us the exceeding bitterness of sin, and upon Him as our Representative laid the Divine resentment against sin, thereby He vindicated the Holiness and Righteousness of God. As the sinner looks at the Cross, there shines forth upon him in dazzling splendour the Father's Love. Calvary is the length of God's Love. Love could do no more. The Cross was the Father's sacrifice also in that He spared not His only Begotten Son. The Saviour's agony in the Garden of Gethsemane was the Father's agony. The desolation of the Cross was also the Father's loneliness. To both the Father and the Son the words in the Lamentations of Jeremiah apply, "Behold, and see if there be any sorrow like unto My sorrow, which is done unto Me" (Lam. i. 12).

Yielding ourselves unto Christ, with the full knowledge and realisation that we are sinners, and therefore upon Him must lay our guilt, we can obtain peace, for the faithful Priest has made the

Marginal notes:
1 Sam. ii. 12–17 ; 22–36. The one perfect Sacrifice for sin.

The Cross reveals the Father's Love.

Lam. i. 12.

How we can obtain peace.

43

1 Sam. ii. 12–17 ; 22–36. full and perfect sacrifice, satisfaction, and expiation for us, and for the whole world. We are accepted before God by virtue of our faith in, and consequent union with, Christ. We can draw near with boldness unto the throne of grace, and know we shall receive mercy, and find grace to help us in our need (Heb. iv. 16). Our trust must be in the "real Saviour of real sinners," keeping close to Him, abiding in Him, and in proportion as we do this shall we be made partakers of His Holiness. He is the Mediator of a new and better Covenant (Heb. xii. 24), confirmed with His own precious blood (St. Luke xxii. 20).

Hophni and Phinehas lost their lives.

Our High Priest gave His Life.

The very different results from each.

Hophni and Phinehas lost their lives in battle, the Ark consigned to their care was taken by the foe, their country was defeated. The faithful High Priest did not lose His Life, but gave it, and there followed the most glorious victory over sin and death the world has ever seen. By His Death He hath purchased to Himself an universal Church, the family of the Redeemed, " *a sure house*," against which the forces of evil rage and do their utmost to prevail, but in vain, for He dwells therein.

" Worthy is the Lamb that hath been slain to receive the power, and riches, and wisdom, and might, and honour, and glory, and blessing."

" Unto Him that sitteth on the throne, and unto the Lamb, be the blessing, and the honour, and the glory, and the dominion for ever and ever " (Rev. v. 12, 13).

IV

SPEAK, LORD; FOR THY SERVANT HEARETH

And the child Samuel ministered unto the LORD before Eli,
And the word of the LORD was precious in those days ; *there
was* no open vision. And it came to pass at that time, when
Eli *was* laid down in his place, and his eyes began to wax dim,
that he could not see ; And ere the lamp of God went out in
the temple of the LORD, where the ark of God *was*, and Samuel
was laid down *to sleep ;* That the LORD called Samuel : and
he answered, Here *am* I. And he ran unto Eli, and said, Here
am I ; for thou calledst me. And he said, I called not ; lie
down again. And he went and lay down. And the LORD
called yet again, Samuel. And Samuel arose and went to Eli,
and said Here *am* I ; for thou didst call me. And he answered,
I called not, my son ; lie down again. Now Samuel did not
yet know the LORD, neither was the word of the LORD yet
revealed unto him. And the LORD called Samuel again the
third time. And he arose and went to Eli, and said, Here *am*
I ; for thou didst call me. And Eli perceived that the LORD
had called the child. Therefore Eli said unto Samuel, Go, lie
down : and it shall be, if he call thee, that thou shalt say,
Speak, LORD ; for thy servant heareth. So Samuel went and
lay down in his place. And the LORD came, and stood, and
called as at other times, Samuel, Samuel. Then Samuel
answered, Speak ; for thy servant heareth.

And the LORD said to Samuel, Behold, I will do a thing in
Israel, at which both the ears of every one that heareth it shall
tingle. In that day I will perform against Eli all *things* which
I have spoken concerning his house : when I begin, I will also
make an end. For I have told him that I will judge his house
for ever for the iniquity which he knoweth ; because his sons
made themselves vile, and he restrained them not. And
therefore I have sworn unto the house of Eli, that the iniquity

of Eli's house shall not be purged with sacrifice nor offering for ever.

And Samuel lay until the morning, and opened the doors of the house of the LORD. And Samuel feared to shew Eli the vision. Then Eli called Samuel, and said, Samuel, my son. And he answered, Here *am* I. And he said, What *is* the thing that *the LORD* hath said unto thee ? I pray thee hide *it* not from me : God do so to thee, and more also, if thou hide *any* thing from me of all the things that he said unto thee. And Samuel told him every whit, and hid nothing from him. And he said, It *is* the LORD : let him do what seemeth him good.

And Samuel grew, and the LORD was with him, and did let none of his words fall to the ground. And all Israel from Dan even to Beer-sheba knew that Samuel *was* established *to be* a prophet of the LORD. And the LORD appeared again in Shiloh : for the LORD revealed himself to Samuel in Shiloh by the word of the LORD.—1 SAM. III.

---

1 Sam. iii.

The evil lives of Eli's sons.

IN contrast to the evil lives of Eli's sons, Samuel is shown as ministering unto the Lord from his earliest days (verse 1). The country was in a most grievous state. The people were being destroyed for lack of knowledge (Hos. iv. 6). "*The word of the Lord was precious,*" or "*rare in those days.*" How could it be otherwise, seeing that the service of God was openly discredited in the eyes of the people by its religious representatives ? Eli in his private life

No open vision in the land.

The preparation of a leader.

was blameless, but he was no leader. Prophecy had ceased in the land, "*there was no open vision.*" Meanwhile God had not forsaken His people altogether ; He was preparing a prophet and a leader hard by the place where His honour was openly flouted and disgraced. Samuel was set apart to carry out, in due time, the Divine will, and to lead the children of Israel back to God.

Samuel is his name.

His call.

Up to the event recorded in this chapter he had

accepted the teaching of Eli without questioning, **1 Sam.** and had rendered implicit obedience to him; but **iii.** now a new experience was to come into his life. God was about to reveal Himself personally to him (verse 7). Hitherto Samuel had known Him indirectly, or at best at second hand.[1] The time had at length arrived when the Lord should come and stand before him, and call him by name (verse 10). Many years of Samuel's life are passed over in silence, but a very detailed account is given of his call; for from that day onward his life took a new direction, and what transpired then enables us to see the principle which governed it. The case of Isaiah is very similar, with this difference, that we know nothing whatever of his history previous to his call to consecration and service. His real life began with that call, and a minute account is given of it. In the spiritual life, the ordinary methods of reckoning time do not apply. The greatest moment in any man's life is when he hears and recognises the Voice of God addressing him for the first time, and makes a personal surrender of himself to Him. He has passed out of death into life (1 St. John iii. 14).

When the call came, Samuel had reached the age **At the age** of twelve years at least. It is not likely that he **of twelve.** left his mother before he was two years old (1 Sam. i. 24). Between that time and his call, three sons and two daughters had been given to Hannah (ii. 21). Samuel therefore would be no longer a

---

[1] We shall return to the consideration of this subject later on.

**1 Sam.
iii.**

**The
adolescent
period.**

child, but a youth. For him the adolescent period, which commences somewhat earlier in the East than in our own country, would have begun. It is a difficult period in any boy's life; changes, both physical and mental, are taking place; but it is also a time when he is most susceptible to the Divine Voice, and a life-long decision for good or for evil may be taken. God is indeed Master of His Own household, and it is not for us to limit the operations of His grace to any one period in human life; but law operates in the spiritual world as well as in what is called the natural world. Experience tends to show that the adolescent period is the most important chapter in life; and therefore it is incumbent upon the Church of God to use all the resources at her disposal to help her younger members to respond to the Voice of the Holy Spirit speaking within their hearts. Parents, too, need to pray for understanding and sympathy, that they may gain the confidence of their children, and thus help them at a critical time. Eli did not understand his children, and the disastrous effects of this are recorded, amongst other reasons, for our learning.

**God speaks
to Samuel
by name.**

Samuel heard God speak to him by name. Four times God addressed him (verses 4, 6, 8, and 10). On the fourth occasion God called him twice: "*Samuel, Samuel!*" The repetition of a name is used, in the Bible, by God alone, and then only on occasions of the gravest importance: "Martha, Martha!" (St. Luke x. 41); Simon, Simon!" (St. Luke xxii. 31); "Saul, Saul!" (Acts ix. 4). In all these instances it is instructive to notice

48

that they prefaced some very solemn announcement. **1 Sam.**
Religion is nothing unless it is personal. The Good **iii.**
Shepherd "Calleth His own sheep by name" **Religion**
(St. John x. 3). St. Paul writes to the Galatians **nothing**
that "it was the good pleasure of God, Who **unless**
separated me, even from my mother's womb, and **personal.**
called me through His grace, to reveal His Son in **Gal. i. 15,**
me" (Gal. i. 15, 16): and in the same letter, he **16.**
speaks of the oneness of his life with Christ: "I have
been crucified with Christ; yet I live; and yet no
longer I, but Christ liveth in me: and that life
which I now live in the flesh I live in faith, the faith
which is in the Son of God, Who loved me, and gave
Himself up for me" (Gal. ii. 20). In the grammar
of the Christian life, little if any progress can be
made until the personal pronouns have been
thoroughly mastered—"Thou," "we," and "our."
In the same connection, we must add that the
importance of two prepositions has also to be learnt,
"for" and "in" : "Christ *for* me," "Christ *in*
me"; "Christ *in* you the hope of glory."

Returning to Samuel's call, it is necessary to **The circum-**
examine with care the circumstances amidst which **stances of**
Samuel heard the Voice of God, if for no other **Samuel's**
reason in order that his example may help us to **call.**
hear the Divine Voice in our own days. The time
is significant. "*Ere the lamp of God went out* . . .
the Lord called Samuel" (verses 3 and 4, A.V.).
It was towards early morning. The seven-branched
candlestick or lampstand, which occupied a position
on the south side of the Holy Place, opposite to the
table of the shewbread (Exod. xxvi. 35), was kept

The First Book of Samuel

1 Sam.
iii.
alight during the night (Ex. xxx. 7, 8), but was
extinguished in the morning. Carlyle has said that
" no man becomes a Saint in his sleep." Certainly
it may be said that, when others are sleeping, the
true servants of God are often to be found wrestling
with God in prayer. It was so with Jacob; he
became " Israel," a Prince with God, when the
day was breaking (Gen. xxxii. 24–28). No hard-
and-fast rule can be laid down. St. Paul bids
masters in his Colossian letter to continue in prayer,
" watching therein," the literal meaning of the
Greek being to keep wide awake, " be wakeful when
you pray " (Col. iv. 2). Some people are freshest at
night; but others are at their best early in the

The im-
portance of
the morning
watch.
morning. The keeping of the morning watch would
make the greatest difference to many people,
especially to those who are called to be ministers
and stewards of the mysteries of God. Was not
one of the secrets of the life of the Son of Man to

St. Mark i.
35.
be found in the fact that " In the morning, a great
while before day (so early that it was still dark),
He rose up and went out, and departed into a desert
place, and there prayed " (St. Mark i. 35) ?

Prayer and
silence.
A very good reason underlies the choice of this
time. People are not yet astir. No sounds can
be heard in the streets. There is no fear of interruption, and nothing to distract the mind from
outside. It was when silence reigned supreme that
Samuel heard God speaking to him. Silence is

Ps. xlvi. 10.
necessary if we are to hear the Voice of God. " Be
still, and know that I am God," was the Psalmist's
experience (Ps. xlvi. 10). Both Elijah and Job

discovered that God could be heard in a "still **1 Sam.**
small voice" (1 Kings xix. 12 ; Job iv. 16, R.V. **iii.**
margin). "The Lord is in His holy Temple ; let
all the earth keep silence before Him !" In the
Hebrew it is an exclamation, "Hush !" (Hab. ii.
20). Both in our public and private worship there
must be times of silence.

> "God Himself is present :
> Heart, be stilled before Him !
> Prostrate, inwardly adore Him !"
> (TEERSTEGEN.)

Too much talking goes on in the Presence of God.
Christian people need to listen as well as to speak.
The advice is sound that, should those who pray
have but three minutes for the purpose, one minute
in silence should be spent in recollecting the presence
of God. In the words of the Sadhu, "God is quiet,
He does not make a noise ; therefore to understand
Him we must be quiet. In the hurry and rush of
life, God is silent ; we have to sit at Christ's feet
if we would feel His blessing, and then Heaven
will be in our heart." Long ago St. Augustine
confessed that "it is not easy to recognise Christ
in the crowd. In order to see Him our mind needs
some retirement and solitude."

Samuel was alone. Christianity is a social
religion. The model prayer which the Saviour
Himself taught us begins with "our Father," not
"my Father." The great Christian rite is a social
Meal, and our Lord's teaching centred round the
Kingdom of God. Personality has been defined as

1 Sam. iii.

a capacity for fellowship. But the complementary truth needs to be maintained. "God loves originals, otherwise He would have made duplicates." The unique personal relationship in which each soul stands to Christ. To be "alone with the great Alone" is an experience which all God's children should endeavour to cultivate and enjoy. "Solitude is to character what space is to the tree." In these days of the daily newspaper, the telephone, the motor car and broadcasting, the best is in danger of being crowded out by the good.

To be alone with the Great Alone.

> "The world is too much with us; late and soon
> Getting and spending we lay waste our powers."

Conferences and Congresses are innumerable. If this stricken and division-torn world in which we live could have been saved by paper and talk, its salvation would have been accomplished during the years which have passed since the Great War. The prime necessity of the age is that Christian men and women should make more time to be alone with Christ, and to listen as well as to speak. If we did this, we should be saved many a mistake, many a failure.

Samuel's habit of obedience.

Samuel's habit of ready obedience stood him in good stead when the Divine Voice called him the third time. Instructed by Eli, the quick response came from his lips, "*Speak; for Thy servant heareth*" (verse 10). Samuel did, however, omit one word, and that was "Lord." This seems to point to the fact that God was evidently to him, yet, but a distant, unrealised Being, and he could not associate a distinct voice as coming from such a One. This looks as though Eli's teaching and example (which had failed utterly with his sons) had been somewhat of a failure in the case of Samuel too ; perhaps consisting of a round of religious duties performed in too perfunctory a fashion. Obedience he had learnt, and thus was he enabled to listen to what God had to say to him. It was with a very heavy heart that he heard the doom pronounced on the house of his spiritual father and friend. *" I am about to do a deed in Israel that will make the ears of all who hear it ring "* (verse 11, Dr. Moffatt).

1 Sam. iii.

Doom pronounced on the house of Eli.

Eli's sons had made themselves *" vile "* or accursed before the Lord, without any serious attempt on Eli's part to check them (verse 13). The day of repentance had passed. No sacrifice or atonement could ever purge their iniquity (verse 14). Later on that morning when Samuel was astir, as a Levite in a subordinate position (1 Chron. xv. 23), it was his duty to open the doors of the House. How easy it would have been for him to excuse himself on the plea of a broken night's rest ! But no experience, overwhelming though it might be, could turn him aside from doing his work. This is as it should be. Whenever any great crisis befalls us, it must never be made a pretext for neglecting our ordinary everyday duties. The closer we live to God, the more conscientious we should be about our work. The oft-quoted saying of Tauler is to the point ; " One

The First Book of Samuel

man can spin, another can make shoes, and all
these are gifts of the Holy Ghost. I tell you, if I
were not a priest, I should esteem it a great gift
that I was able to make shoes, and I would try to
make them so well as to be a pattern to all."

Samuel's painful task, and how he discharged it.

It was very natural that Samuel should hold back
from communicating his vision. Only under pres-
sure from Eli for a complete account, and of his
oath, "*God do so to thee, and more also, if thou hide
anything from me of all the things that He spake unto
thee*" (verse 17 ; cf. 1 Sam. xiv. 44, xx. 13, xxv. 22),
did Samuel reveal to him the whole truth, keeping
nothing back.

The Divine blessing on Samuel.

As the years passed by, and Samuel reached
man's estate, it became clear to all that the Divine
blessing was upon him, and that he was indeed a
Prophet of the Lord (verses 19 and 20). We are
expressly told, "*And the Lord appeared again in
Shiloh*" (verse 21).

God often speaks to men. Not all hear His voice.

God often speaks to men, but not all hear His
Voice. Towards the end of His ministry, after the
meeting with the Greeks, our Lord exclaims,
"Father, glorify Thy Name." At once the Voice
from heaven came, "I have both glorified it, and will

St. John xii. 28, 29.

glorify it again." The Evangelist comments on the
fact that some of those standing by thought that it
thundered, others that an angel spake to Him ; the
Voice of God was not recognised (St. John xii. 28, 29).

When God speaks, there must be on man's part
the capacity to hear. This law applies in the case
of ordinary intercourse between man and man.
Two persons may live together, and yet never really

know each other. Their natures are entirely **I Sam.** different. Their tastes and interests are not the **iii.** same. Each goes his own way. This being so, neither of them can show his real self. Mutual forbearance there may be, but friendship is out of the question. In the same way, to be capable of **On the** hearing God, implies sympathy both on His side **human side,** and ours. Not learning, but lowliness of mind, and **the need of** readiness to obey, enable men to hear God speaking **sympathy.** to their hearts and souls. Wireless telegraphy **An illustra-** illustrates this. The air is full of messages going **tion from** to and fro throughout the world, but they can only **wireless** be picked up by specially prepared instruments. **telegraphy.** The receiver must be perfectly tuned to the transmitter, otherwise it cannot receive the message. Even then the message may come through blurred and indistinct, on account of atmospheric disturbances. In like manner the heavenly message can be heard and received only by the soul made sensitive through waiting upon the Will of God, and acting upon it as it is revealed. Sin produces a disturbing effect, so that intercourse is interrupted. When our minds and wills are fastened upon Christ, then shall we hear.

> " Speak, Lord ; for Thy servant heareth.
> Grant us ears to hear, eyes to see,
> Wills to obey, hearts to love.
> Then declare what Thou wilt,
> Reveal what Thou wilt,
> Command what Thou wilt.
> Demand what Thou wilt."

> (C. ROSSETTI.)

V

THE ARK OF GOD IS TAKEN

And the word of Samuel came to all Israel. Now Israel went out against the Philistines to battle, and pitched beside Ebenezer : and the Philistines pitched in Aphek. And the Philistines put themselves in array against Israel : and when they joined battle, Israel was smitten before the Philistines : and they slew of the army in the field about four thousand men.

And when the people were come into the camp, the elders of Israel said, Wherefore hath the LORD smitten us to day before the Philistines ? Let us fetch the ark of the covenant of the LORD out of Shiloh unto us, that, when it cometh among us, it may save us out of the hand of our enemies. So the people sent to Shiloh, that they might bring from thence the ark of the covenant of the LORD of hosts, which dwelleth *between* the cherubims : and the two sons of Eli, Hophni and Phinehas, *were* there with the ark of the covenant of God. And when the ark of the covenant of the LORD came into the camp, all Israel shouted with a great shout, so that the earth rang again. And when the Philistines heard the noise of the shout, they said, What *meaneth* the noise of this great shout in the camp of the Hebrews ? And they understood that the ark of the LORD was come into the camp. And the Philistines were afraid, for they said, God is come into the camp. And they said, Woe unto us ! for there hath not been such a thing heretofore. Woe unto us ! who shall deliver us out of the hand of these mighty Gods ? these *are* the Gods that smote the Egyptians with all the plagues in the wilderness. Be strong, and quit yourselves like men, O ye Philistines, that ye be not servants unto the Hebrews, as they have been to you : quit yourselves like men, and fight.

And the Philistines fought, and Israel was smitten, and they fled every man into his tent : and there was a very great slaughter ; for there fell of Israel thirty thousand footmen. And the ark of God was taken ; and the two sons of Eli, Hophni and Phinehas, were slain.

The Ark of God is taken

And there ran a man of Benjamin out of the army, and came to Shiloh the same day with his clothes rent, and with earth upon his head. And when he came, lo, Eli sat upon a seat by the wayside watching : for his heart trembled for the ark of God. And when the man came into the city, and told *it*, all the city cried out. And when Eli heard the noise of the crying, he said, What *meaneth* the noise of this tumult ? And the man came in hastily, and told Eli. Now Eli was ninety and eight years old ; and his eyes were dim, that he could not see. And the man said unto Eli, I *am* he that came out of the army, and I fled to day out of the army. And he said, What is there done, my son ? And the messenger answered and said, Israel is fled before the Philistines, and there hath been also a great slaughter among the people, and thy two sons also, Hophni and Phinehas, are dead, and the ark of God is taken. And it came to pass, when he made mention of the ark of God, that he fell from off the seat backward by the side of the gate, and his neck brake, and he died : for he was an old man, and heavy. And he had judged Israel forty years.

And his daughter in law, Phinehas' wife, was with child, *near* to be delivered : and when she heard the tidings that the ark of God was taken, and that her father in law and her husband were dead, she bowed herself and travailed ; for her pains came upon her. And about the time of her death the women that stood by her said unto her, Fear not ; for thou hast borne a son. But she answered not, neither did she regard *it*. And she named the child I-chabod, saying, The glory is departed from Israel : because the ark of God was taken, and because of her father in law and her husband. And she said, The glory is departed from Israel : for the ark of God is taken.— 1 Sam. iv.

WHEN the Israelites took the momentous step of going forth to battle with the Philistines, it was not with the concurrence of Samuel, for the opening words of chapter iv., "*And the word of Samuel came to all Israel*," belong to the last verse of chapter iii.

Far better for the Israelites had they, in Matthew Henry's words, "first repented and reformed, and

1 Sam. iv. Samuel's absence.

The Israelites

57

The First Book of Samuel

1 Sam.
iv.

suffer a
reverse.
In conse-
quence they
hold a
council of
war.
The causes
of defeat
investi-
gated.   The
resolutions
taken.

The Ark is
taken to
battle.

so begun their work at the right end." On this
occasion the Israelites suffered a severe reverse,
but were not put to flight (verse 2).

After the engagement, that same day, a council
of war was held, at which the elders, the representatives of the people, were present. Samuel was not,
however, bidden to attend the assembly (cf. 1 Kings
xxii. 7, 8). An investigation was made into the
causes of defeat; "*Wherefore hath the Lord smitten
us to-day before the Philistines?*" (verse 3). At
length it was resolved that the Ark should be
brought from Shiloh, to be taken along with them
when they next encountered their foes; not only
would it enable them to retrieve their late disaster,
but with it in their midst they would carry all
before them. There was much to be said in favour
of this course. Both history and precedent were
on their side. The Ark, from time immemorial,
had been indissolubly connected with the destinies
of Israel, and in one instance they would consider
that its absence was the cause of their defeat by
the Amalekites (Num. xiv. 42 ff.); while, on the
other hand, that it had led them to victory over
Jericho (Josh. vi. 6–20). They knew, also, that
immediately the Ark made its appearance in the
camp, the *morale* of the people would improve at
the expense of their foes. And this came to pass
(verse 5). No sooner did the Philistines hear the
shouts of the Hebrews, than panic seized them.
But in the end, a courage born of fear fired them
(verse 9). Nor is this surprising, inasmuch as they
also shared the belief that the Ark was associated

with the Divine Presence; and they could not **1 Sam.**
forget that the gods of Israel "*smote the Egyptians* **iv.**
with all manner of plagues in the wilderness"
(verse 8), and, the mighty Pharaoh had been over-
thrown at the Red Sea. But one most important **The one**
factor had been left out in the Israelites' reckoning: **cause left**
the character of the God Whom they professed to **out of**
serve and worship. They had not hearkened unto **reckoning.**
the voice of the Lord their God, and had not
observed His commandments and His statutes
to do them (Deut. xxviii. 15), and for these reasons **Deut. xxviii.**
He would cause them to be smitten before their **15.**
enemies (Deut. xxviii. 25).

The effrontery of Hophni and Phinehas exceeded
all limits, in supposing, as they must have done,
that Jehovah Who "loved righteousness and hated
iniquity" could ever have blessed and prospered
their side. Again, let the absence of Samuel be
noted. The Ark was powerless to save the children
of Israel that day. "Ichabod" had been pro- **Ichabod.**
nounced over the unhappy people (cf. verse 21).
The Glory and Majesty of Jehovah had departed
from them. Just as before the siege of Jerusalem
in A.D. 70, voices were said to have been heard in
the Temple, saying, "Let us go hence" (Euseb. iii.
8), so now God had left His people, and the Ark had
become the symbol of a departed Presence! Terrible **The defeat**
was the defeat which followed. Thirty thousand **which**
men met their death on the field of battle, and the **follows.**
remainder of the army fled in disorder; Hophni and
Phinehas were slain, and the Ark of God fell into
the hands of the Philistines.

The First Book of Samuel

Hereupon follows one of the most tragic scenes in the whole of the Bible : a description of the manner in which Eli and his daughter-in-law received the news. The latter's refusal to be comforted, and death of a broken heart in giving birth to her son, is a sad and pathetic story ; but it is with Eli himself that we are most concerned.

We can picture the scene. He who has been High Priest and judge forty years (verse 18) is sitting " on his official seat by the outer gate of the Tabernacle enclosure " (Prof. Kirkpatrick) ; a piteously forlorn and pathetic figure, blind, infirm, and in failing health by reason of his great age (verse 15). Full of gloomy forebodings and strong presentiments which he cannot shake off, " *for his heart trembled for the Ark of God* " (verse 13), he awaits the issue of the battle. Hour after hour passes, and the silence grows intolerable. At length there steal upon his ears the sounds of uproar and tumult. Already, in the city of Shiloh, there has appeared a man of the tribe of Benjamin, who has run all the way, breathless and bloodstained, from the field of slaughter, with the outward signs of deepest mourning and woe, " *his clothes rent, and with earth upon his head* " (verse 12 ; cf. 2 Sam. iii. 31 ; Rev. xviii. 19). In a thin, quavering voice, Eli inquires the meaning of it all. The messenger is sent for, and through the street, up to where Eli is sitting, he wends his way. To Eli's eager and anxious question, " *How went the matter, my son ?* " (verse 16), the messenger makes reply : " Israel has fled before the Philistines, a great slaughter has

ensued. Thy two sons Hophni and Phinehas have
met their end." Was there here an ominous pause ?
The old man listens motionless—" *The Ark of God
is taken !* " Whereupon before the messenger can
grasp the bowed form, Eli falls back and all is over !
" His heart was broken first, and then his neck "
(verse 18, Matthew Henry). Not to Eli do the
poet's words on old age apply :

" It is to suffer this,
And feel but half, and feebly, what we feel.
Deep in our hidden heart
Festers the dull remembrance of a change,
But no emotion—none."

(MATTHEW ARNOLD.)

Whatever may have been Eli's weakness and
errors, he cared more for the cause of God than for
himself and his sons. His end was a noble one.
The Ark of God was taken ! the cause of God was
lost ! The Israelites believed thus ; the Philistines
were of the same mind. Eli died in the full certainty
of it. But though the Ark was taken God was
not defeated, as subsequent events proved. In
His own good time His glory and honour were
vindicated.

Since then, throughout the centuries, both the
friends and the foes of religion have cried out
in despair or exultation, " The Ark of God is
taken ! "

During the Babylonian captivity, many amongst
the Jews must have felt that events had proved the
falsity of the Hope handed down to them from their

Margin notes:
1 Sam. iv.

The Ark of God is taken ! Eli's death.

His end a noble one.

Friends' and foes' concern for the Ark of God.

The Babylonian Captivity.

1 Sam. iv.

The Lord's second coming.

forefathers. Within a hundred years after our Lord's Ascension, many, who believed that they should see His visible coming, cried out, "Where is the promise of His coming? for, from the day that the fathers fell asleep, all things continue as they were from the beginning of the creation" (2 St. Pet. iii. 4), or sadly exclaimed, that the Lord was "slack concerning His promise" (cf. 2 St. Pet. iii. 9).

The attacks made on religion in our day.

In our own generation men and women have exclaimed, in the face of attacks made upon religion on scientific grounds, or when confronted with novel theories concerning the Inspiration of the Bible, "The Ark of God is taken!" Not every theory is true because it is new, nor can a belief claim to be of God on account of its antiquity. But God's people would be less nervous were they to take long views, and bear in mind that all truth is of God, and therefore cannot be in antagonism to Him.

The Church is God's Church, not ours.

The Church of Christ is His Church, not ours, and He will take care of it. Provided we are faithful, and rely upon the Holy Spirit to lead us into all the Truth (St. John xvi. 13), quietness and confidence shall be our strength. Jesus Christ is "the same yesterday and to-day, yea and for ever" (Heb. xiii. 8).

The prophecies of the downfall of Christianity falsified by history.

Oft has the despairing wail, "Christianity has had her day," been heard in the history of the Church of Christ. But that Church has been well compared to "an anvil which has worn out many hammers." The Ark was taken that day by the Philistines, but came back with renewed honour and glory after a while. Luther's words

are true : " I say to my Lord God, if He cannot **1 Sam.**
keep His Church, we cannot ; and if we thought **iv.**
that we could, we should be the proudest asses under
the sun."

" The grass withereth, the flower fadeth : but
the word of our God shall stand for ever " (Isa. xl. 8).

THE SUPREMACY OF CHRIST

And the Philistines took the ark of God, and brought it from Ebenezer unto Ashdod. When the Philistines took the ark of God, they brought it into the house of Dagon, and set it by Dagon.

And when they of Ashdod arose early on the morrow, behold, Dagon *was* fallen upon his face to the earth before the ark of the LORD. And they took Dagon, and set him in his place again. And when they arose early on the morrow morning, behold, Dagon *was* fallen upon his face to the ground before the ark of the LORD ; and the head of Dagon and both the palms of his hands *were* cut off upon the threshold ; only *the stump of* Dagon was left to him. Therefore neither the priests of Dagon, nor any that come into Dagon's house, tread on the threshold of Dagon in Ashdod unto this day. But the hand of the LORD was heavy upon them of Ashdod, and he destroyed them, and smote them with emerods, *even* Ashdod and the coasts thereof. And when the men of Ashdod saw that *it was* so, they said, The ark of the God of Israel shall not abide with us : for his hand is sore upon us, and upon Dagon our god. They sent therefore and gathered all the lords of the Philistines unto them, and said, What shall we do with the ark of the God of Israel ? And they answered, Let the ark of the God of Israel be carried about unto Gath. And they carried the ark of the God of Israel about *thither*. And it was *so*, that, after they had carried it about, the hand of the LORD was against the city with a very great destruction : and he smote the men of the city, both small and great, and they had emerods in their secret parts.

Therefore they sent the ark of God to Ekron. And it came to pass, as the ark of God came to Ekron, that the Ekronites

The Supremacy of Christ

cried out, saying, They have brought about the ark of the God of Israel to us, to slay us and our people. So they sent and gathered together all the lords of the Philistines and said, Send away the ark of the God of Israel, and let it go again to his own place, that it slay us not, and our people : for there was a deadly destruction throughout all the city ; the hand of God was very heavy there. And the men that died not were smitten with the emerods : and the cry of the city went up to heaven.— 1 SAM. V.

AFTER the complete rout of the Israelites, the Philistines brought the Ark of God to Ashdod, and placed it in the house of Dagon, their national deity. Dagon was originally worshipped, either as a god of the sea (the actual name, it is said, being derived from a word signifying " fish "), or as the god of agriculture, Dagon coming equally well from a word which means " corn." **1 Sam. v.** **The Ark of God brought to Ashdod.**

It must have been a proud day for the Philistines when they brought their enemies' god to their own temple, for so closely did they identify the Presence of Jehovah with the Ark, that in gaining possession of the latter they imagined that He was actually in their power. Thus by placing the Ark beside the image of Dagon, they proclaimed the superiority of their own god to Jehovah. But the Ark was not only a votive offering, inasmuch as the Hebrew word for " *set it by* " Dagon (verse 2) is used elsewhere of " setting upright," *e.g.* in Gen. xxx. 38 and Judges viii. 27 ; and this, according to Professor H. P. Smith, implies that worship was to be offered to the captive God as well as to Dagon. This was a very common practice in those days, and lasted till long after the foundation of Christianity. **The Ark beside Dagon's image.** **Divine honours rendered to Dagon and Jehovah.**

65   E

The First Book of Samuel

Alexander Severus, best of Roman Emperors since the Antonines, who reigned from 222 to 235 A.D., had in his own oratory, not only statues of Orpheus, Alexander the Great and Apollonius of Tyana, but also of Abraham and Jesus Christ. Divine honours were to be rendered unto Dagon and Jehovah.

Dagon upon his face. On the following morning a strange and wondrous sight met the eyes of those who came to visit the shrine. The idol of the Philistines had fallen on its face before the Ark of the Lord. To those who saw it, this accident, though in reality it was no accident, must have caused many disquieting feelings. Some of them may have volunteered a natural explanation. Either some one had come in during the night and committed this outrage, or when last taken down and carried in procession, it had been carelessly put back in its place. But the fact remained that their god "*had fallen upon his face*" before the God of their enemies, as though to pay Him homage. No other course was open to them but to put Dagon back again in his old place (verse 3).

Dagon smashed to pieces. The next morning they revisited the temple, and their eyes lighting upon Dagon smashed to pieces, their worst fears were realised. The head and the palms of the hands, the symbols of his strength and power, were severed from the trunk, lying upon the threshold. "*On the threshold*" where men, entering the temple, might easily and unwittingly spurn them with their feet, or tread upon them, **God's honour vindicated.** thus doing them fresh dishonour! By this means was it shown to them that, whilst the Ark might be in captivity, the power of Jehovah could not be

66

The Supremacy of Christ

bound, but was as irresistible as ever. "The Lord, I **Sam. v.** He is God ; the Lord, He is God " (cf. 1 Kings xviii. 39) ; and, what is more, that in His Presence the existence of another god was impossible.

In order to bring home to the Philistines the Divine displeasure, stroke after stroke was showered upon them. The vines and crops in and around Ashdod were destroyed by a plague of mice (" *He destroyed them*," better, " *He wasted them* " (verse 6, and cf. vi. 5), and terrible diseases broke out amongst the people. After a meeting had been **The Ark is** summoned, to which the lords of the Philistines **sent away.** were invited, it was resolved that the Ark should be sent to Gath, from twelve to sixteen miles east of Ashdod, the place being possibly chosen as having no temple in honour of Dagon. Very similar punishment was meted out to the people of Gath (verse 9). Again the Ark was sent away, this time to Ekron, eleven miles north of Gath. The fame of the Ark had already reached the neighbourhood, and as it drew near, loud and bitter outcries arose against the approach of the dangerous trophy, and a second council of state was held (verses 10 and 11). But it was of no avail, and in their case, not only did a plague break out amongst the inhabitants, but many died from its effects, " *and the cry of the city went up to heaven* " (verse 12).

The sovereignty of Jehovah was vindicated. It **Our Lord** took many centuries of sorrow and discipline for **alone has** the children of Israel to learn this truth ; but when **the right to sit upon the** in the fulness of time God sent His Son, it had been **Father's** engraved upon the heart and consciences of the **throne.**

The First Book of Samuel

chosen people. The Christian Church has lived in and by the same faith. Jesus Christ alone has the right to sit upon the Father's throne, the Lamb of God and the Lion of the tribe of Judah (Rev. v. 5, 6). "All authority hath been given unto Him in heaven and on earth" (St. Matt. xxviii. 18). He has the Name which is above every name (Phil. ii. 9). In Him "dwelleth all the fulness of the Godhead bodily" (Col. ii. 9). None other may share these prerogatives; He is "pre-eminent in all things." In the early centuries of the Christian era, men and women suffered in their thousands and tens of thousands for Christ. The Roman Power had no objection to the existence of Christianity as one religion amongst many. Provided that her adherents consented to render divine honours to the Emperors, she was free to carry on her worship and practices in her own way. Such terms were impossible. Either Christ or Cæsar, but not both. No earthly power could receive the adoration which was due to Jesus Christ. The sole and unique Lordship of Jesus is the faith of the Church, but it must also be the faith of the individual. "Know ye not," writes St. Paul to the Corinthians, "that ye are a temple of God, and that the Spirit of God dwelleth in you? If any man destroyeth the temple of God, him shall God destroy; for the temple of God is holy, which temple ye are" (1 Cor. iii, 16, 17). Christ should reign supreme in the heart. St. John warns his readers to guard themselves against idols (1 St. John v. 21). Whilst to-day the actual bowing down to wood and

Either Christ or Cæsar, but not both.

68

The Supremacy of Christ

stone may constitute but little danger to the intelligent and educated men and women of our country, yet Dagon may and does reappear in other forms. Not only vice, but pleasure, money, even human affection (none of them save vice wrong in themselves), may usurp the first place, and thus lead to idolatry. Human love is a gift from God; but if in the enjoyment of the gift we lose sight of the Giver, the sacredness and true beauty of love are lost. The Bible does not condemn money as such, but it does condemn the love of money for its own sake, without due consideration of the responsibilities which the possession of it involves. "A guinea held too near the eye blocks out the sun," is an old saying, but money consecrated to the service of God, and regarded as a solemn trust, will ever bless the giver and those upon whom it is bestowed. If Christ is to enter the heart, and to abide there, it can only be on the condition that the owner is willing that He should take full control of his life and all its concerns; there must be no secret chamber to which He is forbidden entrance. The Christian's one endeavour and prayer will be to bring every thought into captivity unto the obedience of Christ. This emphatic truth has been finely expressed in the words of the late Professor Huxley, "Any man can be a Christian, but it takes all that he has to be one."

I Sam. v. The reappearance of the worship of Dagon in other forms.

Christ must take full control of the heart.

PRAYER

"Cramped is the dwelling of my soul; do Thou expand it, that Thou mayest enter in. It is in

69

1 Sam. v. ruins, restore Thou it. There is that about it which must offend Thine eyes; I confess and know it, but who will cleanse it? or to whom shall I cry but to Thee? Cleanse me from my secret sins, O Lord, and keep Thy servant from those of other men" (St. Augustine, *Confessions*, Bk. I. v. 6).

VII

UNLAWFUL CURIOSITY, OR THE SIN OF INDIFFERENCE

And the ark of the LORD was in the country of the Philistines seven months. And the Philistines called for the priests and the diviners, saying, What shall we do to the ark of the Lord ? tell us wherewith we shall send it to his place. And they said, If ye send away the ark of the God of Israel, send it not empty ; but in any wise return him a trespass offering : then ye shall be healed, and it shall be known to you why his hand is not removed from you. Then said they, What *shall be* the trespass offering which we shall return to him ? They answered, Five golden emerods, and five golden mice, *according to* the number of the lords of the Philistines : for one plague *was* on you all, and on your lords. Wherefore ye shall make images of your emerods, and images of your mice that mar the land ; and ye shall give glory unto the God of Israel : peradventure he will lighten his hand from off you, and from off your gods, and from off your land. Wherefore then do ye harden your hearts, as the Egyptians and Pharaoh hardened their hearts ? when he had wrought wonderfully among them, did they not let the people go, and they departed ? Now therefore make a new cart, and take two milch kine, on which there hath come no yoke, and tie the kine to the cart, and bring their calves home from them : And take the ark of the LORD, and lay it upon the cart ; and put the jewels of gold, which ye return him *for* a trespass offering, in a coffer by the side thereof ; and send it away, that it may go. And see, if it goeth up by the way of his own coast to Beth-shemesh, *then* he hath done us this great evil : but if not, then we shall know that *it is* not his hand *that* smote us ; it *was* a chance *that* happened to us.

And the men did so : and took two milch kine, and tied them to the cart, and shut up their calves at home : And they laid the ark of the LORD upon the cart, and the coffer with the mice of gold and the images of their emerods. And the kine took the straight way to the way of Beth-shemesh, *and* went along the highway, lowing as they went, and turned not aside *to* the right hand or *to* the left; and the lords of the Philistines went after them unto the border of Beth-shemesh. And *they of* Beth-shemesh *were* reaping their wheat harvest in the valley: and they lifted up their eyes, and saw the ark, and rejoiced to see *it.* And the cart came into the field of Joshua, a Beth-shemite, and stood there, where *there was* a great stone: and they clave the wood of the cart, and offered the kine a burnt offering unto the LORD. And the Levites took down the ark of the LORD, and the coffer that *was* with it, wherein the jewels of gold *were,* and put *them* on the great stone: and the men of Beth-shemesh offered burnt offerings and sacrificed sacrifices the same day unto the LORD. And when the five lords of the Philistines had seen it, they returned to Ekron the same day. And these *are* the golden emerods which the Philistines returned *for* a trespass offering unto the LORD; for Ashdod one, for Gaza one, for Askelon one, for Gath one, for Ekron one; And the golden mice, *according to* the number of all the cities of the Philistines *belonging* to the five lords, *both* of fenced cities, and of country villages, even unto the great *stone of* Abel, whereon they set down the ark of the LORD: *which stone remaineth* unto this day in the field of Joshua, the Beth-shemite.

And he smote the men of Beth-shemesh, because they had looked into the ark of the LORD, even he smote of the people fifty thousand and threescore and ten men: and the people lamented, because the LORD had smitten *many* of the people with a great slaughter. And the men of Beth-shemesh said, Who is able to stand before this holy LORD God? and to whom shall he go up from us?

And they sent messengers to the inhabitants of Kirjath-jearim, saying, The Philistines have brought again the ark of the LORD; come ye down, *and* fetch it up to you.—1 SAM. VI.

1 Sam. vi.

The Philistines decline to send the Ark away.

IN spite of the judgements of God the national pride of the Philistines would not admit of their sending away the Ark of the Lord. For seven months it remained in their land. Far from softening their hearts, the punishments which God had inflicted upon them had just the reverse effect (verse 6);

Unlawful Curiosity

like Pharaoh of old they refused to see the hand of God in all the calamities they had experienced.
Suffering embitters some, making them hard and
rebellious (Rev. xvi. 9). It ennobles others (Ps. cxix.
67), enabling them to see the folly of their ways,
and return in penitence and humility to Him Whose
laws they have broken (Heb. xii. 6). The same sun
will both melt ice and harden clay.

1 Sam.
vi.
Punishment
hardens
them.

Eventually the Philistines sought the advice
of their priests and magicians, as to what they
should do with their trophy, and where to send
it, should they suffer it to depart from their
hands.

Eventually
they seek
advice.

The diviners and soothsayers of the Philistines
were credited with great ability in finding out the
will of Heaven, and in the interpretation of omens
(cf. Isa. ii. 6). The fame of their oracle at Ekron
had spread far and wide (2 Kings i. 2). Such
customs were an abomination to the Lord (Deut.
xviii. 9–12), and the children of Israel were forbidden
to practise them (Lev. xix. 26 ; Mic. v. 12). Christianity has adopted a very similar attitude, on the
ground that they engender a morbid curiosity with
regard to the Unknown, and foster restlessness and
anxiety concerning the future, which the servant
of Christ should avoid, believing as he does that
the world is ruled by an All-Wise, All-Loving Father
Whose will is to be discovered in the daily exercise
of prayer and Christian discipleship. " He has
beset us behind and before " (Ps. cxxxix. 5). He
goes in front to clear the way. He remains behind
to clear up our mistakes.

The fame
of their
diviners and
soothsayers.

The Chris-
tian
attitude
towards the
same.

Ps. cxxxix.
5.

The First Book of Samuel

**The advice
given to the
Philistines.**

The Philistines were bidden by their religious leaders to send away the Ark of God, and with it some expression on their part that they had sinned and done amiss—a trespass offering must be made (verse 3). The form it was to take consisted in five representations in gold, one for each city of the Philistines (cf. verses 17, 18), of the disease from which they had been suffering, together with five golden mice. The latter had been chosen on account of the terrible ravages which their crops had sustained from field mice (verse 4). Ample acknowledgment, also, was to be made of the Source from whence all these evils and troubles had come (verse 5). Besides all this, they must send the Ark away upon a new cart which had never seen previous service, to be drawn by "*two milch kine on which there had come no yoke*" (verse 7), and in a coffer by the side of the Ark was to be placed the sin offering.

The test.

Further, the following test was suggested : " In order to discover whether these recent ills have happened to you by chance or not, we make the following proposal. If these kine, unaccustomed as they are to bear the yoke, should, contrary to their natural instincts, their calves being left behind them (verse 7), betake themselves to Beth-shemesh, the nearest Israelitish town, then you may rest assured that it is the hand of Jehovah which has smitten our land " (verse 9).

**Chance or
Providence.**

These suggestions were carried out to the letter, and the Ark, drawn by two kine, made its way direct to Beth-shemesh. The lords of the Philistines also went out of their way to satisfy themselves as to what should occur, and

Unlawful Curiosity

the writer simply states, "*and when the five Lords* **1 Sam.**
of the Philistines had seen it, they returned" (verse 16). **vi.**
Once more through the chequered history of man,
God had been working out His purpose.

Following the Ark, we are informed that it was **The Ark's**
the time of wheat harvest when it arrived at **arrival at**
Beth-shemesh, which must have been either at the **Beth-shemesh.**
end of May or the beginning of June. Imagine
the feelings of delight with which the Israelites
beheld the Ark once more in their midst. To them
it implied that God had returned to bless and guard
His people. But unfortunately they had forgotten
a most important command of their God, and this
gives the impression that they had derived but
little profit from their past defeats. Instead of,
with befitting reverence, covering the Ark, thereby
securing it from the public gaze, they looked into
it with profane curiosity, although they must have
known that even the Levites were not allowed to
enter into the Holy of Holies on pain of death
(Num. iv. 19, 20). In consequence of this many of
the people lost their lives. Their joy was turned **Joy turned**
into mourning; they had been guilty of irreverent **into**
curiosity. **sorrow.**

Curiosity is not wrong in itself. It is an instinct **Curiosity a**
which man partly shares with the lower animals, **true and**
but he alone asks the why and wherefore of the **proper**
world, himself included. This insatiable curiosity **instinct.**
is the secret of all progress. To the earnest spirit
of inquiry, manifested by our greatest scientists,
is due the wonderful advance mankind has made,
especially within the last one hundred and fifty

75

The First Book of Samuel

Christians must not be afraid of inquiry.

All investigation should be conducted in a spirit of reverence.

A much-needed caution.

years. Whilst all those who believe in the truth of Christianity should be the first to welcome every reverent and honest investigation of its claims, no other position is possible for those who adopt the teaching of the Reformation. Entirely useless is it on our part " to build a wall around certain districts of thought and forbid all access therein." Prepared we must be to give " a reason for the hope that is within us," but it presupposes the sanctifying of the Lord God in our hearts, and that our curiosity be blended with the spirit of meekness and fear (1 St. Pet. iii. 15). To take up the latest attack against Christianity, to see what the other side has to say against her, in a careless offhand fashion, may be to court disaster. On the other hand, should we feel impelled to look into her credentials, for the sake of our own personal faith, or to succour the faith of others, then we may take it as an indication of the leading of the Spirit Who will guide us into all truth. To master any subject requires much time and patience, and in the highest of all subjects, Religion, this is most emphatically true. It must also be remembered that the pure in heart alone can see God, and that in order to see God we must veil our faces. The truth of God can only be apprehended on our knees, and by living it out in the life. " That which sees must also be kindred and similar to its object, before it can see it. The eye could never have beheld the sun, had it not become sunlike. The mind could never have perceived the beautiful, had it not first become beautiful itself," so wrote Plotinus ; and that is only another way of saying " spiritual things must be spiritually discerned " (cf. 1 Cor. ii. 11–16).

1 Sam. vi.

Thus a reverent search into the things of God is to be commended, but just as the inhabitants of that Israelitish town sent messengers to the men of Kirjath-jearim that they should come and take the Ark away, in like manner profane curiosity has driven the Saviour from many a heart.

1 Cor. ii. 11–16.

Profane curiosity may drive the Saviour away.

But there is another rendering of this story, the point of which is in strong contrast to that with which we have been dealing. Dr. Moffatt translates the nineteenth verse thus : " The sons of Jeconiah, however, did not rejoice along with the men of Beth-shemesh when they saw the Ark of the Eternal : so he struck [fifty thousand] seventy of them. . . . And the folk mourned because the Eternal had smitten the folk with a heavy slaughter"; and this reading is also given in the margin of the Revised Version. According to this rendering, the sons of Jeconiah were guilty of the sin of indifference towards the most holy object in the Israelitish worship—the visible symbol of God's Presence in the midst of His people. The afflictions visited upon their country had made so little religious impression upon them that they abstained from taking any outward part in the celebrations which attended the Ark's return.

Another rendering of verse 19.

The sin of indifference.

Indifference, rather than hostility, is the prevailing temper evinced by large masses of the people to-day towards the claims of the spiritual world. Immersed in the pursuit of pleasure or business they are deaf to any religious appeal, or, on the plea

Its prevalence to-day.

of broadmindedness and tolerance, assert that all religions are equally true, frequently with the mental reservation that all religions are of slight importance. Breadth of mind is a virtue not to be claimed by the individual for himself; he should leave it to others to decide whether or not he is so fortunate as to possess it. What right has a man to call himself broad-minded respecting any subject upon which he has not taken the trouble to enlighten himself? And this is true in the case of the highest and most vital of all subjects.

Its claim to broad-mindedness denied.

Bitter was the feeling towards the countries which adopted a neutral attitude during the Great War, because those in the midst of that awful experience knew the stupendous issues at stake, and considered it intolerable that any should stand aside and take no part in the struggle for life or death. Whatever broad-mindedness may be, it is not to be confused with lukewarmness.

The indifferent cannot avoid making a choice.

The indifferent, however, do make a choice. No man can take up a neutral position towards God, or Christ. He who stands on one side, by that very fact, implies that to him the conflict between good and evil is of little moment, the salvation won by the Saviour for mankind of small value, and that in his view God does not count in the affairs of men to-day. The Gallios (Acts xviii. 17) of this world, and they are many, have in effect chosen a course, and walk therein. The issues of life and death placed by Christ before the human soul are so vast and momentous that He does not hesitate to say,

St. Matt. xii. 30. "He that is not with Me is against Me" (St. Matt.

The Sin of Indifference

xii. 30). Dante's description of those who in life **I Sam.** incurred neither infamy nor praise is severe, but **vi.** should not fall on our ears unheeded.

"Heaven, not to be less fair, did these expel,
  Nor will the deep Inferno them receive,
  For they would cause some boast to those in Hell:
     *   *   *   *   *   *
  The world permits no fame of theirs to grow,
  Mercy and Justice hold them in disdain,
  Speak not of them, but glance and past them go.

                    (*Inferno*, vii. 40–42, 49–51.)

"From the sin of indifference, from the dread sentence against those who are neither cold nor hot, Good Lord, deliver us."

VIII

AN ANCIENT WAR MEMORIAL

And the men of Kirjath-jearim came and fetched up the ark of the LORD, and brought it into the house of Abinadab in the hill, and sanctified Eleazar his son to keep the ark of the LORD. And it came to pass, while the ark abode in Kirjath-jearim, that the time was long; for it was twenty years: and all the house of Israel lamented after the LORD.

And Samuel spake unto all the house of Israel, saying, If ye do return unto the LORD with all your hearts, *then* put away the strange gods and Ashtaroth from among you, and prepare your hearts unto the LORD, and serve him only: and he will deliver you out of the hand of the Philistines. Then the children of Israel did put away Baalim and Ashtaroth, and served the LORD only. And Samuel said, Gather all Israel to Mizpeh, and I will pray for you unto the LORD. And they gathered together to Mizpeh, and drew water, and poured *it* out before the LORD, and fasted on that day, and said there, We have sinned against the LORD. And Samuel judged the children of Israel in Mizpeh And when the Philistines heard that the children of Israel were gathered together to Mizpeh, the lords of the Philistines went up against Israel. And when the children of Israel heard *it*, they were afraid of the Philistines. And the children of Israel said to Samuel, Cease not to cry unto the LORD our God for us, that he will save us out of the hand of the Philistines.

And Samuel took a sucking lamb, and offered *it for* a burnt offering wholly unto the LORD: and Samuel cried unto the LORD for Israel; and the LORD heard him. And as Samuel was offering up the burnt offering, the Philistines drew near to battle against Israel: but the LORD thundered with a great thunder on that day upon the Philistines, and discomfited them; and they were smitten before Israel. And the men of Israel went out of Mizpeh, and pursued the Philistines, and smote them, until *they came* under Beth-car. Then Samuel took a

An Ancient War Memorial

stone, and set *it* between Mizpeh and Shen, and called the name of it Eben-ezer, saying, Hitherto hath the LORD helped us.

So the Philistines were subdued, and they came no more into the coast of Israel : and the hand of the LORD was against the Philistines all the days of Samuel. And the cities which the Philistines had taken from Israel were restored to Israel, from Ekron even unto Gath ; and the coasts thereof did Israel deliver out of the hands of the Philistines. And there was peace between Israel and the Amorites. And Samuel judged Israel all the days of his life. And he went from year to year in circuit to Beth-el, and Gilgal, and Mizpeh, and judged Israel in all those places. And his return *was* to Ramah ; for there *was* his house ; and there he judged Israel ; and there he built an altar unto the LORD.—1 SAM. VII.

THE Ark of God remained in Kirjath-jearim, but no improvement in the fortunes of Israel took place for many years. The country continued in subjection to the Philistines. " The public worship of Jehovah was intermitted : for the Tabernacle seems to have been dismantled, and the Ark was in a private house. The people sank into gross idolatry " (Prof. Kirkpatrick). At length the dawn of a better day could just be faintly seen. " *All the house of Israel lamented* " or sighed " *after the Lord* " (verse 2). *[margin: 1 Sam. vii. Israel's desperate condition.]*

The way was thus paved for the appearance of Samuel. For the first time, he received a hearing from the nation. He did not mince matters. He declined to prophesy smooth things. " You have forsaken God," he says in effect to them, you must return to Him in no half-hearted fashion, but " *with all your heart . . . and serve Him only* " (verse 3). *[margin: Samuel appears on the scene. His plain speaking.]*

The first step in their return would be to put away the Baalim and the Ashtaroth, the gods and

81   F

The First Book of Samuel

1 Sam. vii.

The insufficiency of a mere negative reformation.

goddesses of the Canaanites, with all the licentiousness inseparable from their worship. But a mere negative reformation would not suffice. As in the case of our Lord's parable concerning the swept and garnished heart, it was taken possession of by wicked spirits because it was empty (St. Matt. xii. 43–45) ; unless something better should take the place of idolatry, they, the men of Israel, would only slip back again into their evil ways. Therefore let them set their hearts steadfastly towards Jehovah (verses 3 and 4).

The people follow Samuel's guidance.

They assemble at Mizpeh.

The people were now ready to follow Samuel, and carry out his injunctions. Idolatry was put away ; obedience rendered unto Jehovah (verse 4). But inasmuch as there had been a national apostasy, so must there be set apart a day of national humiliation and confession. In pursuance of Samuel's orders, Israel gathered together on the very spot where they underwent their terrible defeat about twenty years before, at Mizpeh (Neby Samwîl), five miles north-west of Jerusalem. As a symbol of their contrition " *They drew water, and poured it out before the Lord* " (verse 6). As Cornelius a Lapide says, " We would desire on account of our sins to shed so many tears as there are drops in the bucket ; but because we are unable to do this, nor have we tears to our hands, hence we pour out water in their stead."

Mr. Wet-eyes.

Whoever has read Dr. Alexander Whyte's chapter on " Mr. Wet-eyes " in his *Bunyan's Characters*, will appreciate the point of this ritual performed by the children of Israel that day. Dr. Whyte turns

An Ancient War Memorial

round on his reader and asks, "Did you ever weep 1 Sam.
so much as one good tear-drop for pure sin? one vii.
true tear? not because your sins have found you
out, but for secret sins that you know can never
find you out in this world? And still better, did
you ever weep in secret places, not for sin, but for
sinfulness—which is a very different matter? Did
you ever weep to yourself and to God alone over
your incurably wicked heart? If not, then weep
for that with all your might, night and day."

We have greater cause to be moved to penitent
tears, or their equivalent, than had the Israelites.
For when we look at the Broken Figure on that
Tree erected outside the city wall, and realise,
though it be ever so little, that it was not the nails,
but the love of Christ in contact with our sin, that
kept Him there, a penitence too deep for tears
should pierce our hearts. This penitence of the
Israelites was accompanied with fasting, a good
and wholesome practice pursued by the Puritans
and early Evangelicals, though not very popular
with their successors to-day; those, however, who
wish to deepen their penitence, and discipline their
lives, should not dispense with it altogether. And Public con-
of more importance than fasting, this sorrow for sin, fession of sin.
enjoined by Samuel at Mizpeh, was accompanied by Amendment
open confession and amendment of life. "*We* of life.
*have sinned against the Lord. And Samuel judged
the children of Israel in Mizpeh*" (verse 6). Justice,
which in the East is so often deflected from its true
course by bribery and corruption (1 Sam. viii. 3),
was carried out, and idolatry punished.

The First Book of Samuel

1 Sam.
vii.

The suspicions of the Philistines aroused.

They assemble at Mizpeh.

During this time the suspicions of the Philistines had been aroused. News of a vast concourse had reached their leaders (verse 7), and this in their estimation was tantamount to open rebellion. Without delay, they proceeded to Mizpeh with the purpose of putting it down with a ruthless hand. God's people were entirely unarmed, and when they saw the hosts of their ancient foes gathered together against them, in their distress they implored Samuel to beseech of God to intervene on their behalf. Samuel proceeded at once to offer up a sacrifice of expiation, a burnt offering unto the Lord (verse 9)— a foreshadowing of the great Sacrifice of the Son of God, Who alone can take away sin, and cause the sinner to enjoy a daily triumph over himself and the forces of evil, by virtue of his union with the

God delivers His people.

victorious Lord. Whilst engaged in the very act of sacrifice, God graciously interposed for His people's sake. "*The Lord thundered with a great thunder.*" Whereupon a panic ensued. The Philistines betook themselves to flight, pursued by the victorious Israelites as far as Bethcar. After this, peace reigned in the land; and during the days of Samuel's active judgeship they had rest both from the Philistines (verse 13) and the Amorites (verse 14).

The Prophet's War Memorial.

One very significant action performed by Samuel must now receive attention, namely, the War Memorial which he raised on the field of battle between Mizpeh and Shen (verse 12), to commemorate the glorious victory vouchsafed by God to His people.

An Ancient War Memorial

The actual memorial was without any artistic 1 Sam. vii. merit. Seeing how prone the Israelites were to idolatry at the time, this was an advantage rather than otherwise. This does not hinder us to-day from erecting beautiful statues, monuments, buildings, as thankofferings for past mercies, whether national or individual. Anything conceived in bad taste, or which is ugly, is objectionable to God. Dante sees in the world of appearances a reflection of the Divine Beauty:

> "All things created—both of heaven and earth
> Are but the beam of His idea, who
> By love paternal calls them into birth."

Nothing can be too good to offer to God; it need **Nothing too** not be elaborate, for simplicity has a charm and a **good for** beauty all its own. Care must also be taken that **God.** any monument, or work of art of a religious character, should not attract the observer to itself, causing him to be so lost in wonder and admiration at the beauty of conception and design, as to lose sight of Him to whose honour it has been erected. Those who have had the privilege of spending an afternoon in the cloisters of St. Mark's at Florence, and have gazed on the frescoes and pictures of Fra Angelico, cannot fail to have been uplifted by the sight and drawn closer to God. Fortunate are the people who have an architect, a sculptor, a painter, of whom it may be said that he never undertook any work without prayer. Vasari records **The angelic** this of Fra Angelico, and that he could not depict **painter.** the Crucifixion without tears running down his

1 Sam. vii.

cheeks, and that it was a saying of the artist, " He who would do the work of Christ, must live continually with Him."

The suitability of the War Memorial at Mizpeh. What it suggested to future generations.

Samuel's War Memorial was just what was wanted for the time. It was a perpetual reminder to the Israelite of what God had wrought on behalf of his country. It would not convey the slightest suggestion of national glorification or arrogant pride. When the Jewish mother explained to her child how it came there, she could not fail to mention that when the children of Israel were attacked by the Philistines, they were entirely unarmed, so that the victory was not due to their own prowess, but to God, and God alone. Quite naturally would she also allude to the terrible defeat the Israelites had experienced on identically the same spot, although they were well armed and the sacred Ark was in their midst. By these examples would she impress on the youthful mind that " there is no restraint to the Lord to save by many or by few " (1 Sam. xiv. 6 ; cf. Judges vii. 2). He is not always " on the side of the biggest battalions," but those who love righteousness and mercy and serve God with all their hearts, He will come down to deliver.

The name of the Memorial.

The spectator would also remember the name of the stone, " Ebenezer " : " HITHERTO HATH THE LORD HELPED US." It is not only on rare occasions that God's help is bestowed, nor is He limited to any one particular event or time. His help is continuous. Most buildings and monuments carry their date upon them. The practised eye takes in

at a moment's glance the century or period to which **1 Sam. vii.**
the particular work may be assigned. But this
stone of Samuel could have been put up in any age,
and therefore belongs to every age.

When God appeared to Moses in the wilderness God's help
in the burning bush, He revealed to him His name. continues.
" *I* am that I am " (Exod. iii. 14). One of the Exod. iii.
greatest of Old Testament scholars, the late Dr. 14.
Davidson, would translate the words, " I will be
what I will be." What He will be is left unex-
pressed, for each generation, that is faithful to Him,
will discover what a Helper, Strengthener, Deliverer,
He will prove to be to them according to their
special needs. God is the Living One. " Our
fathers have declared unto us the noble works that
He did in their days and in the old time before
them " ; but we too have seen His glory in our
days. He has helped us, and will help again
(Ps. cxv. 12). We have not been saved FROM the Is. xliii. 2.
fire, but we have been saved IN the fire (Isa. xliii. 2).
Experience has proved that, in the case of those
who have set the Lord always before them, He has
been at their right hand (Ps. xvi. 8) to bless and
sustain them. Thus we dare to face the future.
Our defeats, in the light of subsequent events, may Our defeats
prove to have been manifestations of God's help. turned into
After that bitter hour of self-humiliation, when we victories.
had given way to some temptation, and felt as if
we could never look up again, we learnt to be very
distrustful of ourselves, and in place of our former
confidence and pride, we came to lean more upon
Christ's redeeming grace and power. Thus was

**1 Sam.
viii.**

our defeat turned into victory, so that, though for
some unfaithfulness God may have withdrawn His
help, yet He has not forsaken us, but has raised us
up again (Ps. xxxvii. 24).

Our help is in the Name of the Lord ;
Who hath made heaven and earth.
Blessed be the Name of the Lord,
Henceforth, world without end.

THE DIVINE RESPECT FOR HUMAN FREEDOM AND ACTIVITY

And it came to pass, when Samuel was old, that he made his sons judges over Israel. Now the name of his firstborn was Joel; and the name of his second, Abiah : *they were* judges in Beer-sheba. And his sons walked not in his ways, but turned aside after lucre, and took bribes, and perverted judgment. Then all the elders of Israel gathered themselves together, and came to Samuel unto Ramah, and said unto him, Behold, thou art old, and thy sons walk not in thy ways : now make us a king to judge us like all the nations.

But the thing displeased Samuel, when they said, Give us a king to judge us. And Samuel prayed unto the Lord. And the Lord said unto Samuel, Hearken unto the voice of the people in all that they say unto thee : for they have not rejected thee, but they have rejected me, that I should not reign over them. According to all the works which they have done since the day that I brought them up out of Egypt even unto this day, wherewith they have forsaken me, and served other gods, so do they also unto thee. Now therefore hearken unto their voice : howbeit yet protest solemnly unto them, and shew them the manner of the king that shall reign over them.

And Samuel told all the words of the Lord unto the people that asked of him a king. And he said, This will be the manner of the king that shall reign over you : He will take your sons, and appoint *them* for himself, for his chariots, and *to be* his horsemen ; and *some* shall run before his chariots. And he will appoint him captains over thousands, and captains over fifties ; and *will set them* to ear his ground, and to reap his harvest, and to make his instruments of war, and instruments of his chariots. And he will take your daughters *to be* confectionaries, and *to be*

89

The First Book of Samuel

cooks, and *to be* bakers. And he will take your fields, and your vineyards, and your oliveyards, *even* the best *of them*, and give *them* to his servants. And he will take the tenth of your seed, and of your vineyards, and give to his officers, and to his servants. And he will take your menservants, and your maidservants, and your goodliest young men, and your asses, and put *them* to his work. He will take the tenth of your sheep : and ye shall be his servants. And ye shall cry out in that day because of your king which ye shall have chosen you ; and the LORD will not hear you in that day.

Nevertheless the people refused to obey the voice of Samuel ; and they said, Nay ; but we will have a king over us ; That we also may be like all the nations ; and that our king may judge us, and go out before us, and fight our battles. And Samuel heard all the words of the people, and he rehearsed them in the ears of the LORD. And the LORD said to Samuel, Hearken unto their voice, and make them a king. And Samuel said unto the men of Israel, Go ye every man unto his city.—1 SAM. VIII.

I Sam. viii.

Samuel's old age.

His sons share his labours.

Their scandalous lives and methods cause widespread discontent.

THE narrative is silent as to the number of years during which Samuel judged Israel after the battle of Mizpeh, but a considerable time must have elapsed, for when the Prophet is next mentioned, he appears on the scene as an old man (verse 1). He is obliged to call in the help of his sons. A division of labour follows. To them is allotted the southern district of Palestine centring on Beersheba, while Samuel still keeps the north in his own hands (verse 2).

The names of his sons were Joel and Abiah, " Jehovah is my God " ; " Jah is my Father." Doubtless these names were chosen as a protest against the prevailing idolatry, but in their case, as with Eli's sons, they departed from the precepts of their father and walked not in his ways (verse 3). Their scandalous misgovernment caused widespread'

Divine Respect for Human Freedom

discontent and disaffection, and gave an excellent **1 Sam.** handle to those who desired to have a different **viii.** form of government.

At length events came to a head at Ramah, In consequence the when the elders, the representatives of the tribes people and cities, without any warning to Samuel, demanded demand a that a king should be appointed over them (verse 5). king. Two reasons were given for this serious step. The Their first was the bribery and corruption which character- reasons for a visible ised the judicial methods pursued by Samuel's sons. king. How strange it is that the sons of both Eli and Samuel should have been bad men ! Were Eli and Samuel too much taken up with their " religious " duties, to attend to the right bringing up and spiritual care of their own children, thus neglecting the first of all religious duties ?

Secondly, there was the desire of the people to be like the other nations whose kings judged them, and went out before them, and fought their battles (verse 20).

Naturally Samuel felt aggrieved at their request. How Their ingratitude wounded him to the quick. All Samuel takes their that he had done for them was put on one side, and request. his past services were forgotten. Instead, however, He refers of thwarting them, he adopted the very wise course to God. of referring their petition to Almighty God : " *And Samuel prayed unto the Lord* " (verse 6) ; and here in his intercourse with God, we note how the Prophet's personal feelings gradually retired into the background.

The whole dispute was raised to a very much higher level than that of Samuel's individual

1 Sam.
viii.

thoughts and feelings on the subject: *Did this demand of the people meet with God's approval?* Instead of being carried away by feelings of resentment and wounded pride, he was enabled calmly and quietly to marshal the arguments against the change in the constitution of Israel's government, and thus place the whole subject in its proper light. When men ascend into the mount of God, their own personal concerns assume a relative unimportance, and they come to view human affairs in their proper perspective. They breathe a purer air, which braces them, and enables them better to cope with the trials and difficulties of the valley beneath.

He acquaints the people with the Divine Will.

Samuel was not slow in acquainting the people with the Divine Will (verse 10), "*Hearken unto the voice of the people in all that they say unto thee, Not thee, their judge have they rejected, but Me their true King have they rejected from reigning over them*" (verse 7). The pronouns *thee* and *Me* are most emphatic.

The demand for a visible Head very natural.

This demand for a strong centralised government with an outward visible Head was a very natural one to make, and in after times it arose in the Christian Church. A Church which is subservient to the State may enjoy its prestige and favour, but cannot assert her independence, and, as in the case of Prussia before the war, may tend to become a department of the State. Or, as in the case of the Roman Catholic Church, she may grow into a strong well-knit body, wonderfully effective in certain respects, whilst crushing with an iron hand any assertion of individual independence or freedom of **1 Sam.** thought. **viii.**

Israel was intended to be a Theocracy, recognising Israel and God as her sole Head. Christ alone is the Head of the His Church; she is ever to depend on her unseen Christian Church. Lord; herein lies her freedom, and her power. St. Paul makes use of a very bold expression concerning the relation between the Church and her Lord. Following Dr. Armitage Robinson's translation, "The Church which is His Body," "the Eph. i. 23. fulness of Him who all in all is being fulfilled" (Eph. i. 23). May we reverently say that Christ is mystically incomplete apart from His Church? To quote Dr. Robinson once more : "His feet and hands no longer move and work in our midst, as once they moved and wrought in Palestine. But St. Paul affirms that He is not without feet and hands on earth : the Church is His Body." [1] We are in a very real sense necessary to Him. None the less He is the inspiring, directive, governing Power. The Church must take her orders from Him, her very life depends upon Him ; in fact, He is her life. The more she looks up instead of around, the better will she be equipped to carry on His work. By fulfilling these conditions through the indwelling power of the Holy Spirit does she render visible to the world her unseen Lord and Master.

This truth is concealed in this Old Testament story of the desire manifested on the part of Israel

[1] *St. Paul's Epistle to the Ephesians*, pp. 57, 58. Macmillan & Co., London, 1923.

The First Book of Samuel

for a visible king, but it is blazoned forth in the New Testament.

Samuel, as we have seen, cast all personal feelings and prejudices on one side. Having made known the Divine disapproval of the step his countrymen were taking, he proceeded to point out to them the consequences which should follow it.

Samuel points out to his countrymen the consequences of their having a king.

Their king would be a tyrant after the oriental pattern. There would be a form of universal conscription, from which not even the women-kind would be exempt. He would compel their daughters to be confectionaries (or rather to serve as perfumers), to be cooks and bakers (verse 13). Their men would not only have to serve in the army, but in the days of peace he would force them to plough his ground ("to ear his ground," A.V.), and to reap his harvest. More than this, heavy exactions would be levied, often unjust (verse 14), and a very comprehensive form of tithing demanded, which few would be able to avoid or evade (verse 17).

The Israelites persist in their demand.

Notwithstanding this gloomy picture of the future drawn by the Prophet, the people remained unconvinced ; they adhered to their previous demands for a king, and God gave way in the person of His servant.

God permitting man to have his own way.

Here we have a striking instance of God permitting man to assert his own independence by the adoption of courses other than He intended. Never is the Divine Power exercised except with a due regard to human freedom. Just as in a game of chess, a player proves his skill by checkmating his opponent in spite of any moves the latter may

Divine Respect for Human Freedom

determine to make, and yet scrupulously observes 1 Sam. the rules of the game, so God, while never ceasing viii. to conform to the limitations of His activity, self-imposed when He created man after His own image, without haste and without rest, pursues His victorious way in spite of the moves which man makes contrary to His desire and plans. Should then any situation arise which runs counter to the Divine Will, its effect is the more to call out the resources and energies of the Divine love and patience, with the result that even man's sins become contributory to the honour and glory of God. " He maketh the wrath of man to praise Him."

Regarding a wrong choice from the human side, *When man* it is right that we should ask what happens to one *declines to* who has a clear indication of the Divine Will, and *carry out* declines to act upon it ? The words of Mordecai to *Will, what* Esther will suffice for our answer. Should Esther *happens ?* have refused to take her life in her hands and go in to Ahasuerus, to defend her people against the machinations of Haman, who had arranged to bring about their massacre on a certain day, deliverance would have arisen to the Jews from another quarter ; but her refusal to act would have involved both her and her father's house in ruin (Esther iv. 14). In other words, God's cause would have been upheld, but the particular instrument of which He had intended to make use, would have suffered irreparable loss. *The Will of*

The great aim of all our lives should be to find out *Christ* the Will of Christ. Do we wish to gain our own *should be* ends, irrespective of God, we may be allowed even *our lives.*

95

The First Book of Samuel

1 Sam.
viii.

to succeed for a while. On the other hand, do we make God's business our chief concern, not of necessity shall we be successful as the world counts success, nor be spared sorrow or pain, but we shall attain a blessedness higher than happiness, for there is no joy or peace to be compared with the sure knowledge that we are doing the will of God. " In His Will is our peace " (Dante).

X

SAUL IN SEARCH OF HIS FATHER'S ASSES FINDS A KINGDOM

Now there was a man of Benjamin, whose name *was* Kish, the son of Abiel, the son of Zeror, the son of Bechorath, the son of Aphiah, a Benjamite, a mighty man of power. And he had a son, whose name *was* Saul, a choice young man, and a goodly : and *there was* not among the children of Israel a goodlier person than he : from his shoulders and upward *he was* higher than any of the people. And the asses of Kish Saul's father were lost. And Kish said to Saul his son, Take now one of the servants with thee, and arise, go seek the asses. And he passed through mount Ephraim, and passed through the land of Shalisha, but they found *them* not : then they passed through the land of Shalim, and *there they were* not : and he passed through the land of the Benjamites, but they found *them* not. *And* when they were come to the land of Zuph, Saul said to his servant that *was* with him, Come, and let us return ; lest my father leave *caring* for the asses, and take thought of us. And he said unto him, Behold now, *there is* in this city a man of God, and *he is* an honourable man ; all that he saith cometh surely to pass ; now let us go thither ; peradventure he can shew us our way that we should go. Then said Saul to his servant, But, behold, *if* we go, what shall we bring the man ? for the bread is spent in our vessels, and *there is* not a present to bring to the man of God : what have we ? And the servant answered Saul again, and said, Behold, I have here at hand the fourth part of a shekel of silver : *that* will I gave to the man of God, to tell us our way. (Beforetime in Israel, when a man went to enquire of God, thus he spake, Come, and let us go to the seer : for *he that is* now *called* a Prophet was beforetime called a Seer.) Then said Saul to his servant, Well said ; come, let us go. So they went unto the city where the man of God *was*.

97   G

The First Book of Samuel

And as they went up the hill to the city, they found young maidens going out to draw water, and said unto them, Is the seer here ? And they answered them, and said, He is ; behold, *he is* before you : make haste now, for he came to day to the city ; for *there is* a sacrifice of the people to day in the high place : As soon as ye be come into the city, ye shall straightway find him, before he go up to the high place to eat : for the people will not eat until he come, because he doth bless the sacrifice ; *and* afterwards they eat that be bidden. Now therefore get you up ; for about this time ye shall find him. And they went up into the city : *and* when they were come into the city, behold, Samuel came out against them, for to go up to the high place.

Now the LORD had told Samuel in his ear a day before Saul came, saying, To morrow about this time I will send thee a man out of the land of Benjamin, and thou shalt anoint him *to be* captain over my people Israel, that he may save my people out of the hand of the Philistines : for I have looked upon my people, because their cry is come unto me. And when Samuel saw Saul, the LORD said unto him, Behold the man whom I spake to thee of ! this same shall reign over my people. Then Saul drew near to Samuel in the gate, and said, Tell me, I pray thee, where the seer's house *is*. And Samuel answered Saul, and said, I *am* the seer : go up before me unto the high place ; for ye shall eat with me to day, and to morrow I will let thee go, and will tell thee all that *is* in thine heart. And as for thine asses that were lost three days ago, set not thy mind on them ; for they are found. And on whom *is* all the desire of Israel ? *Is it* not on thee, and on all thy father's house ? And Saul answered and said, *Am* not I a Benjamite, of the smallest of the tribes of Israel ? and my family the least of all the families of the tribe of Benjamin ? wherefore then speakest thou so to me ? And Samuel took Saul and his servant, and brought them into the parlour, and made them sit in the chiefest place among them that were bidden, which *were* about thirty persons. And Samuel said unto the cook, Bring the portion which I gave thee, of which I said unto thee, Set it by thee. And the cook took up the shoulder, and *that* which *was* upon it, and set *it* before Saul. And *Samuel* said, Behold that which is left ! set *it* before thee, *and* eat : for unto this time hath it been kept for thee since I said, I have invited the people. So Saul did eat with Samuel that day.

And when they were come down from the high place into the

city, *Samuel* communed with Saul upon the top of the house. And they arose early : and it came to pass about the spring of the day, that Samuel called Saul to the top of the house, saying, Up, that I may send thee away. And Saul arose, and they went out both of them, he and Samuel, abroad. *And* as they were going down to the end of the city, Samuel said to Saul, Bid the servant pass on before us, (and he passed on,) but stand thou still a while, that I may shew thee the word of God.

Then Samuel took a vial of oil, and poured *it* upon his head, and kissed him, and said, *Is it* not because the LORD hath anointed thee *to be* captain over his inheritance ?—1 SAM. IX. and x. 1.

So far, Samuel has been the principal character of the book. He has not appeared in every scene, but on these occasions his absence is felt. Not yet do we bid him farewell, but he tends to recede into the background to make way for a lesser man, Israel's first king. *1 Sam. ix. and x. 1. Samuel retires into the background.*

St. John the Baptist proved his humility and disinterestedness by his noble disclaimer of being the promised Messiah, and his assertion that he was nothing more than a voice proclaiming the close Advent of the expected One (St. John i. 23). But, at least, he had the joy of being the Bridegroom's friend, and making way for One, " the latchet of whose shoes he was not worthy to unloose " (St. John i. 27). For Samuel there was no such consolation. *St. John the Baptist did the same.*

Convinced as he was that the people were making a most tragic mistake, he was persuaded of God that there was no other course but to comply with their wishes. *Samuel convinced that the people are mistaken.*

The aged Prophet's loyalty, alike both to God and His Anointed, is one of the finest traits in his *Saul is to be chosen king.*

99

1 Sam.
ix. and
x. 1.

A young
man.

He is
looking for
his father's
asses.

character. The Divine choice falls upon one Saul
(asked-of-God), the son of Kish, of the smallest of
the tribes of Israel, the tribe of Benjamin (verse 1).
Saul makes his first appearance on the stage of his
country's history in the prime of life (" *a young man*,"
verse 2), engaged in a search for his father's asses,
which had strayed away and whose whereabouts
no one knew. This was not a matter of small
moment to an Eastern household; for asses were
valuable property, and were used for riding (1
Sam. xxv. 20–23; 2 Sam. xvii. 23, xix. 26), carrying
burdens (1 Sam. xvi. 20, xxv. 18; 2 Sam. xvi. 1),
and also for ploughing. A long and wearisome
journey is undertaken both by Saul and his servant,
but all to no purpose. When they find themselves
in Zuph, probably the land about Ramah, Saul
announces his decision to give up the search, on
the ground that their long-continued absence would
cause his father to entertain fears concerning their
safety (verse 5). The servant is not of the same
opinion. In the city hard by " *There is*," he says,
" *a man of God, and he is a man that is held in honour ;
all that he saith, cometh surely to pass* " (verse 6).
It was more than likely that he would give all the
needed information. Whereupon Saul changes his
mind, though he has to borrow of his servant a
quarter of a silver shekel; for none in his position
could go to the prophet empty-handed (verse 8).

Finds his
way to
Samuel.

Towards evening they make their ascent to the city
(verse 11), and in answer to their inquiries as to
where the Seer might be, they are bidden to make
haste, for on that very day Samuel had come to

Saul finds a Kingdom

bless the sacrifice (verses 12 and 13); and, on
entering the city, they would be certain to see him.
Nor were they disappointed, for once within the city,
who should come out to meet them from the opposite
direction but the Prophet himself (verse 14).
No sooner do the eyes of Samuel light upon Saul,
than he is assured by God that he is face to face
with Israel's future king (verse 17). When, therefore, Saul asks him if he could direct him to the
Seer's house, Samuel at once makes himself known.

**1 Sam.
ix. and
x. 1.**

The Prophet loses no time in inviting Saul to be
his guest, and proceeds to pay him honour by
insisting on his going in front of him to the sacrifice
(verse 19). As for the asses, Saul may set his mind
at rest; they have been found. Matters of far
greater moment must now engage his attention.
In Samuel's own words, " *I will tell thee all that is in
thine heart* " (verse 19). Those longings of yours to
free the country from the oppression of the Philistines, and the part you wish to take in the struggle,
are about to be realised. The most desirable things
of Israel are about to be placed within your grasp.
" *And for whom is all that is desirable in Israel? is
it not for thee, and for all thy father's house?* " (verse
20). To put it quite plainly, Saul will be Israel's
king.

Saul the
guest of the
Prophet.

Saul told
that he is
to be king.

Forthwith, Samuel brings him to the chamber in
the high place where the sacrificial meal was
partaken of. On his arrival, there is accorded to
him " *the chiefest place* " in the presence of all the
other thirty guests, and at the banquet itself a
special portion (verse 23), to quote Josephus's words,

He receives
a royal
portion.

101

The First Book of Samuel

1 Sam.
ix. and
x. 1.

Samuel anoints him king.

Doing his simple duty he found a kingdom.

"a royal portion," is set before him. Thus did Samuel delight to show him honour. Not content with this, the Prophet takes him to the roof of his own house, and there in view of the people, that all may see, he treats Saul as an honoured and distinguished guest. At dawn on the following day, after Saul's servant had been dismissed, on the confines of the city, Samuel takes a vial of oil and anoints him king.

For us it is interesting, not only as an historical fact, but still more as a record of how one who was doing a simple duty, found a kingdom. It is a parable of life. We may compare it with Lovell's vision of Sir Launfal. The good knight starts in gilded mail to seek in every clime the Holy Grail. As he passes on this quest from the gates of his castle, hard by there crouches a leper who sues for alms. Whereat Sir Launfal's heart stands still like a frozen waterfall, and a loathing comes over him. He tosses him a piece of gold, but the leper raises not the gold from the dust. He wanders far through England's broad demesnes, France's fair fields, Italy's ancient cities, and still further South to sunnier climes. The years pass by, and now another occupies his ancestral halls. But the quest seems a hopeless one, not a glimpse of the Holy Grail is given to him. Back to his old home he returns, and there in the selfsame spot he beholds once more the leper in the desolate horror of his disease. This time the knight parts in twain his single crust, and breaks the ice to give him water to drink, and lo, and behold a light shone round

about the place, and the Christ stood before him. **1 Sam.**
Thereupon Sir Launfal awoke. **ix. and**

x. 1.

"The Grail in my castle here is found."

Saul and Sir Launfal discover each his kingdom,
not in the pursuit of adventure, but in treading the
ordinary path of his daily life.

In the case of Our Lord's Mother, a simple village
maiden, we are told (St. Luke i. 28) Gabriel "came
in unto her:" very likely she was engaged in
commonplace household duties at the time. Hence
the romance of the Christian Life. Only to the few,
to the very exceptional few, is granted the thrill
and excitement of attempting to scale the heights
of Mount Everest, or to discover the whereabouts
of the North or South Pole, but to all there is given
the possibility of finding that kingdom which is
within each one of us, created after God's pattern,
and for His indwelling.

The discovery comes, sometimes after long and **All of us**
painful wanderings, sometimes in a flash across the **may have a**
soul. A leafless tree may be the messenger of God, **similar**
as in the case of Brother Lawrence. The well-known **experience.**
novel, *Adam Bede*, by George Eliot, herself not
a Christian, may bring the revelation, as it did to
a clergyman of our acquaintance; or it may be
some shattering experience when the spirit "is
stabbed broad awake."

But in more ways than one does this story of **Man never**
how Saul came into his kingdom suggest man's **satisfied.**
search after that true heritage for which God
created him. Man has ever craved for something,

The First Book of Samuel

often he knew not what. The complaint is loud in certain quarters that he is never satisfied. No sooner does he attain to one object, or one goal of ambition, than he reaches after another. His wants are never ended. Should we be surprised at this? Man is the offspring of the Infinite One; he has an infinite capacity. Can aught but the Infinite satisfy him? As Christopher Harvey, the friend of Izaak Walton, exclaimed,

> "The whole round world is not enough to fill
> The heart's three corners; but it craveth still:
> Onely the Trinity, that made it, can
> Suffice the vast-triangled heart of man."

Saul also dissatisfied with his lot.

We may infer from the words of Samuel, "*I will tell thee all that is in thine heart*" (verse 19), that Saul was dissatisfied with the inactive part he was playing, and desired a wider field of action; this desire inflamed by the sorrows and humiliations his country was undergoing at the hands of its enemies. This desire was now to be gratified. He was to enter into his kingdom. When Christ came He taught men what it was they unconsciously sought, nothing less than a kingdom, and, moreover, pointed out to them the way thereto, even Himself, "I am the Way."

Saul is crowned by Samuel. The Christian crowned by Christ.

God gave Saul his crown by the hand of Samuel; to the Christian He gives his crown through Christ. Herein is Samuel also a type of our Lord. Three times is the chord struck in the Book of the Revelation, of the royal dignity and priestly service which have been conferred upon mankind through the

Saul finds a Kingdom

1 Sam. ix. and x. 1.

Sacrifice of Christ (Rev. i. 6, v. 10, xx. 6 ; cf. St. Matt. v. 3 ; 1 Cor. iv. 8). As we have already observed, this kingdom is within man, but man only finds it, and thus his true self, in Christ (St. Luke xv. 17), and is found of Him.

The manner of the meeting between Samuel and Saul should not escape our notice. It was not Saul who discovered the Prophet, but the Prophet who revealed himself to Saul when on his way to bless the sacrifice. Sooner or later in the quest of the seeking soul she is confronted by the Cross, and there beholds the great Sacrifice for sin. Jesus bends down and makes Himself known to her in His saving power and redeeming grace ; then only does she begin to enter upon the kingdom which is destined for her by God. Thus is the Christ both the Way and the Door into the Way. Looking at the Cross of Jesus, and realising by faith that He was bruised for our iniquities, that the chastisement of our peace was upon Him, and that on Him hath been laid the iniquity of us all (Isa. liii. 5, 6), she realises that her own sins and shortcomings are included, and that full atonement has been made for them.

The manner of Samuel's and Saul's meeting.

How Christ meets us.

All this is the prelude to the invitation to the Feast, when He invites her to sup with Him and feeds her with the royal dainties of heaven.

The Christian Eucharist.

Samuel takes a lower place than Saul so that all may see to what great height God had raised him. As an old teacher of the Church, St. Irenæus, has phrased it, " Jesus Christ our Lord, Who, because of His great love, was made what we are, that He

1 Sam.
ix. and
x. 1.

might bring us to be even what He is Himself." Better still, St. Paul, " For ye know the grace of our Lord Jesus Christ, that, though He was rich, yet for your sakes He became poor, that ye through His poverty might become rich " (2 Cor. viii. 9 ; cf. v. 21). And in the Eucharist the Feast of praise and thanksgiving, we are ever reminded of that perfect Sacrifice made on our behalf, and are honoured, beyond all words, with the intimate friendship of the unseen Lord, Who comes to humble and believing souls, feeding them with the Bread of Heaven, and is Himself the Life of their life, and the joy and hope of their existence.

The part played by Saul's servant.

The use of very humble instruments.

Fain would we linger a little longer on this story of Saul, but we must content ourselves with suggesting thoughts on which the reader can meditate at his own leisure. Notice the part Saul's servant played, humble though he was ; without him, Saul might never have come across Samuel. The Holy Spirit makes use of the humblest instruments to bring men and women to Christ. The British and Foreign Bible Society owed its inception to a little Welsh girl ; the famous Lord Shaftesbury, his conversion with its far-reaching consequences, to the teaching and faithful witness of his old nurse.

Nevertheless, Samuel dismissed the servant before the actual anointing took place (verse 27). Here we have a picture of the great truth, that no human eye may witness the scene when the Lord, with the sanctifying grace of the Holy Spirit, anoints man **Gen. xlv. 1.** king ; he must be alone with his Master (cf. Gen. xlv. 1).

Saul finds a Kingdom

To receive such a high and noble honour man 1 Sam. ix. and x. 1. must bend himself in lowliest humility, and feel as Saul who exclaimed in astonishment: "*Am not I a Benjamite, of the smallest of the tribes of Israel? and my family the least of all the families of the tribe of Benjamin? Wherefore then speakest Thou to me after this manner?*" (verse 21). Then will the Saviour run and fall on his neck, and tenderly kiss him (St. Luke xv. 20 ; cf. 1 Sam. x. 1). Humility.

There will be indeed joy in heaven, and, above all, what joy to the King of Kings! for " the place that Jesus taketh in our soul He shall never remove it, without end as to my sight : for in us is His home-liest home, and His endless dwelling " (Lady Julian).

107

XI

THE IMPORTANCE OF ATMOSPHERE

When thou art departed from me to day, then thou shalt find two men by Rachel's sepulchre in the border of Benjamin at Zelzah; and they will say unto thee, The asses which thou wentest to seek are found: and, lo, thy father hath left the care of the asses, and sorroweth for you, saying, What shall I do for my son? Then shalt thou go on forward from thence, and thou shalt come to the plain of Tabor, and there shall meet thee three men going up to God to Beth-el, one carrying three kids, and another carrying three loaves of bread, and another carrying a bottle of wine: And they will salute thee, and give thee two *loaves* of bread; which thou shalt receive of their hands. After that thou shalt come to the hill of God, where *is* the garrison of the Philistines: and it shall come to pass, when thou art come thither to the city, that thou shalt meet a company of prophets coming down from the high place with a psaltery, and a tabret, and a pipe, and a harp, before them; and they shall prophesy: And the Spirit of the LORD will come upon thee, and thou shalt prophesy with them, and shalt be turned into another man. And let it be, when these signs are come unto thee, *that* thou do as occasion serve thee; for God *is* with thee. And thou shalt go down before me to Gilgal; and, behold, I will come down unto thee, to offer burnt offerings, *and* to sacrifice sacrifices of peace offerings: seven days shalt thou tarry, till I come to thee, and shew thee what thou shalt do.

And it was *so*, that when he had turned his back to go from Samuel, God gave him another heart: and all those signs came to pass that day. And when they came thither to the hill, behold, a company of prophets met him; and the Spirit of God came upon him, and he prophesied among them. And it came to pass, when all that knew him beforetime saw that, behold, he prophesied among the prophets, then the people said one to another, What *is* this *that* is come unto the son of Kish? *Is*

The Importance of Atmosphere

Saul also among the prophets ? And one of the same place answered and said, But who *is* their father ? Therefore it became a proverb, *Is* Saul also among the prophets ? And when he had made an end of prophesying, he came to the high place.

And Saul's uncle said unto him and to his servant, Whither went ye ? And he said, To seek the asses : and when we saw that *they were* no where, we came to Samuel. And Saul's uncle said, Tell me, I pray thee, what Samuel said unto you. And Saul said unto his uncle, He told us plainly that the asses were found. But of the matter of the kingdom, whereof Samuel spake, he told him not.

And Samuel called the people together unto the LORD to Mizpeh ; And said unto the children of Israel, Thus saith the LORD God of Israel, I brought up Israel out of Egypt, and delivered you out of the hand of the Egyptians, and out of the hand of all kingdoms, *and* of them that oppressed you : And ye have this day rejected your God, who himself saved you out of all your adversities and your tribulations ; and ye have said unto him, *Nay,* but set a king over us. Now therefore present yourselves before the LORD by your tribes, and by your thousands. And when Samuel had caused all the tribes of Israel to come near, the tribe of Benjamin was taken. When he had caused the tribe of Benjamin to come near by their families, the family of Matri was taken, and Saul the son of Kish was taken : and when they sought him, he could not be found. Therefore they enquired of the LORD further, if the man should yet come thither. And the LORD answered, Behold, he hath hid himself among the stuff. And they ran and fetched him thence : and when he stood among the people, he was higher than any of the people from his shoulders and upward. And Samuel said to all the people, See ye him whom the LORD hath chosen, that *there is* none like him among all the people ? And all the people shouted, and said, God save the king. Then Samuel told the people the manner of the kingdom, and wrote *it* in a book, and laid *it* up before the LORD. And Samuel sent all the people away, every man to his house.

And Saul also went home to Gibeah ; and there went with him a band of men, whose hearts God had touched. But the children of Belial said, How shall this man save us ? And they despised him, and brought him no presents. But he held his peace.

Then Nahash the Ammonite came up, and encamped against

Jabesh-gilead : and all the men of Jabesh said unto Nahash, Make a covenant with us, and we will serve thee. And Nahash the Ammonite answered them, On this *condition* will I make *a covenant* with you, that I may thrust out all your right eyes, and lay it *for* a reproach upon all Israel. And the elders of Jabesh said unto him, Give us seven days' respite, that we may send messengers unto all the coasts of Israel : and then, if *there be* no man to save us, we will come out to thee.

Then came the messengers to Gibeah of Saul, and told the tidings in the ears of the people : and all the people lifted up their voices, and wept. And, behold, Saul came after the herd out of the field ; and Saul said, What *aileth* the people that they weep ? And they told him the tidings of the men of Jabesh. And the Spirit of God came upon Saul when he heard those tidings, and his anger was kindled greatly. And he took a yoke of oxen, and hewed them in pieces, and sent *them* throughout all the coasts of Israel by the hands of messengers, saying, Whosoever cometh not forth after Saul and after Samuel, so shall it be done unto his oxen. And the fear of the LORD fell on the people, and they came out with one consent. And when he numbered them in Bezek, the children of Israel were three hundred thousand, and the men of Judah thirty thousand. And they said unto the messengers that came, Thus shall ye say unto the men of Jabesh-gilead, To morrow, by *that time* the sun be hot, ye shall have help. And the messengers came and shewed *it* to the men of Jabesh ; and they were glad. Therefore the men of Jabesh said, To morrow we will come out unto you, and ye shall do with us all that seemeth good unto you. And it was *so* on the morrow, that Saul put the people in three companies ; and they came into the midst of the host in the morning watch, and slew the Ammonites until the heat of the day : and it came to pass, that they which remained were scattered, so that two of them were not left together.

And the people said unto Samuel, Who *is* he that said, Shall Saul reign over us ? bring the men, that we may put them to death. And Saul said, There shall not a man be put to death this day : for to day the LORD hath wrought salvation in Israel. Then said Samuel to the people, Come, and let us go to Gilgal, and renew the kingdom there. And all the people went to Gilgal ; and there they made Saul king before the LORD in Gilgal ; and there they sacrificed sacrifices of peace offerings before the LORD ; and there Saul and all the men of Israel rejoiced greatly.—1 SAM. x. 2–xi.

The Importance of Atmosphere

Saul had been privately anointed King by Samuel; his public coronation had yet to come. Before the latter ceremony could take place, further signs must be given to Saul to prove that Samuel's choice was not of his own devising, but was directed by God.

1 Sam. x. 2–xi.

Saul's public coronation yet to follow.

The son of Kish had found a great kingdom, but a life of ease and magnificence was not to be his apportioned lot. Nay, rather was he raised up for the express purpose of "*saving his people out of the hand of the Philistines*" (ix. 16).

No life of ease before Saul.

For this task Saul's heart must undergo some preparation. His character needed to be disciplined by obedience. He was a man of moods and sudden impulses. To free the land of Israel from its foes, a leader was required who knew how to bide his time, and then, when the opportunity presented itself, to strike hard, without fear and without hesitation.

His heart must be prepared.

Soon after Saul had been acclaimed king by the people (x. 24) he went home to Gibeah, and there he must have remained a month (cf. x. 27, R.V. margin) before messengers arrived from Jabesh-Gilead with a cry for help, on account of the humiliating demands imposed upon its inhabitants by Nahash the Ammonite.

Saul's return home.

A cry of distress from Jabesh-Gilead.

Saul was following the oxen from the field when he heard the tidings of the desperate plight of the city of Jabesh-Gilead.

The time since he was made king had been long enough for him to resume his old life, and thereby learn to possess his soul in patience. The Lord's

Saul back at his old work.

1 Sam. x. 2–xi.

He needs to learn patience.

disciples had to undergo a very similar experience. After that first Easter Day, for a time the Risen Lord remained away from them. How they must have chafed at His absence! At last tired of waiting and inactivity, at Peter's suggestion they return to their old work of fishing. And whilst they were engaged in this occupation on the sea of Tiberias, the Lord again made His appearance. When men have found the kingdom, then it is that their real life-work begins. They may, and should, have peace of soul, but they are engaged in a continual warfare, from which there is no discharge on earth, with the foes which are still lurking within their own hearts, and with the problems, both social and spiritual, belonging to the city, the land, and the world, with all their crying needs.

There are times when, to all outward appearances, they must remain inactive, or be content just to lead a more or less commonplace existence. Years of preparation may precede the moment when a good blow is struck for God's cause, and those years call forth the utmost patience and endurance of which men are capable (cf. Exod. iii. 1 and Acts vii. 23–30).

And also enthusiasm.

Saul also needed enthusiasm. Patience and enthusiasm are not always linked together. Some natures will exert all their powers in a mighty effort, and then sink back, weary and exhausted, after their labours, and refuse to do anything more.

A steady enthusiasm is needed for God's work. Our Lord demands from His disciples a heart on fire, a heart wherein His love burns steadily, not

with fitful flicker, affording no reliable light or 1 **Sam. x.**
warmth. Saul must be filled with a steady and **2–xi.**
burning indignation against his country's oppressors,
if he is to infuse that feeling into others, and thus
be able to inspire them to come together as "*one
man*" (xi. 7). There is "virtue in a good hot
fire." Men are often despondent and inactive when
left to themselves; but once let those same men be
fired with enthusiasm for a righteous cause, and
under proper leadership they will carry all before
them. It was the Divine anger in Saul (xi. 6), Saul rallies
accompanied by the threat of the destruction of his
their oxen should the men prove defaulters, country-
symbolised by the hewing in pieces of the yoke of men.
oxen, which filled the people with a new spirit,
enabling them to smite the Ammonites and scatter
them in all directions, "*so that two of them were not
left together*" (xi. 11).

How was this enthusiasm engendered in the How the
case of Saul? The last of the three signs foretold enthusiasm
by Samuel after the anointing of Saul, and fulfilled was en-
as the new king returned to his home, will furnish gendered in
us with the answer to this question. Saul is Saul.
informed that no sooner shall he arrive at the hill
of God, where is the garrison of the Philistines,
than he shall meet a band of prophets coming down
from the high place (x. 5), and in their company the
Spirit of the Lord shall come mightily upon him,
and he shall be "*turned into another man.*"

Breathing for a time in their atmosphere, he will The
catch their spirit, and become such as they are. prophets.
Samuel's prediction came to pass, and the change

**1 Sam. x.
2–xi.**

**The effect
they pro-
duced on
Saul.**

wrought in Saul's character was of so remarkable a nature, that it became a proverb amongst the Israelites, when any man appeared in a new character, or assumed an unexpected rôle, "*Is Saul also among the prophets ?* " (cf. x. 12, xix. 24 ; cf. St. Matt. xiii. 54–57).

It may sound rather startling to compare these wandering prophets to the Flagellants of the Middle Ages, or to the Dervishes of to-day. (Dr. Moffatt, in his translation of 1 Sam. x., substitutes Dervishes for prophets ; cf. verses 5, 10, 11, and 12.) Of the latter, the late Professor Bliss wrote " that, through the quaint tales of a gentle-eyed sheikh in Jerusalem, he learnt past all forgetting, that in spite of the wild demonstration which travellers witness for a fee in Constantinople and Cairo, the controlling motive of the dervish life is the hunger and thirst after righteousness." [1] Be that as it may, lowly as the origins of prophecy may in some cases have been amongst the Israelites, it only throws into stronger relief the heights to which prophecy attained when fully controlled and educated by the Spirit of God, which drew from Lotze, one of the greatest thinkers of the nineteenth century, the remark, " Among the theocratic nations of the East, the Hebrews appear to us like sober men among drunkards. To the ancient world they doubtless seemed like dreamers among waking men."

These bands of wandering prophets were stirred

---

[1] *The Religions of Modern Syria and Palestine.* T. and T. Clark, Edinburgh, 1912. Preface, xi.

by a sense of their country's wrongs to a condition 1 Sam. x. almost bordering on frenzy, and thus kept alive 2—xi. the smouldering ashes of discontent, fanning into The con- a living flame the hope of freedom amongst a despair- tagion of ing people. Samuel foresaw that in their company their spirit. the new king's desire to save his country would be increased a hundredfold. No one who was with them for long could fail to be affected by their spirit. Their spiritual atmosphere was contagious (cf. xix. 20 ff.).

For God's work and for His cause the importance Importance of atmosphere cannot be overestimated. As in of atmo- the natural world a good healthy atmosphere is sphere. necessary for the growth of human beings and of trees, so is its spiritual counterpart equally necessary for the development of the soul's life. This truth may be illustrated in the spheres of the Home, the School, and the Church.

Man is born into a family. The earlier part of Seen in life is spent in a home. Parents are in duty bound the home. to talk to their children judiciously, and at the right time to tell them what is right and what is wrong in the conduct of their everyday lives, to instil into them firm principles of honour, truth, and godliness, in the practice of which lies the road to happiness ; and the inevitable consequences of an opposite course. This is quite a different thing from continual fault-finding, and merely " improving the occasion," which are exceedingly irritating to the child, and do not cease to be so when the child is grown up ! But the wisest talk from the most sympathetic parent is of no good if it stand alone.

1 Sam. x. 2–xi. It is the life of the parents, their unconscious as well as conscious acts, their words and ways when *off their guard ;*—it is these things which have the most telling effect upon their boys and girls. And moreover, they are often influenced the most when entirely unaware that they are being influenced at all. No word may have been consciously directed towards their " improvement." And it is the *spirit* of the place that tells ; and not only are the inmates thus affected, all those who are sensitive to their surroundings can soon feel when they enter a particular house whether it is a Christian home or otherwise, whether the spirit of peace and goodwill, or of discord and restlessness pervades the atmosphere. This will depend on the kind of people who rule the house. If their lives are hid with Christ in God, His Spirit will overshadow the place, and all within its influence will be encouraged and helped to follow in the way they should go.

The school. The same applies to the School. The *esprit de corps*, the tone of the school, are only different ways of saying that those who belong to it are being educated in a high moral atmosphere. In after years those same boys or girls, now grown up, may remember little of what they learnt, but they will be the first to attribute much of the good in them, and their attitude towards life, to the influences brought to bear upon them in those same school days.

The church. The church a man attends has also its particular kind of atmosphere. In some places of worship, irreverence, formality, the critical spirit, descend

116

The Importance of Atmosphere

upon their members and weigh them down. The
contrary may be the case. There is real devotion,
and it is easy on account of the stillness of the place
to know that it is indeed a House of Prayer. The
congregation is devout, and somehow the Living
Christ seems to be very near and very real.

1 Sam. x. 2–xi.

But in the last resort spiritual atmosphere depends
on the individual. Margaret in Goethe's *Faust*
says of Mephistopheles, though she does not know
who he is :

Spiritual atmosphere depends on the individual.

> " His presence chills my blood,
>   Towards all beside I have a kindly mood ;
>   That he's a villain my conviction's strong !
>   May heaven forgive me, if I do him wrong."

She feels depressed in his atmosphere. Others, like
St. Columba of old, need speak no word ; their very
presence in the fields or in a room brings with it
sunshine and peace.

Each Christian should carry with him an atmosphere which enables others to feel the nearness of
Christ, and perceive the beauty of goodness. This
is possible only when he has learnt to live habitually
in the Presence of God ; he may find it difficult to
express his inmost thoughts, but if he is living with
Christ, he will, more effectively than by many
sermons or much talking, help others to embrace his
Master's cause with enthusiasm and devotion.

What the Christian atmosphere should be.

XII

THE SUBLIMATION OF FEAR

And Samuel said unto all Israel, Behold, I have hearkened unto your voice in all that ye said unto me, and have made a king over you. And now, behold, the king walketh before you : and I am old and gray-headed ; and, behold, my sons *are* with you : and I have walked before you from my childhood unto this day. Behold, here I *am :* witness against me before the LORD, and before his anointed : whose ox have I taken ? or whose ass have I taken ? or whom have I defrauded ? whom have I oppressed ? or of whose hand have I received *any* bribe to blind mine eyes therewith ? and I will restore it you. And they said, Thou hast not defrauded us, nor oppressed us, neither hast thou taken ought of any man's hand. And he said unto them, The LORD *is* witness against you, and his anointed *is* witness this day, that ye have not found ought in my hand. And they answered, *He is* witness.

And Samuel said unto the people, *It is* the LORD that advanced Moses and Aaron, and that brought your fathers up out of the land of Egypt. Now therefore stand still, that I may reason with you before the LORD of all the righteous acts of the LORD, which he did to you and to your fathers. When Jacob was come into Egypt, and your fathers cried unto the LORD, then the LORD sent Moses and Aaron, which brought forth your fathers out of Egypt, and made them dwell in this place. And when they forgat the LORD their God, he sold them into the hand of Sisera, captain of the host of Hazor, and into the hand of the Philistines, and into the hand of the king of Moab, and they fought against them. And they cried unto the LORD, and said, We have sinned, because we have forsaken the LORD, and have served Baalim and Ashtaroth : but now deliver us out of the hand of our enemies, and we will serve thee. And the LORD sent Jerubbaal, and Bedan, and Jephthah, and Samuel, and delivered you out of the hand of your enemies on every side,

118

and ye dwelled safe. And when ye saw that Nahash the king of the children of Ammon came against you, ye said unto me, Nay; but a king shall reign over us: when the LORD your God *was* your king. Now therefore behold the king whom ye have chosen, *and* whom ye have desired! and, behold, the LORD hath set a king over you. If ye will fear the LORD, and serve him, and obey his voice, and not rebel against the commandment of the LORD, then shall both ye and also the king that reigneth over you continue following the LORD your God: But if ye will not obey the voice of the LORD, but rebel against the commandment of the LORD, then shall the hand of the LORD be against you, as *it was* against your fathers.

Now therefore stand and see this great thing, which the LORD will do before your eyes. *Is it* not wheat harvest to day? I will call unto the LORD, and he shall send thunder and rain; that ye may perceive and see that your wickedness *is* great, which ye have done in the sight of the LORD, in asking you a king. So Samuel called unto the LORD; and the LORD sent thunder and rain that day: and all the people greatly feared the LORD and Samuel. And all the people said unto Samuel, Pray for thy servants unto the LORD thy God, that we die not: for we have added unto all our sins *this* evil, to ask us a king.

And Samuel said unto the people, Fear not: ye have done all this wickedness: yet turn not aside from following the LORD, but serve the LORD with all your heart; And turn ye not aside: for *then should ye go* after vain *things*, which cannot profit nor deliver; for they *are* vain. For the LORD will not forsake his people for his great name's sake: because it hath pleased the LORD to make you his people. Moreover as for me, God forbid that I should sin against the LORD in ceasing to pray for you: but I will teach you the good and the right way: Only fear the LORD, and serve him in truth with all your heart: for consider how great *things* he hath done for you. But if ye shall still do wickedly, ye shall be consumed, both ye and your king.—1 SAM. XII.

THE public coronation of Israel's first king having **1 Sam.** been performed with all the impressive and religious **xii.** rites and ceremonies befitting such an occasion, in the presence of the assembled multitudes of the children of Israel, Samuel felt it incumbent upon

The First Book of Samuel

1 Sam.
xii.

Samuel's
solemn
farewell to
the people.

him to take a solemn farewell of the people. He had
handed over the reins of office to another, from
henceforth he would be in retirement, only to return
to public life at very rare intervals, when the king
and country felt their need of his wise statesman-
ship. The people might always rely upon him for
his best advice and his prayerful sympathy :
" *Moreover as for me, God forbid that I should sin
against the Lord in ceasing to pray for you : but
I will instruct you in the good and right way* "
(verse 23).

He passes in review his own tenure of office,
putting himself on trial, not without first alluding
to the reasons which determined the people to
choose a king. These were his increasing years,
and the government of his sons (verse 2), whose
misconduct is not spoken of in so many words, but
is just hinted at in the words " *and behold my sons
are with you.*"

Samuel stands at the bar of the people, with God
and " *His Anointed* " as the Judges. This reminds
us of another famous trial, which has been called
by Ewald " the great arraignment " ; it occurs in
the first chapter of Isaiah. In this case the positions
are reversed. It is the people who are on trial.
God is still the Judge ; He is also the Accuser,
speaking through the mouth of His servant and
prophet Isaiah.

The principles of justice are the same in both
cases. Stress is laid on righteousness, not ritual.
Samuel challenges the court to instance a single
occasion on which the perversion of justice has taken

120

place with his connivance. Can an example be **1 Sam.**
given, he asks, where he has been known to take a **xii.**
bribe ? " *Whose ox have I taken ? or whose ass have*
I taken ? " Contrary to the practice which pre-
vails in Eastern countries, he has never been known
to take advantage of his position, and give judgement
in favour of the rich as against the poor, thereby
laying himself open to the charge of fraud and
oppression, steadfastly refusing to receive gifts in
any form, according to the Septuagint even to the
extent " of a pair of shoes " ; that is, however small
and paltry the bribe might be (verse 3), the acceptance of which must " blind the eyes " of the receiver
(cf. Ex. xxiii. 8), every case which has come before
him he has striven to judge on its own merits, and
to deliver thereupon a just verdict. Should a
single instance of justice going astray be laid at his
door, he is prepared to make free and ample
restitution. Whereas in the second trial, related by
Isaiah, flagrant examples of injustice and oppression
were too well known for any attempt to be made at
defence, judgement went by default. In that of
Samuel, on the contrary, his contemporaries bore
testimony to his unfailing integrity and irreproach-
able character.

Samuel cared but little what the people might **His reasons**
think of him ; he would have subscribed with all **for this.**
his heart to the solemn truth that in the last resort
a man is not judged by his fellow-men, but stands
at the bar of God, and there receives His final
verdict. He was prompted to review his life before
the nation by his anxiety for their future welfare,

The First Book of Samuel

and that they should remain firm in their allegiance to God.

His real humility.

The charge of egotism cannot with justice be brought against Samuel. He who lives very closely to God loses all thought of self. He can declare what God has wrought in and through himself with perfect lack of bias or self-consciousness, with sense of due proportion, in the same spirit as he can relate the Divine dealings with another. The heights of humility rise nearest to the Throne of God. He who was the perfect pattern of humility said, " I do always those things which please Him," and " which of you convinceth Me of sin ? "

Samuel then proceeds to turn their thoughts away from himself to themselves. It was for this purpose that he desired them to pass an opinion on his rule. Everything that he had so far said was intended to lead up to this end.

He bids the people look back at their past history.

He bids them look back. What were the lessons their past history could teach them ? The figure of the trial is retained, but it is Samuel now who is conducting the case for the prosecution, the people have to stand on their defence. Samuel will reason with them before the Lord (verse 7). God is ever willing to reason with His people (Isa. i. 18). Unlike the god, or " allah," proclaimed by Muhammed, whose character resembles that of an Arabian chieftain or Oriental despot, Jehovah pleads with His children. His decisions, far from being arbitrary, exhibit His righteousness and mercy. Indifference, not reason, is the great foe of religion. It is better to think wrongly rather than not at all.

The Sublimation of Fear

The complaint is true now, as it was in the days of old. " My people doth not consider " (Isa. i. 3). Therefore it behoves us to stand still and listen awhile to that still small Voice pleading within our hearts (1 Kings xix. 12), and also to look out into the world at large and survey the course of human history, pondering over in our minds the moral order as witnessed to by the events of the world, the violation of which brings disaster in its train, and its acceptance, blessing and peace, so that we can exclaim, " Doubtless there is a God that judgeth the earth."

1 Sam. xii.

Isa. i. 3.

In pleading with his countrymen, Samuel insistently appeals to the marvellous deliverances wrought for them by the Hand of God, especially through Moses and Aaron, and subsequently by the Judges, raised up by Him for the ruling and salvation of His chosen people (verses 6–12).

Let them think of their great deliverances.

To the Israelite of those times (and to his successor of to-day), the freeing of his forefathers from the cruel bondage of Egypt has ever appeared to be the crowning act of God's redeeming mercy and power. The bare recital of it would kindle his faith anew, and raise his hopes, as well as inspire him to fresh courage and endeavour, no matter how the heathen might furiously rage around him, and the forces of evil threaten to overwhelm his land or his people. The remembrance of what took place at the Red Sea enabled God's people to view the events of the world around them at whatever epoch in their true perspective.

The Deliverance from Egypt.

Let us look at this now from the Christian stand-

1 Sam.
xii.

The
Christian's
great De-
liverance.

Via Crucis,
Via Lucis.

point, and see the "reasonable" effects of the far
greater Deliverance wrought for all the world, when
Christ our Passover was sacrificed for us, and by
virtue of His Death and Resurrection became our
Leader through this world's wilderness, to the
Heavenly Land, the Conqueror over every foe.

Via Crucis, Via Lucis. Many things blurred and
confused to us, when read in the light of that great
Sacrifice, become clear and plain. In recent years
the remark has frequently been made, Why did not
God stop the war? why should so many innocent
people suffer? they have done no wrong. This
difficulty is centuries old. Very similar language
was used at Calvary, "If Thou be the Son of God,
come down from the Cross, and we will believe"
(St. Matt. xxvii. 40). "He trusted in God, let
Him deliver Him now, if He will have Him: for
He said, I am the Son of God" (St. Matt. xxvii.
43). God will not and cannot save men from sin
and its consequences *in spite of themselves*, and by
violent methods: His way is to appeal to their
higher and better selves to lead the life of love
issuing forth in self-sacrifice. Had men pondered
more deeply upon the message and meaning of
that great Deliverance wrought upon the Altar of
the Cross, at least they would have learnt that God
does not stand aside and view the sin of the world
as an unconcerned spectator, but that He has
entered into the world's agony and sin, and bears
its burden and weight upon His heart. Jesus Christ
has drained to its dregs the world's cup of misery
and woe: "In all their afflictions He was afflicted."

The Sublimation of Fear

He, the Holy and Just One, has suffered for the unjust (1 St. Pet. iii. 18). Not in letters of gold, but of blood, the truth has been written, that the world lives by the vicarious death of the just and the innocent. As a modern writer on ethics, the late Professor Paulsen, has observed, " The text to the sermon which is called the history of mankind, is the text to the Good Friday sermon from the fifty-third chapter of the Prophet Isaiah." [1]

1 Sam. xii.

The vicarious death of the just and innocent.

The Cross, as nothing else can, quickens the conscience. As we come to the Holy Communion, and partake of the Holy Bread and poured-out Wine, peace comes to our hearts, unutterable peace, from the sense of sins forgiven, for our inquity is laid upon Him, our Ransomer and Ransom, our High Priest and Sacrifice. Our consciences are purged and quickened, and we go away in the strength of that most sacred of all memories, and of that Divine Food, to battle anew with the forces without and within us. This peace and inspiration of the Christian are, as we well know, not confined to any holy time or season, but are, should be, always with us. The Cross is no silken cushion on which the Christian may recline and take his rest, but rather may it be likened unto the cordial given to weary men, strengthening them afresh to fight the battles of their Lord.

The Cross no silken cushion.

The children of Israel having been reminded of their great Deliverance, Samuel proceeds to tell them how short-lived were the memories of their

Samuel revives the people's memories.

---

[1] *A System of Ethics.* London : Kegan Paul, Trench, Trübner & Co., Ltd. 1899. E. T. p. 159.

The First Book of Samuel

forefathers, " *They forgat the Lord* " (verse 9) ; the result being that degeneration and decay set in which sapped their national vigour and powers of resistance. Beset as they were by enemies on all sides, they could not withstand them : " *He sold them into the hand of Sisera, captain of the host of Hazor, and into the hand of the Philistines, and into the hand of the King of Moab* " (verse 9). Then they cried unto the Lord, and on their true repentance He heard them in their distress. Jerubbaal or Gideon, Bedan, probably Barak, Jephthah and Samuel himself (verse 11) were raised up by God to breathe fresh courage into their hearts, and lead them on to victory.

His allusion to their past faithlessness.
Once more Samuel alludes to their faithlessness in insisting upon a king to reign over them. " *Nay, but a king shall reign over us : when the Lord your God was your king* " (verse 12).

The great lesson their history teaches them.
At length Samuel reaches the great lesson which their past history had proved, and which, if learnt, would provide them with their best security for the future. Fear the Lord and serve Him in truth with all your heart, and obey His Voice (verses 14, 24), and you will have nothing to fear (cf. verse 20).

Should, however, the fear of God be lost sight of in your national life, you will have reason then to know what fear is, for you will be faced with utter destruction, both ye and your king (verse 25).

Samuel's call upon God.
Then comes the climax. Samuel calls upon God to attest to the truth of his words. During May and June, the time of the wheat harvest in Palestine, rain very rarely fell. Thunder and rain were sent.

The Sublimation of Fear

Thus was pronounced the Divine Amen to the message of the aged Prophet.

1 Sam. xii.

"*The fear of God.*" How continually that phrase meets us in the Bible! a long history lies behind the conception. In its lower form, of the terror inspired by the threat of severe punishment for disregarding, and acting against, the Divine Commands, we meet it in this chapter. As time went on, however, the people would discover that Samuel's words were susceptible of a higher interpretation. The fear would be turned into awe and reverence. It will then denote the attitude befitting a son who looks up to his father with the deepest respect and love. The bare thought of what his father will think will act as a restraint, should he be inclined to yield to temptation. To him the severest punishment will not be any pain or penalties which his parent may inflict upon him, but the sorrow and shame his unfilial conduct will bring upon him who is his best friend. The memory of that look which the Master bestowed upon Peter when he had denied Him, must often have acted as a restraining or compelling influence upon the Apostle in after years. In fact, if we desire to learn, and still more to practise, the virtue of Holy Fear, we cannot do better than turn to the Epistle which bears his name. By him are we bidden to pass the time of our sojourning here in fear (1 St. Pet. i. 17), and whilst honouring all men, and loving the brotherhood, we are exhorted to fear God (ii. 17).

The Fear of God has various meanings.

Holy Fear and the First Epistle of St. Peter.

One of the great mistakes of to-day is that so many people consider that the world has outgrown

The necessity of

The First Book of Samuel

1 Sam.
xii.
the appeal
to the lower
form of fear
not yet
abolished.

It is found
in Christ's
teaching.

the necessity of the appeal to the lower form of
fear. Our Lord did not hesitate to make use of it
(St. Matt. x. 28; St. Luke xii. 5), not only once,
but both in the Sermon on the Mount, and in His
parables, *e.g.* the Rich Man and Lazarus, and the
Talents. We dare, at our peril, to trifle with Him
with Whom we have to do. Nature has no mercy
on those who presume to take liberties with her.
If a man plays with dynamite, he must be prepared to pay the price should his amusement cost
him his life. The God of Nature and of Revelation
is one God. There are not two Gods.

Robert Burns may write that—

> "The fear o' hell's a hangsman whip
> To haud the wretch in order,"

but well had it been for him had he possessed that
fear; it would have saved his life from ending in
misery and ruin.

But it is Fear in its highest form, a holy Austerity,
which is clean and endureth for ever (Ps. xix. 9).
The verse of the old hymn may not be, as the Dean
of Chester, Dr. Bennett, remarks: "very good
poetry, but it is very good science":

> "Fear Him, ye Saints, and you will then
> Have nothing else to fear;
> Make you His service your delight,
> Your wants shall be His care."

In modern phrasing, the best fear of God will be
the sublimation of all fear.

128

The Sublimation of Fear

To-day we are reminded that every instinct is 1 Sam. xii. primarily directed towards a definite and specific end which is of real value to the animal's life. But Sublimation: its meaning. in course of time, as man has advanced in civilisation, some of those ends have become more easily attained than they could be in past ages. The result is that the full strength of the original instinct has not been used, because not required, hence the large amount of primitive energy which is " going loose." This surplus, which a boy or a man has at his disposal, may be treated of in three different ways.

It may be squandered on objects both harmful to himself and to his fellow-beings. Or it may be hidden away " repressed." But at any moment the temptation may prove irresistible, and the repressed force surge from the depths of the subconscious life, to be flung broadcast, regardless of consequences. The remaining alternative is to reinvest this surplus energy in purposes of lasting benefit to the individual concerned, and to society at large. This last is called the process of sublimation.[1]

Fear is an instinct of inestimable value and im- Fear is an instinct. portance. Without it, primitive man, beset on all sides by innumerable dangers, could never have survived the struggle for existence. As society developed, she was able to exercise an ever-increasing protection over her members, and thereby reduce to an extraordinary extent the grounds for fear,

[1] Cf. the chapter on Sublimation in *Psychology and Morals*, by J. A. Hadfield (J. Methuen & Co., London, 1924), 4th edition, which has been largely made use of in this part of our chapter.

The First Book of Samuel

Civilisation cannot destroy it.

hard for us to realise who live in a civilised and well-ordered community. But this primitive instinct of dread will always remain with us.

"Through the Jungle very softly
    Flits a shadow and a sigh—
    He is fear, O little hunter, he is fear !
    Very softly down the glade runs a waiting, watching
        shade,
    And the whisper spreads and widens far and near,
    And the sweat is on thy brow, for he passes even now—
    He is fear, O little hunter, he is fear."

Which of us does not appreciate these lines of Mr. Rudyard Kipling's ? But further, in consequence of our increased protection against external foes, many of us have a large surplus of fear at our disposal.

It appears in many forms.

Too often we expend it, almost against our will, on unworthy objects. It may be an inordinate fear of what other people may say, fear of the unknown, fear of the future, fear of what may happen to those we love, fear of responsibility, not to mention all those " phobias, like agoraphobia (the fear of open spaces), claustrophobia (the fear of closed spaces), and a thousand other fears for which the Greek language is impotent to provide names." [1] The best method is to redirect all these fears to God, by transforming them into that alertness of mind and will which is bent on His service, and reposes on His watchful care and guidance.

Redirect our fears to God.

How He transforms them.

Fear of the unknown. Science has not abolished

[1] Cf. Hadfield, *op. cit.*, p. 154.

it, for death is to her a great mystery, the secrets 1 Sam. xii. of which she is powerless to unveil, but with regard to this we may quote Samuel's words, "*The Lord will not forsake His people for His great Name's sake*" (1 Sam. xii. 22). Christ has come, and has Himself abolished death and brought light and immortality to light through the Gospel (2 Tim. i. 10). He has assured us that in His Father's house are many mansions (St. John xiv. 2). Through the valley of the shadow of death we shall be accompanied by Him Who is the Resurrection and the Life, and therefore we need not be afraid.

Again, as to the fear of what others may say, When man ceases to be afraid. the saying of an old writer is true : " It is the fear of God that makes men fearless, and the fear of man that makes men cowards." Samuel is an illustration of this ; he was not afraid of the people because he feared God. Continual seeking after God's approval makes us more and more independent of man's praise, so that when necessary we shall not be afraid to take the unpopular line, if only we can be assured that it is right.

It is told of Charles Spurgeon that once on driving home to Clapham, he suddenly, and without any assignable cause, burst out into a fit of hilarious laughter. It had suddenly struck him how absurd it was to be filled with apprehension and worry, as he had been that morning, when he had such a splendid word as this upon which to lean : " My grace is sufficient for thee." Man ceases to be afraid when he hears the Son of Man say, " It is I ; be not afraid." And who has a better right to say

**1 Sam.
xii.**

Heb. v. 7.

these words, seeing that " in the days of His flesh, having offered up prayers and supplications with strong crying and tears unto Him that was able to save Him from death," He was " heard for His godly fear " ? (Heb. v. 7).

XIII

OBEDIENCE AND WORSHIP

Saul reigned one year; and when he had reigned two years over Israel, Saul chose him three thousand *men* of Israel; *whereof* two were with Saul in Michmash and in mount Beth-el, and a thousand were with Jonathan in Gibeah of Benjamin: and the rest of the people he sent every man to his tent. And Jonathan smote the garrison of the Philistines that *was* in Geba, and the Philistines heard *of it*. And Saul blew the trumpet throughout all the land, saying, Let the Hebrews hear. And all Israel heard say *that* Saul had smitten a garrison of the Philistines, and *that* Israel also was had in abomination with the Philistines. And the people were called together after Saul to Gilgal.

And the Philistines gathered themselves together to fight with Israel, thirty thousand chariots, and six thousand horsemen, and people as the sand which *is* on the sea shore in multitude: and they came up, and pitched in Michmash, eastward from Beth-aven. When the men of Israel saw that they were in a strait, (for the people were distressed,) then the people did hide themselves in caves, and in thickets, and in rocks, and in high places, and in pits. And *some of* the Hebrews went over Jordan to the land of Gad and Gilead. As for Saul, he *was* yet in Gilgal, and all the people followed him trembling.

And he tarried seven days, according to the set time that Samuel *had appointed:* but Samuel came not to Gilgal; and the people were scattered from him. And Saul said, Bring hither a burnt offering to me, and peace offerings. And he offered the burnt offering. And it came to pass, that as soon as he had made an end of offering the burnt offering, behold, Samuel came; and Saul went out to meet him, that he might salute him.

And Samuel said, What hast thou done? And Saul said, Because I saw that the people were scattered from me, and

The First Book of Samuel

that thou camest not within the days appointed, and *that* the Philistines gathered themselves together at Michmash; Therefore said I, The Philistines will come down now upon me to Gilgal, and I have not made supplication unto the LORD: I forced myself therefore, and offered a burnt offering. And Samuel said to Saul, Thou hast done foolishly: thou hast not kept the commandment of the LORD thy God, which he commanded thee: for now would the LORD have established thy kingdom upon Israel for ever. But now thy kingdom shall not continue: the LORD hath sought him a man after his own heart, and the LORD hath commanded him *to be* captain over his people, because thou hast not kept *that* which the LORD commanded thee. And Samuel arose, and gat him up from Gilgal unto Gibeah of Benjamin. And Saul numbered the people *that were* present with him, about six hundred men. And Saul, and Jonathan his son, and the people *that were* present with them, abode in Gibeah of Benjamin: but the Philistines encamped in Michmash.

And the spoilers came out of the camp of the Philistines in three companies: one company turned unto the way *that leadeth to* Ophrah, unto the land of Shual: and another company turned the way *to* Beth-horon: and another company turned *to* the way of the border that looketh to the valley of Zeboim toward the wilderness.

Samuel also said unto Saul, The LORD sent me to anoint thee *to be* king over his people, over Israel: now therefore hearken thou unto the voice of the words of the LORD. Thus saith the LORD of hosts, I remember *that* which Amalek did to Israel, how he laid *wait* for him in the way, when he came up from Egypt. Now go and smite Amalek, and utterly destroy all that they have, and spare them not: but slay both man and woman, infant and suckling, ox and sheep, camel and ass. And Saul gathered the people together, and numbered them in Telaim, two hundred thousand footmen, and ten thousand men of Judah. And Saul came to a city of Amalek, and laid wait in the valley.

And Saul said unto the Kenites, Go, depart, get you down from among the Amalekites, lest I destroy you with them: for ye shewed kindness to all the children of Israel, when they came up out of Egypt. So the Kenites departed from among the Amalekites. And Saul smote the Amalekites from Havilah *until* thou comest to Shur, that *is* over against Egypt. And he

134

Obedience and Worship

took Agag the king of the Amalekites alive, and utterly destroyed all the people with the edge of the sword. But Saul and the people spared Agag, and the best of the sheep, and of the oxen, and of the fatlings, and the lambs, and all *that was* good, and would not utterly destroy them : but every thing *that was* vile and refuse, that they destroyed utterly.

Then came the word of the LORD unto Samuel, saying, It repenteth me that I have set up Saul *to be* king : for he is turned back from following me, and hath not performed my commandments. And it grieved Samuel ; and he cried unto the LORD all night. And when Samuel rose early to meet Saul in the morning, it was told Samuel, saying, Saul came to Carmel, and, behold, he set him up a place, and is gone about, and passed on, and gone down to Gilgal. And Samuel came to Saul : and Saul said unto him, Blessed *be* thou of the LORD : I have performed the commandment of the LORD. And Samuel said, What *meaneth* then this bleating of the sheep in mine ears, and the lowing of the oxen which I hear ? And Saul said, They have brought them from the Amalekites : for the people spared the best of the sheep and of the oxen, to sacrifice unto the LORD thy God ; and the rest we have utterly destroyed. Then Samuel said unto Saul, Stay, and I will tell thee what the LORD hath said to me this night. And he said unto him, Say on. And Samuel said, When thou *wast* little in thine own sight, *wast* thou not *made* the head of the tribes of Israel, and the LORD anointed thee king over Israel ? And the LORD sent thee on a journey, and said, Go and utterly destroy the sinners the Amalekites, and fight against them until they be consumed. Wherefore then didst thou not obey the voice of the LORD, but didst fly upon the spoil, and didst evil in the sight of the LORD ? And Saul said unto Samuel, Yea, I have obeyed the voice of the LORD, and have gone the way which the LORD sent me, and have brought Agag the king of Amalek, and have utterly destroyed the Amalekites. But the people took of the spoil, sheep and oxen, the chief of the things which should have been utterly destroyed, to sacrifice unto the LORD thy God in Gilgal. And Samuel said, Hath the LORD *as great* delight in burnt offerings and sacrifices, as in obeying the voice of the LORD ? Behold, to obey *is* better than sacrifice, *and* to hearken than the fat of rams. For rebellion *is as* the sin of witchcraft, and stubbornness *is as* iniquity and idolatry. Because thou hast rejected the word of the LORD, he hath also rejected thee from *being* king.

The First Book of Samuel

And Saul said unto Samuel, I have sinned : for I have transgressed the commandment of the LORD, and thy words : because I feared the people, and obeyed their voice. Now therefore, I pray thee, pardon my sin, and turn again with me, that I may worship the LORD. And Samuel said unto Saul, I will not return with thee : for thou hast rejected the word of the LORD, and the LORD hath rejected thee from being king over Israel. And as Samuel turned about to go away, he laid hold upon the skirt of his mantle, and it rent. And Samuel said unto him, The LORD hath rent the kingdom of Israel from thee this day, and hath given it to a neighbour of thine, *that is* better than thou. And also the Strength of Israel will not lie nor repent : for he *is* not a man, that he should repent. Then he said, I have sinned : *yet* honour me now, I pray thee, before the elders of my people, and before Israel and turn again with me, that I may worship the LORD thy God. So Samuel turned again after Saul ; and Saul worshipped the LORD.

Then said Samuel, Bring ye hither to me Agag the king of the Amalekites. And Agag came unto him delicately. And Agag said, Surely the bitterness of death is past. And Samuel said, As thy sword hath made women childless, so shall thy mother be childless among women. And Samuel hewed Agag in pieces before the LORD in Gilgal.

Then Samuel went to Ramah : and Saul went up to his house to Gibeah of Saul. And Samuel came no more to see Saul until the day of his death : nevertheless Samuel mourned for Saul : and the LORD repented that he had made Saul king over Israel.
—1 SAM. XIII. and XV.

1 Sam. xiii. and xv.

Saul's standing army.

Hostilities break out between the Israelites and the Philistines.

AFTER Saul had reigned for some years he took the important step of forming the nucleus of a standing army. It only numbered three thousand strong, two-thirds of which he placed under his own command in Michmash, north of Jerusalem, and the remainder under Jonathan at Gibeah (xiii. 2).

Hostilities broke out afresh between the Israelites and the Philistines, owing to Jonathan, in pursuance of his father's orders, having smitten the garrison of the Philistines in Geba (verse 3). This was the

136

Obedience and Worship

beginning of the campaign against the Philistines 1 Sam.
which continued throughout Saul's reign (xiv. 52), xiii. and
and it also formed the rallying cry for the assembling xv.
of the Israelites at Gilgal, close to Jericho, where
they gathered together after Saul (xiii. 4).

In the meanwhile the enemy did not remain idle. The
Enormous forces were gathered together, which have strength of
been computed at thirty thousand chariots (but a the Philis-
lower number is more probable, three thousand or tines.
even a thousand chariots), and six thousand horsemen, the infantry being so numerous that they were
compared to the sand on the seashore. This vast
host took up its position at Michmash, probably
because Saul had felt it advisable to withdraw any
troops he had there, and concentrate on Gilgal.

As it was, the *morale* of the Israelites was The morale
thoroughly shaken. They felt quite unable to of the
encounter such vast numbers. Many of them, in Israelites.
consequence, took refuge in any hiding-places they
could find (verse 6), others crossed the River Jordan
to Gad and Gilead, whilst of those who were with
Saul, each day that passed by saw their numbers
diminish, so that in the end the thousands had
dwindled to hundreds (verse 15).

When Samuel anointed Saul to be king, after he Samuel's
had foretold to him what should immediately injunctions
follow, he admonished him as to the steps he should to Saul.
take. He was to meet him at Gilgal, tarrying for
him seven days, when he, Samuel, would come and
offer up burnt offerings and peace offerings, and
show him what he should do. On no account must
Saul make any move independent of Samuel (x. 8).

137

The First Book of Samuel

1 Sam.
xiii. and
xv.

Saul's
critical
position.

The first part of Samuel's command had been carried out by Saul. He had gone to Gilgal, and, what is more, had waited for him seven days. Still there was no appearance of Samuel, and as each day passed by, Saul saw that his position was becoming more and more critical. Desertions from his army on a large scale were of constant occurrence. Within a few miles of him were assembled the forces of the opposing side. The situation had become desperate. Strike, Saul felt he must, and at once, otherwise soon no fighting men would be left to

He disobeys
Samuel.

him. He must proceed to take the law into his own hands, he would entreat the Lord to favour their cause, and, contrary to Samuel's instructions, offer up the necessary sacrifices.

In this he
acts
foolishly.

By so doing Saul acted foolishly. He was a soldier, and ought to have known that an order was an order, and that the command of a superior must be carried out in spite of consequences. To Samuel, under God, he owed his kingdom. Further, he should have remembered the past history of his nation. He had forgotten Gideon, whose example Samuel had cited in his farewell speech (xii. 11), how his army of twenty-two thousand men had been reduced to three hundred, and had to oppose the Midianites, " like locusts for multitude, and their camels without number, and their army as the sand

God is left
out of his
reckoning.

which is on the sea shore " (Judges vii. 12). Nevertheless the Lord had discomfited the hosts of Midian, and delivered them into the hands of Gideon. What God had wrought for His people in those days, He could accomplish now for Saul. Good had it been for Saul had he prayed the prayer of a certain king, when about to engage an army five times as great as his own : " O Lord, take away from me the sense of numbers." 1 Sam. xiii. and xv.

But even if the entire available strength of his country could have been placed at Saul's disposal, his army would have remained very inferior to that of the enemy. His sole hope of success lay in the introduction of another factor, and that factor was Almighty God. With Him as shield and rereward, there could be nothing to fear.

At length Samuel arrived at Gilgal, and in the answer to his inquiry, " *What hast thou done ?* " (verse 11), his worst fears concerning the fitness of Saul for the work entrusted to him by God were confirmed. Under such a king the country could not prosper, it could not receive the Divine Blessing. A people chosen by God must have a ruler in sympathy with God. The Kingdom then could not continue in Saul's family (verse 14). It must be given to another. Samuel's arrival at Gilgal.

Sternly Samuel pronounced sentence : " *Thy kingdom shall not continue : The Lord hath sought Him a man after His own heart, and the Lord hath appointed him to be prince over His people* " (verse 14). The sentence was severe, but not too severe when viewed in the light of Saul's reign as a whole. His sentence upon Saul.

No actual battle is recorded, but the oppression of the Israelites by the Philistines continued to be very grievous, and their military domination over the land was complete.

Let it be noted here that Saul's sacrifice at Gilgal The uselessness of

The First Book of Samuel

1 Sam.
xiii. and
xv.

Saul's
sacrifice at
Gilgal.

Saul's
encounter
with the
Amalekites.

was rendered useless by his disobedience. Worship and obedience must go hand-in-hand. The first without the second is worse than useless : " If I regard iniquity in my heart, the Lord will not hear " (Ps. lxvi. 18).

Besides the Philistines, Saul had to contend with other foes, and in this direction his efforts were attended with a considerable amount of success. The sacred writer contents himself with giving a short summary of his wars, not going into any detail (xiv. 47–49, 52), with one exception—Saul's encounter with the Amalekites.

Their utter
destruction
is com-
manded.

In accordance with Samuel's instructions he was to go up against the Amalekites, and inflict upon them such a crushing defeat as they should never be able to recover, thus would they cease to be a source of trouble to God's people for ever (1 Sam. xv.). Measures of the most extreme kind were commanded. No prisoners were to be taken, no quarter allowed. He was bidden " *utterly to destroy all that they have, and spare them not* " (xv. 3). The word translated " utterly destroy " literally means " devote." This refers to the " sacred ban " (Heb. ḥérem) by which the enemies of the community, and their god, were devoted to destruction. It included " the utter destruction, not only of the persons involved, but of their property ; and only metals, after they had passed through the fire, were added to the treasure of the sanctuary (Josh. vi. 24, vii. 24 ; 1 Sam. xv.)." [1]

The
" sacred
ban."

[1] Professor Robertson Smith, *Lectures on the Religion of the Semites*. First Series. London : Adam & Charles Black. New and revised edition, 1907, p. 454.

Obedience and Worship

Terrible to us as is this "sacred ban"; it con- tained within it the promise of better days, when xiii. and war should be no more. A religious war must xv. never be prosecuted for the sake of material gain, or the acquirement of treasure. It lent itself to the idea that war could only have any shadow of justification when waged for the purposes of defence, or to prevent grave injustices from arising. It cut at the root of many wars which have been waged in the interests of high finance.

In the past the Amalekites had gone out of their The cruelty way in their hostility and cruelty towards the chosen of the people. When the Israelites were come out of Amalekites in the past. Egypt, the Amalekites, taking advantage of their weakness and weariness, had swooped down upon them, cutting off any stragglers and defenceless Israelites who happened to be separated from the main body (Deut. xxv. 18).

At Telaim or Telem in the south of Judah, Saul Saul defeats gathered together a strong army (1 Sam. xv. 4), the went up against the city of Amalek, and utterly Amalekites. routed the enemy. He had previously warned the Kenites who dwelt amongst them to separate themselves from them. Saul could not forget the kindness the Kenites had shown to his countrymen in the past (verse 6).

The victory over the Amalekites was complete. Agag and Saul, however, spared Agag, and the best of the the best of the spoil are sheep, oxen and fatlings, destroying only everything spared. that was vile and refuse (verse 9). Once more Not from Saul disobeyed Samuel, not from feelings of motives of humanity, be it observed, for the women and humanity.

141

1 Sam. xiii. and xv.

children were not spared.[1] Saul believed, equally with Samuel, that the complete extermination of the Amalekites had been decreed by Almighty God, and to neither of them would this command constitute the serious moral difficulty that it does to us. The inwardness of Saul's action consisted in his wilful disobedience of the Divine command as he conceived it to be, and the rejection by God which ensued, turned on this, and this alone. Saul was knowingly false to the light given to him. He had set up his own will in opposition to the Will of God as it had been declared to him. Herein lay the heinousness of his offence.

Saul's wilful disobedience.

Samuel's second arrival at Gilgal.

As soon as Samuel learnt of Saul's disobedience, he set out with a heavy heart to meet Saul and acquaint him of the Divine displeasure. For the second time he was the harbinger of judgement and doom.

Saul's excuses of no avail.

It was at Gilgal that the historic encounter between Saul and the aged Prophet took place. Saul hastened to greet him with the news that he had performed the commandment of the Lord. Hardly had the words escaped his lips, than Samuel sternly demanded the meaning of the sounds which reached his ears : " *What meaneth then this bleating of the sheep in mine ears, and the lowing of the oxen which I hear ?* " (verse 14). Saul was taken aback, and stammered out the excuse that the people were to blame, disclaiming, as he had no right to do, any responsibility for their action ; and urging that the spoil had been spared " *to sacrifice unto the Lord*

Cf. Professor Peake's *Commentary on the Bible*, p. 280.

Obedience and Worship

thy God" (verse 15). These excuses were brushed 1 **Sam.**
on one side by the Prophet, and when again brought **xiii.** and
forward by Saul, Samuel was inspired to formulate **xv.**
the law which underlies all spiritual worship, in
language which will never be forgotten, so long as
the Bible is studied and honoured. "*Hath the Lord* The Prophet
as great delight in burnt offerings and sacrifices, as in enunciates
obeying the voice of the Lord? Behold, to obey is an eternal
better than sacrifice, and to hearken than the fat of truth.
rams. For rebellion is as the sin of witchcraft, and
stubbornness is as idolatry and teraphim" (verses 22,
23).

This reply is cast in a rhythmical form, and considering its importance we give Professor H. P.
Smith's translation :

"Does Yahweh delight in offerings and sacrifices
  As in obedience to the voice of Yahweh ?
  Behold, obedience is better than sacrifice,
  And to hearken than the fat of rams.
  For rebellion is the sin of soothsaying,
  Obstinacy is the iniquity of Teraphim.[1]
  Because thou hast rejected the word of Yahweh,
  He has rejected thee from ruling over Israel."

Saul had been rejected by God, and at once he Saul is
acknowledged his guilt, and alleged that his trans- rejected by
gression was due to fear of the people. Coupled God.
with his confession was the request that Samuel
would both pardon his sin, and accompany him that
he might worship the Lord. The Prophet refused

[1] Teraphim were images associated with divination. Yahweh
is the more correct form of Jehovah.

The First Book of Samuel

to go with him, and as he turned away Saul laid hold of his skirt or tunic, "*and it rent*" (verse 27). *And Samuel said to him, The Lord hath rent the kingdom of Israel from thee this day, and hath given it to a neighbour of thine, that is better than thou*" (verse 28). But from pity for the rejected king (for Samuel possessed a very tender heart, cf. "*nevertheless Samuel mourned for Saul*," verse 35), he consented to go back and worship with him in the presence of the people (verse 31).

Agag is slain.

After this Samuel commanded that Agag should be brought before him. The latter came to him "delicately," or, according to Dr. Moffatt's excellent translation, "*with tottering footsteps*" (verse 32). There and then Agag met his death at the hands of Samuel.

Saul's disobedience on both occasions connected with worship.

Twice had Saul disobeyed God, and on both occasions his disobedience was connected with worship. His conduct in each case manifests the eternal truth, which the passing of the ages illumines rather than obscures, that in man's approach to God it is his attitude of mind and will that counts beyond all else.

Outward forms and ceremonies have their rightful place, but in importance they are far exceeded by the moral disposition and state of heart of the worshipper.

Worship, its meaning in general terms.

Worship is a very large subject, and as it does not appear in the First Book of Samuel under the particular form of adoration where the worshipper forgets himself and his needs in the realisation " of the full nearness of God's majesty in its beatitude

Obedience and Worship

and awefulness," [1] (an experience, however, by no means unknown to the Old Testament saints,) it will not be touched upon here.

I Sam. xiii. and xv.

Without attempting a definition of the word, worship, in general terms, includes all practices of prayer, intercession, thanksgiving, and praise offered up to God by the individual in private, or by the congregation. Three elements, essential to all true spiritual worship, are borne in upon the reader by a study of this first book of Samuel.

Three essential elements in worship.

First, that the worshipper entertain a true conception of God (cf. Heb. xi. 6). In this fifteenth chapter of the first book of Samuel occur these words, " *The Strength* (' The splendour,' Dr. Moffatt) *of Israel will not lie nor repent : for He is not a man, that He should repent* " (verse 29). Unlike the heathen gods, the One and only true God is not capricious, at one time gracious, at another displeased for no reason. Nor is He changeable, as a man whose moods vary from day to day, even from hour to hour (Num. xxiii. 19 ; Isa. xlv. 5, lv. 8, 9 ; Mal. iii. 6 ; Rom. xi. 29). He is ever the same (Ps. cii. 27 ; 1 Cor. xii. 5), and in the perfect Disclosure of Himself to man, Jesus Christ, we know that " He is the same yesterday and to day, yea and for ever " (Heb. xiii. 8).

(1) A true conception of God.

But now we are brought face to face with the greatest difficulty in the book. Is the God, Who through Samuel directed Saul utterly to destroy the Amalekites, and not even to spare their women

We are faced by a moral difficulty.

[1] R. Otto, *The Idea of the Holy*, E. T. (Humphrey Milford, Oxford University Press, 1923), p. 220.

**1 Sam.
xiii. and
xv.**

and children, the same God revealed to us in the Person of our Blessed Lord ? Could the Saviour Himself have given such an order ? The question has only to be stated to receive its most emphatic denial.

God's character is ever the same, but man's understanding of that character is progressive. The education of the human race in the knowledge of God is of very slow growth. As truth has to be adapted to the intelligence of the child, as distinct from that of the man, in like manner that which is suitable to the childhood of the race will not be quite the same in its more developed stages.

Neither Samuel nor Saul would consider the individual, apart from the tribe or clan to which he belonged. When the mandate went forth that the Israelites should go and subdue the Amalekites, it would be interpreted by Samuel as tantamount to ordering their entire destruction from off the face of the earth.

**The Divine
Message
and the
human
medium.**

The human medium does affect the Divine message through which it passes. The most perfect musician is dependent upon the quality and tone of his instrument, and God has willed to submit Himself to similar conditions when He uses human instruments for the expression of His purposes. Hence the necessity and reasonableness of the Incarnation. A life without spot or flaw alone can be the perfect medium for the supreme Revelation of the nature and character of God vouchsafed to man : " God, having of old time spoken unto the fathers in the prophets by divers portions and in

Obedience and Worship

divers manners, hath at the end of these days spoken unto us in His Son " (Heb. i. 1, 2).

The question of humanity, and the respect for women and children belonging to the enemy, would Heb. i. 1, 2. never enter into the mind of the writer of the book of Samuel, any more than it would suggest itself to his contemporaries. The central fact to his consciousness was this, that the demand of all others which God lays upon His people is obedience; short of that, all is of no avail.

Secondly, worship and daily life do not belong (2) Worship to two separate departments. They must act and and daily react upon each other. That worship should be life. suffused with emotion cannot be denied, but that is not to say they are one and the same. Benevuto Cellini, guilty of murders and the vilest excesses, yet recounts, with evident sincerity, the delights he experienced during his devotions in the nearness of God. Such a case would receive no encouragement from the Old Testament prophets. Never were they weary of insisting that worship, however elaborate, when divorced from righteousness, mercy, and judgement, was worse than useless; it was a mockery of God, an offence in His sight (Isa. i. 10–17; Jer. vii. 21–23; Amos v. 21–24; Mic. vi. 6–8). The story is told of a sturdy Scot, valiant in speech as in deed, English ambassador to the court of Prussia, at the table of Frederick the Great, then meditating a war whose sinews were to be mainly formed of English subsidies. Round the table sat French wits of the infidel sort, and they and the king made merry over decadent

The First Book of Samuel

superstitions, the follies of the ancient faith. Suddenly the talk changed to war and war's alarms. Said the long-silent Scot, " England would, by the help of God, stand by Prussia." " Ah ! " said infidel Frederick, " I did not know that you had an ally of that name " ; and the infidel wits smirked applause. " So please your Majesty," was the swift retort, " He is the only ally to whom we do not send subsidies." [1] God is not one whose alliance can be bought with bribes or sacrifices however costly, but there is one condition He imposes upon those who seek His help, and that is, the lifelong devotion of the contrite heart. The principal worship He requires from His followers is that they should love mercy, do justice, and walk humbly before Him.

God's
alliance.

(3) Worship
not only
outward but
inward as
well.

Thirdly, worship is not merely an external act, it is inward as well. God looketh not at the outward appearance, but on the heart (1 Sam. xvi. 7) ; not on the costliness of the gift, but on its cost to the giver ; not on the magnificence of the act of worship, but on the love and reverence which lie behind it. These are what God looks at, and considers.

St. John iv.
24.

Thus Samuel's teaching prepared the way for Him Who alone offered up the " one sacrifice for sins for ever " acceptable in God's sight (Heb. x. 12), and Who demands of His worshippers that they worship Him in spirit and in truth (St. John iv. 24).

---

[1] The story is told in the *City of God*, by Dr. A. M. Fairbairn (London : Hodder & Stoughton, 1897), 6th ed., pp. 85, 86.

XIV

FALSE POSITIONS

Now there was no smith found throughout all the land of Israel: for the Philistines said, Lest the Hebrews make *them* swords or spears : But all the Israelites went down to the Philistines, to sharpen every man his share, and his coulter, and his axe, and his mattock. Yet they had a file for the mattocks, and for the coulters, and for the forks, and for the axes, and to sharpen the goads. So it came to pass in the day of battle, that there was neither sword nor spear found in the hand of any of the people that *were* with Saul and Jonathan : but with Saul and Jonathan his son was there found. And the garrison of the Philistines went out to the passage of Michmash.

Now it came to pass upon a day, that Jonathan the son of Saul said unto the young man that bare his armour, Come, and let us go over to the Philistines' garrison, that *is* on the other side. But he told not his father. And Saul tarried in the uttermost part of Gibeah under a pomegranate tree which *is* in Migron : and the people that *were* with him *were* about six hundred men ; And Ahiah, the son of Ahitub, I-chabod's brother, the son of Phinehas, the son of Eli, the LORD'S priest in Shiloh, wearing an ephod. And the people knew not that Jonathan was gone.

And between the passages, by which Jonathan sought to go over unto the Philistines' garrison, there was a sharp rock on the one side, and a sharp rock on the other side : and the name of the one *was* Bozez, and the name of the other Seneh. The forefront of the one *was* situate northward over against Michmash, and the other southward over against Gibeah. And Jonathan said to the young man that bare his armour, Come, and let us go over unto the garrison of these uncircumcised : it may be that the LORD will work for us : for *there is* no restraint to the LORD to save by many or by few. And his armourbearer said unto him, Do all that *is* in thine heart : turn thee ; behold, I *am* with thee according to thy heart. Then said Jonathan,

The First Book of Samuel

Behold, we will pass over unto *these* men, and we will discover ourselves unto them. If they say thus unto us, Tarry until we come to you; then we will stand still in our place, and will not go up unto them. But if they say thus, Come up unto us; then we will go up: for the LORD hath delivered them into our hand: and this *shall be* a sign unto us. And both of them discovered themselves unto the garrison of the Philistines: and the Philistines said, Behold, the Hebrews come forth out of the holes where they had hid themselves. And the men of the garrison answered Jonathan and his armourbearer, and said, Come up to us, and we will shew you a thing. And Jonathan said unto his armourbearer, Come up after me: for the LORD hath delivered them into the hand of Israel. And Jonathan climbed up upon his hands and upon his feet, and his armourbearer after him: and they fell before Jonathan; and his armourbearer slew after him. And that first slaughter, which Jonathan and his armourbearer made, was about twenty men, within as it were an half acre of land, *which* a yoke *of oxen might plow*. And there was trembling in the host, in the field, and among all the people: the garrison, and the spoilers, they also trembled, and the earth quaked: so it was a very great trembling. And the watchmen of Saul in Gibeah of Benjamin looked; and, behold, the multitude melted away, and they went on beating down *one another*. Then said Saul unto the people that *were* with him, Number now, and see who is gone from us. And when they had numbered, behold, Jonathan and his armourbearer *were* not *there*. And Saul said unto Ahiah, Bring hither the ark of God. For the ark of God was at that time with the children of Israel.

And it came to pass, while Saul talked unto the priest, that the noise that *was* in the host of the Philistines went on and increased: and Saul said unto the priest, Withdraw thine hand. And Saul and all the people that *were* with him assembled themselves, and they came to the battle: and, behold, every man's sword was against his fellow, *and there was* a very great discomfiture. Moreover the Hebrews *that* were with the Philistines before that time, which went up with them into the camp *from the country* round about, even they also *turned* to be with the Israelites that *were* with Saul and Jonathan. Likewise all the men of Israel which had hid themselves in mount Ephraim, *when* they heard that the Philistines fled, even they also followed hard after them in the battle. So the LORD saved Israel that day: and the battle passed over unto Bethaven.

False Positions

And the men of Israel were distressed that day : for Saul
had adjured the people, saying, Cursed *be* the man that eateth
any food until evening, that I may be avenged on mine enemies.
So none of the people tasted *any* food. And all *they of* the land
came to a wood ; and there was honey upon the ground. And
when the people were come into the wood, behold, the honey
dropped ; but no man put his hand to his mouth : for the
people feared the oath. But Jonathan heard not when his
father charged the people with the oath : wherefore he put
forth the end of the rod that *was* in his hand, and dipped it in
an honeycomb, and put his hand to his mouth ; and his eyes
were enlightened. Then answered one of the people, and said,
Thy father straitly charged the people with an oath, saying,
Cursed *be* the man that eateth *any* food this day. And the
people were faint. Then said Jonathan, My father hath
troubled the land : see, I pray you, how mine eyes have been
enlightened, because I tasted a little of this honey. How much
more, if haply the people had eaten freely to day of the spoil of
their enemies which they found ? for had there not been now a
much greater slaughter among the Philistines ? And they
smote the Philistines that day from Michmash to Aijalon : and
the people were very faint. And the people flew upon the
spoil, and took sheep, and oxen, and calves, and slew *them* on
the ground : and the people did eat *them* with the blood.

Then they told Saul, saying, Behold, the people sin against
the LORD, in that they eat with the blood. And he said, Ye
have transgressed : roll a great stone unto me this day. And
Saul said, Disperse yourselves among the people, and say unto
them, Bring me hither every man his ox, and every man his
sheep, and slay *them* here, and eat ; and sin not against the
LORD in eating with the blood. And all the people brought
every man his ox with him that night, and slew *them* there.
And Saul built an altar unto the LORD : the same was the first
altar that he built unto the LORD.

And Saul said, Let us go down after the Philistines by night,
and spoil them until the morning light, and let us not leave a
man of them. And they said, Do whatsoever seemeth good
unto thee. Then said the priest, Let us draw near hither unto
God. And Saul asked counsel of God, Shall I go down after
the Philistines ? wilt thou deliver them into the hand of Israel ?
But he answered him not that day. And Saul said, Draw ye
near hither, all the chief of the people : and know and see
wherein this sin hath been this day. For, *as* the LORD liveth,

which saveth Israel, though it be in Jonathan my son, he shall surely die. But *there was* not a man among all the people *that* answered him. Then said he unto all Israel, Be ye on one side, and I and Jonathan my son will be on the other side. And the people said unto Saul, Do what seemeth good unto thee. Therefore Saul said unto the LORD God of Israel, Give a perfect *lot.* And Saul and Jonathan were taken : but the people escaped. And Saul said, Cast *lots* between me and Jonathan my son. And Jonathan was taken. Then Saul said to Jonathan, Tell me what thou hast done. And Jonathan told him, and said, I did but taste a little honey with the end of the rod that *was* in mine hand, *and,* lo, I must die. And Saul answered, God do so and more also : for thou shalt surely die, Jonathan. And the people said unto Saul, Shall Jonathan die, who hath wrought this great salvation in Israel ? God forbid : *as* the LORD liveth, there shall not one hair of his head fall to the ground ; for he hath wrought with God this day. So the people rescued Jonathan, that he died not. Then Saul went up from following the Philistines : and the Philistines went to their own place.— 1 SAM. XIII. 19–XIV. 46.

1 Sam. xiii. 19– xiv. 46.

The Philistines' subjugation of Israel very complete.

THE subjugation of Israel by the Philistines must have been very thorough, as the victors were able to enforce a general disarmament throughout the country. With the exception of Saul and Jonathan not a single fighting man among the Israelites was allowed to possess either a sword or a spear (xiii. 22) ; and to prevent the possibility of any uprising, the extreme measure was taken of removing the smiths from the land, so that the people were obliged to go to their enemies to sharpen some of their agricultural implements. Both the present and the future looked very dark for God's people. Hope, however, must still have burned brightly in many a patriot's heart, and not least in that of Saul's eldest son, Jonathan.

The Philistines were occupying Michmash, " the

False Positions

very citadel of Israel's hill country." It happened **1 Sam. xiii. 19– xiv. 46.** on a certain day, that Jonathan and his armour-bearer surprised some of the garrison in an outpost close to that place, and this set in motion a series of important events. A panic ensued which infected the enemies' entire army. And to make matters worse, from their point of view, there came an earthquake, *" and the earth quaked,"* *" a trembling of God "* (R.V. margin, xiv. 15), which still further confounded them. The confusion which pervaded their camp had not escaped the notice of Saul's watchman in Gibeah (Jeba, verse 16), and he at once acquainted the king, or the captain of the host, with what had happened.

Jonathan surprises an outpost of the Philistines.

A panic in their army.

Saul grasped the situation in a moment, and perceived that the time for instant action had arrived. After having discovered the absence of Jonathan and his armourbearer, he requested Ahijah to bring hither the Ephod. Our Authorised and Revised Versions relate that the Ark was sent for, but it is best to follow the Septuagint Version of verse 18, *" Bring hither the Ephod. For he wore the Ephod at that time before Israel "* (R.V. margin), the Ark never having been used for the purpose of ascertaining the Divine Will. While the priest was preparing to seek counsel and direction from God, the tumult in the camp of the Philistines increased to such an extent that Saul could brook no further delay. He felt that he and his men must make full use of their present opportunity, and there and then strike a blow against their enemy. Thus was he led into making a fatal mistake. He gave the

Saul takes advantage of this.

The Ephod is brought.

Saul too impatient to await instructions.

153

The First Book of Samuel

1 Sam. xiii. 19– xiv. 46.

order to Ahijah : "*Withdraw thine hand*" (verse 19), that is to say, in his opinion the time for waiting upon God was passed ; they must be up and doing. It was not the moment for prayer, but for action ; they could not tarry to hear the Divine instructions.

Saul's army receives reinforcements.

Meanwhile Saul's army was being reinforced by renegade Israelites, designated in this chapter as "Hebrews" (verse 21), to distinguish them from those of their countrymen who had refused to submit to the Philistine yoke. These men had seen how the tide had turned in favour of their country. To their surprise the invincible army of the Philistines had become an ill-disciplined mob, "*every man's sword was against his fellow*" (verse 20). These and "*likewise all the men of Israel which had hid themselves in the hill country of Ephraim, when they heard that the Philistines fled, even they also followed hard after them in the battle. So the Lord saved Israel that day*" (verses 22 and 23). The enemy were

The rout of the army.

driven back to the north-west of Michmash beyond the pass of Beth-Horon, on the way to Ajalon.

Saul's order.

That same morning Saul had issued the order that none of his men should under any consideration touch food that day until the evening, death being

Why he issued it.

the penalty for disobedience. The motive prompting Saul to such a course may have been fear that, once discipline had been relaxed, and leave granted to obtain food, the soldiers might desist from pursuing the foe, and that there would not be a fight to a finish. Another reason has been alleged to account for Saul's strange action at this time, which is, that he shared the prevailing belief of his age that the

154

False Positions

Divine help would be granted and continued by 1 Sam. xiii. 19–xiv. 46. imposing a food taboo on his people ; that to fast, and to offer up the firstfruits of victory, would be the means of procuring for their arms the favour of the God of Battles. If this is so, the real reasons which impelled Saul to give such an order were religious reasons. Be that as it may, we would insist, that had Saul restrained his impatience, and allowed Ahijah to wait for Divine guidance and help, the order would never have been given.

The consequences of Saul's prohibition were very Its consequences. different from those he had either intended or expected. Had the people possessed the needful energy, a much greater slaughter of the Philistines would have been the result. Famished, their strength failed, they *" were distressed that day "* (verse 24), and unable to reap the full fruit of their victory (verse 30).

Subsequently, when the prohibition was removed, The people's sin. the people in their desperation *" flew upon the spoil, and took sheep, and oxen, and calves, and slew them on the ground,"* and what is more *" did eat them with the blood "* (verse 32). From the days of the patriarch Noah, the eating of blood had been forbidden (Gen. ix. 4), and according to the Mosaic Law it was punishable with death (Lev. xvii. 10, 11, 14 ; Deut. xii. 16, 23, 24, xv. 23). In consequence of this, Saul was compelled to take prompt measures, and to command the people to bring each man his ox or his sheep, and slay it under proper inspection, *" and eat and sin not against the Lord."*

From Saul's point of view the worst has yet to

155

The First Book of Samuel

**1 Sam.
xiii. 19–
xiv. 46.**

Jonathan
unwittingly
disobeys his
father.

His dis-
obedience is
discovered.

Saul's
terrible pre-
dicament.

His false
position.

be related. As Jonathan was passing through one
of the woods in that district, whilst the battle was
still raging, he happened to see a comb of honey
hanging on one of the trees, and in entire ignorance
of his father's command, he dipped the end of his
rod into the honeycomb, tasted it, and at once felt
refreshed.

Jonathan's transgression might have passed
unnoticed but for the following incident. Saul
had erected an altar in thanksgiving for victory
(verse 35). He then suggested that the pursuit
of the enemy should be continued throughout the
night, in the hope that on the following morning
not a man of them would be left alive (verse 36).
Whereupon the priest pointed out that they should
take counsel of God. He may have felt qualms
that he had allowed Saul to interrupt him whilst
waiting to receive instructions from God. This
time Ahijah prevailed. But the Lord gave him
no answer. At once both he and Saul concluded
that Israel had, as a nation, incurred the Divine
displeasure, and Saul swore "*as the Lord liveth*,"
though it were his own son who had committed the
sin, he should be put to death.

By means of casting lots, the possible offenders
were narrowed down to Saul and Jonathan, and then
"*Jonathan was taken*." Thus was Saul placed in
the terrible predicament of having to sentence his
own son to death, which accordingly he did, Jonathan
escaping only by the intervention of the people,
"*God forbid . . . for he hath wrought with God this
day*" (verse 45). Saul had placed himself in a false

156

False Positions

position. He is not the only person in the Bible **1 Sam. xiii. 19– xiv. 46.** who has found himself in very similar circumstances.

Darius, at the instigation of the enemies of Daniel, Others in false positions. Herod. Darius. having passed a decree that no one in his kingdom should ask a petition of any god or man for thirty days save of himself, unwittingly betrayed his truest friend and wisest counsellor. And in the New Testament we have the rash oath of Herod to Herodias, resulting in the death of John the Baptist.

These three men, Saul, Darius, and Herod, need never thus have compromised themselves. Darius should have suspected that unscrupulous courtiers sought to take advantage of his pride and vanity in order to compass their own ends, and have refused to pass such a decree. And as for Herod, to pledge himself in advance to an action quite beyond his ken, and of such possible magnitude, reveals the recklessness and dissoluteness of his character.

It may be laid down as a spiritual law, that if we Make as few promises as possible. rely upon the Holy Spirit's guidance, and walk circumspectly, we shall never find ourselves in a position, from which to extricate ourselves a sin has to be committed. It is always advisable to make as few promises as possible, and those promises should be of such a character that it is possible to see, within reasonable limits, what they are likely to involve, and whether therefore they can be kept. If, however, owing to lack of prudence and neglect of prayer, we find ourselves in a false position, we

The First Book of Samuel

should confess our mistake, and choose the lesser of the two evils.

In the cases of both Darius and Herod, they should rather have broken their word than have hounded an innocent man to his death. Saul, also, should have confessed before God, and his people, that he had adopted a mistaken policy, and expressed before the Divine Presence his contrition for having failed to seek His help and guidance.

An important rendering of verse 41.

Before we bring this chapter to a close, we would draw attention to the particular method by which Saul and Ahijah discovered that Jonathan had disobeyed his father's command. A very interesting translation, based on the Septuagint, has been given of the forty-first verse, and has met with almost universal favour amongst modern scholars : "*And Saul said, O Yahweh ; God of Israel, why hast Thou not answered Thy servant this day ? If this iniquity be in me or in my son Jonathan, O Yahweh, God of Israel, give Urim ; but if it be in Thy people Israel give Thummin. And Jonathan and Saul were taken and the people escaped*" (verse 41 ; cf. Principal Bennett in Peake's *Commentary*, and cf. 1 Sam. xxviii. 6). If this rendering is accepted, it proves that the guilty party was discovered by the Urim and the Thummin, which were also closely connected with the Ephod.

The meanings of the Ephod.

Confining ourselves to the two books of Samuel, the Ephod occurs in certain passages which clearly prove that it was a priestly garment, probably made of linen, and was not confined to any one individual. Samuel " was girded with a linen ephod " (1 Sam. ii.

158

18). It was worn by the eighty-five priests at
Nob (xxii. 18), and David also wore an Ephod when
he danced before the Ark (2 Sam. vi. 14). This
must be distinguished from the Ephod worn or
carried by a particular individual, and which, when
referred to, is for the most part associated with the
ascertainment of the Divine Will (1 Sam. ii. 28 ;
xiv. 3, 18 ; xxi. 9 ; xxiii. 9–12 ; xxx. 7–8). By
many scholars this is thought to refer to the particular garment worn by the High Priest, to which
was attached the pouch containing the Urim and
Thummin, though it should be borne in mind that
the possibility of it as an oracle of some kind in
itself is also entertained (cf. Judg. viii. 26 f.), the
Urim and the Thummin having some intimate but
as yet undiscovered connection with it.

The meaning of the Urim and the Thummin is
also exceedingly obscure. It may be said that
according to chapter xiv. they were the recognised
medium for discovering the guilt or innocence of
suspected parties, but that they were used ex-
clusively for this particular purpose is more than
doubtful ; for it is mentioned that before Saul went
to consult the witch at Endor he made use of the
Urim, and received no answer. It would appear
when Urim fell, the answer was " Yes," when
Thummin, " No." Living as we do under the New
Testament dispensation, such methods have passed
away. " He taketh away the first, that He may
establish the second " (Heb. x. 9). A time comes
when the race, as well as individuals, must put
away childish things (1 Cor. xiii. 11), in malice we

Marginal references:
1 Sam.
xiii. 19–
xiv. 46.

The Urim
and the
Thummin.

Heb. x. 9.

The First Book of Samuel

1 Sam.
xiii. 19–
xiv. 46.

Under the New Testament dispensation.

Knowledge of the Divine Will can be universal.

The Holy Spirit's help continuous.

His work within the heart.

are to be babes, but in mind men (1 Cor. xiv. 20). On the other hand, we are under far more favourable conditions, for the Holy Spirit has been given to us. On Him we can lean, and He will guide us aright. The superiority in privilege, which the Christian has over the ancient Israelite, is manifest.

The knowledge of the Divine Will is not confined to men like Ahijah, Abiathar, or to just a favoured few, but is open to all. " They shall all know Me, from the least of them unto the greatest of them " (Jer. xxxi. 34 ; Heb. viii. 11), " and they shall all be taught of God " (St. John vi. 45). To all alike, provided they make it their endeavour to do the Will of God, it is promised that they shall know " of the teaching whether it be of God " (St. John vii. 17).

Besides this, Urim and Thummin were made use of on important occasions only, and at rare intervals. The Holy Spirit's guidance is continuous. " He is ever making intercession for us with groanings which cannot be uttered," our very prayers He purifies and brings into harmony with the Mind of God, and therefore to those who love God all things must work together for good.

Finally, the use of Urim and Thummin was largely mechanical and quite external to the inquirer. The Holy Spirit works within the heart and sanctifies the possessor, causing him to realise his Divine sonship, and bestowing upon him the liberty which belongs to the children of God. " And as for you, the anointing which ye received of Him abideth in you, and ye need not that any one teach

False Positions

1 Sam.
xiii. 19–
xiv. 46.

you; but as His anointing teacheth you concerning
all things, and is true, and is no lie, and even as it
taught you, ye abide in Him " (1 St. John ii. 27).
In St. Augustine's beautiful words, " He that
teacheth the heart, hath His chair in Heaven."

XV

GOD'S STANDARD OF HUMAN MEASUREMENT

And the LORD said unto Samuel, How long wilt thou mourn for Saul, seeing I have rejected him from reigning over Israel ? fill thine horn with oil, and go, I will send thee to Jesse the Beth-lehemite : for I have provided me a king among his sons. And Samuel said, How can I go ? if Saul hear *it*, he will kill me. And the LORD said, Take an heifer with thee, and say, I am come to sacrifice to the LORD. And call Jesse to the sacrifice, and I will shew thee what thou shalt do : and thou shalt anoint unto me *him* whom I name unto thee. And Samuel did that which the LORD spake, and came to Beth-lehem. And the elders of the town trembled at his coming, and said, Comest thou peaceably ? And he said, Peaceably : I am come to sacrifice unto the LORD : sanctify yourselves, and come with me to the sacrifice. And he sanctified Jesse and his sons, and called them to the sacrifice.

And it came to pass, when they were come, that he looked on Eliab, and said, Surely the LORD's anointed *is* before him. But the LORD said unto Samuel, Look not on his countenance, or on the height of his stature ; because I have refused him : for *the LORD seeth* not as man seeth ; for man looketh on the outward appearance, but the LORD looketh on the heart. Then Jesse called Abinadab, and made him pass before Samuel. And he said, Neither hath the LORD chosen this. Then Jesse made Shammah to pass by. And he said, Neither hath the LORD chosen this. Again, Jesse made seven of his sons to pass before Samuel. And Samuel said unto Jesse, The LORD hath not chosen these. And Samuel said unto Jesse, Are here all *thy* children ? And he said, There remaineth yet the youngest, and, behold, he keepeth the sheep. And Samuel said unto Jesse, Send and fetch him : for we will not sit down till he come

God's Standard of Measurement

hither. And he sent, and brought him in. Now he *was* ruddy, *and* withal of a beautiful countenance, and goodly to look to. And the LORD said, Arise, anoint him : for this *is* he. Then Samuel took the horn of oil, and anointed him in the midst of his brethren : and the Spirit of the LORD came upon David from that day forward. So Samuel rose up, and went to Ramah.—1 SAM. XVI. 1–13.

SAUL had been rejected. Samuel felt so keenly the judgement he had been commanded by God to pronounce upon Israel's first king, that it is quite possible he sank into a lethargy of mind and soul which could only be overcome by his being sent on some difficult and dangerous errand. Sometimes that is God's method of enabling His servant, not " to get over," but, as a Master in the spiritual life has expressed it, " to ' get into ' sorrow, and find right in the heart of it the dearest of all human beings—the Man of Sorrows," [1] Samuel must bestir himself, be taken out of himself, and do some active work for God.

1 Sam. xvi. 1–13.

Samuel and Saul's rejection.

The Divine judgement was unalterable. " I have rejected him from being king over Israel." The Prophet was bidden straightway to go to Bethlehem, carrying with him the horn filled with oil, the actual horn, it may be, wherewith he anointed Saul king, and to seek out the house of Jesse, a man belonging to that village, and grandson of Ruth the Moabitess (Ruth iv. 17–22).

The Prophet goes to Bethlehem.

One of the sons of Jesse had been marked out in the Divine Counsels as the successor of Saul.

In order that Saul's suspicions might not be aroused, Samuel was commanded to conceal the

He conceals the purport of his journey.

[1] Forbes Robinson's *Letters to his Friends.*

163

1 Sam.
xvi. 1—
13.

real purport of his mission. Ostensibly he was to go there to sacrifice unto the Lord. "Concealment of a good purpose for a good purpose is clearly justifiable."

The Prophet's arrival in Bethlehem seems to have given rise to some misgivings on the part of the elders of the city; they met him with "*trembling*" (verse 4).

On some occasions, in days gone by, he had come to the cities and villages in order to deliver judgement, and to correct abuses. This time he had come on a peaceful errand, and he allayed their fears by bidding them make the usual preparations for offering a sacrifice. They were commanded to sanctify themselves, whilst in Jesse's case he himself insisted on superintending the preparations, so that opportunity might be afforded him for a private interview with Jesse and the members of his household.

His arrival at Jesse's house.

Hereupon follows an account of the choice from among Jesse's sons of Israel's second king.

Jesse's sons pass before Samuel.

The narrative is not a mere bald summary of these young men passing before Samuel, each in turn to be rejected until the youngest had been sent for and anointed as the future king. It is much more than this. We are permitted to hear the Voice of God speaking in the Prophet's soul, as the candidates are brought forward. We are given to understand that Israel's first king had been the people's choice, the finest-looking and strongest man in Israel (1 Sam. ix. 2). The Prophet imagined that just such another would be designated as Saul's

God's Standard of Measurement

successor. When therefore Eliab, Jesse's eldest son, stood before him, Samuel said to himself, "*Surely the Lord's anointed is before Him*" (verse 6). At once the thought arose in his mind, prompted by God, that the standard by which he was measuring human fitness was not God's standard. He was not to look on his countenance or on the height of his stature. An altogether different standard was required, the standard of moral fitness; the character must be according to the mind of God; this king was to be a man after His own heart. To use a quaint phrase of Matthew Henry's, "mind, not mien," is the supreme requirement. 1 Sam. xvi. 1–13.

God's standard of human fitness.

Abinadab the second son was also rejected. As regards the other sons who passed before Samuel, he was possessed by the certainty that on none of these did there rest the Divine approval.

At length David was summoned from the fields, "fresh with the dew of God's morn in his golden hair." If Prof. H. P. Smith's translation is followed, "He was ruddy, a youth of fine eyes and goodly appearance." The eyes are the most expressive part of the face, and something in David's look attracted Samuel at once. Generous, true and strong did the shepherd lad appear that day to the aged Prophet. And at once there came the swift command, "*Arise, anoint him : for this is he*," and Samuel without hesitation "*anointed him in the midst of his brethren*" (verses 12 and 13). It may be that none of those present understood the significance of the ceremony. They may have thought that David was being chosen to be a prophet. David is summoned from the fields.

He is anointed.

I Sam.
xvi. 1–
13.

Samuel's
action
justified by
history.

David, a
man after
God's own
heart.

Yet far from
being
perfect.

History has fully confirmed the validity of Samuel's action, and the reason is not far to seek. David complied with God's standard of measurement, and yet he was very far from being a perfect character. He was guilty of sins, which if committed to-day would bring the most brilliant career to an abrupt termination.

Due allowance must be made for the different moral standard which prevailed in the world before the coming of our Lord Jesus Christ. The Divine education of mankind is progressive, and man can only assimilate that which is suited to his mental and moral capacity. But God's moral Law must be obeyed and justified ; judgement fell upon David, and punishment was meted out to him with no sparing hand.

Freedom from the grosser forms of sin does not qualify a man to be accepted before God. We have our Lord's own warrant for saying that many whose sins have brought them low in the eyes of men, may be nearer the gate of repentance than those who feel no need of pardon (St. Matt. xxi. 31).

Direction of
a man's
life all-
important.

Not what we are, but what we shall be, is the important matter in God's sight. The common saying " deeds, not words " can be improved upon thus, substitute " direction " for " deeds," and " deeds " for " words," and we have " direction, not deeds." As it is not implied in the case of " deeds, not words " that words are of little consequence (cf. St. Matt. xii. 36, 37), but merely that in comparison to action, they are very much inferior, in like manner, from the Christian standpoint, the

God's Standard of Measurement

accent is laid more upon the actual direction a 1 Sam. xvi. 1– 13. man's life is taking than on his concrete perform- ance. A musician hears a piece played by a child on the piano. Many are the mistakes the child may make, but to his trained ear they matter but little, sure as he is in his own mind that the child has it in him to become a first-rate pianist, given time and proper training—he recognises the latent capacity.

God knew that David's life would be far from perfect. No attempt is made to gloss over his sins, but David was the kind of man whom God could mould to His Will, for at the very outset of his career he placed his fortunes in God's hands. David fell grievously, but as soon as his sin was brought home to him, he turned to God in repentance. Men and women are accounted righteous How men and women are accepted before God. before God, not because they are righteous in His sight, but on account of their acceptance " in the Beloved," and of their acceptance of Him. Believing that, through the Love of God, the death of Christ embraces not merely the righteous, but ALL in whatever sinful state (cf. Rom. v. 6 ff.), they are prepared and willing to leave in Christ's hands the direction of their lives, fully confident that He who began the good work in them will perfect it until the day of Jesus Christ (Phil. i. 6). This imputed righteousness is not a fiction, for God sees the end in the beginning. When the human heart responds to the Holy Spirit of God, the processes of lifegiving power and grace are set in motion, which ultimately lead to attainment of the measure of the stature of the fulness of Christ.

1 Sam.
xvi. 1—
13.
The road to
Heaven is
paved with
good
intentions.

The Christian man, too, may yield to some severe and terrible temptation, but when he rises again, it is discovered that he is standing by the Cross.

The road to Hell may be paved with good intentions, that to Heaven has a very similar pavement. But in the second case the longings after holiness are not mere pious expressions, or half-hearted aspirations, but take the form of ideals, towards which the man is ever looking, and after which he is striving. He is on the road which must ultimately arrive at God's ideal.

"Thoughts hardly to be packed into a narrow act,
   Fancies that broke through language and escaped;
      All I could never be,
      All, man ignored in me,
   This, I was worth to God, whose wheel the pitcher
      shaped."

(ROBERT BROWNING.)

XVI

RELIGION AND MUSIC

But the Spirit of the LORD departed from Saul, and an evil spirit from the LORD troubled him. And Saul's servants said unto him, Behold now, an evil spirit from God troubleth thee. Let our lord now command thy servants, *which are* before thee, to seek out a man, *who is* a cunning player on an harp : and it shall come to pass, when the evil spirit from God is upon thee, that he shall play with his hand, and thou shalt be well. And Saul said unto his servants, Provide me now a man that can play well, and bring *him* to me. Then answered one of his servants, and said, Behold, I have seen a son of Jesse the Beth-lehemite, *that is* cunning in playing, and a mighty valiant man, and a man of war, and prudent in matters, and a comely person, and the LORD *is* with him.

Wherefore Saul sent messengers unto Jesse, and said, Send me David thy son, which *is* with the sheep. And Jesse took an ass *laden* with bread, and a bottle of wine, and a kid, and sent *them* by David his son unto Saul. And David came to Saul, and stood before him : and he loved him greatly ; and he became his armourbearer. And Saul sent to Jesse, saying, Let David, I pray thee, stand before me ; for he hath found favour in my sight. And it came to pass, when the *evil* spirit from God was upon Saul, that David took an harp, and played with his hand : so Saul was refreshed, and was well, and the evil spirit departed from him.

And it came to pass on the morrow, that the evil spirit from God came upon Saul, and he prophesied in the midst of the house : and David played with his hand, as at other times : and *there was* a javelin in Saul's hand. And Saul cast the javelin ; for he said, I will smite David even to the wall *with it.* And David avoided out of his presence twice.

And the evil spirit from the LORD was upon Saul, as he sat

in his house with his javelin in his hand : and David played
with *his* hand. And Saul sought to smite David even to the
wall with the javelin ; but he slipped away out of Saul's presence,
and he smote the javelin into the wall : and David fled, and
escaped that night.—1 SAM. XVI. 14–23 ; XVIII. 10–11 ; XIX.
9–10.

**I Sam.
xvi. 14–
23 ;
xviii. 10–
11 ; xix.
9–10.**

**David as a
harpist.**

**The value
of music to
Martin
Luther.**

NOT long after Samuel had anointed David king,
he appeared at court as a "*cunning player on the
harp*" (xvi. 16). In that capacity he was introduced to Saul. The latter, according to Professor
Macalister, was suffering "from recurrent par-
oxysmal mania, rather than from melancholia," and,
in his opinion, the influence of music would be of a
most calming and soothing nature in such a case.

The great Reformer Martin Luther, who suffered
much from attacks of depression, valued Music
particularly as the means of driving away the devil
and his temptations, and testified to its wonderful
power of softening and refining the human spirit.
"The heart," he said, "grows satisfied, refreshed
and strengthened by music." He went even
further, and regarded it as one of the most precious
gifts that God has bestowed on mankind. David
has ever been regarded as the sweet Psalmist of
Israel (2 Sam. xxiii. 1). In his case music must
have helped and intensified his religious life. It
will not therefore be out of place here to consider

**Music the
handmaid
of Religion.**

Music as the handmaid of Religion, especially as
we have abundant testimony that it was owing to
David that stringed instruments were introduced
into the service of the sanctuary (1 Chron. xxiii. 5 ;
2 Chron. xxix. 25, 26 ; Neh. xii. 36 ; Amos vi. 5).

In a most impressive manner Music indicates

Religion and Music

that we belong to a spiritual order. Has there
ever been one amongst the great masters of Music,
who avowed himself to be a materialist ? If so, what
mechanical explanation could he give of Music, and
the effect it has upon the human spirit ; how would
he explain his own productions in terms of matter ?
Consider also what Music can effect with such
slender means at her disposal. She has less material
ready to hand with which to work than have her
sister Arts, as Browning in his poem " Abt Volger,"
has put it.

> " Consider it well : each tone of our scale in itself is nought ;
> It is everywhere in the world—loud,
> Soft, and all is said :
> Give it to me to use ! I mix it
> With two in my thought :
> And, there ! Ye have heard and seen :
> Consider and bow the head ! "

At one moment, those who hear are snatched up
into the seventh heaven, and experience what
Handel did when composing his wonderful chorus ;
He saw the heavens opened, and the holy angels,
and the great God Himself sitting on His Throne.

At another, they find themselves plunged into the
depths of despair, the gates of Paradise closed
against them. The most sublime emotions can be
awakened, or deeply stirred, terror, agony, joy,
sorrow, peace. Music can interpret them all as
no human words have the power to do, yes, and the
longing and yearning for the Infinite God. " Can
it be," writes the late Cardinal Newman, " that the
mysterious stirrings of the heart and keen emotions,

Margin notes:
1 Sam.
xvi. 14–
23 ;
xviii. 10–
11 ; xix.
9–10.
Its witness
to a
spiritual
order.
What it can
effect with
very
slender
means.

Music the
great
interpreter.

1 Sam.
xvi. 14–
23 ;
xviii. 10–
11 ; xix.
9–10.

and strange yearnings after we know not what, and awful impressions from we know not whence, should be wrought in us by what is unsubstantial and comes and goes and begins and ends in itself ? It is not so, it cannot be. No. They have escaped from some higher sphere. They are the outpourings of eternal harmony in the medium of created sound." Very early amongst the Greek Philosophers, long before Plato arrived on the scene, the idea was held that the seven moving, and therefore vibrating, planets formed a heptachord, but that men did not notice this Music of the spheres because they always heard it. Music is Divine ; at its highest and its best it is an intimation of the Eternal Harmony which appertains to the Being and Nature of God, " The Master of all Music, The Master of all singing " (Hiawatha).

It is an intimation of the Eternal Harmony.

Music the universal language of mankind.

Music is the universal language of mankind, more so even than Poetry. Tennyson is English, Dante Italian, Victor Hugo French, in a way in which neither Bach nor Beethoven is specifically German. There are, of course, national schools of music ; but those who have the right to speak assure us that the musical creations of the world have nothing provincial about them. The Music of Christendom is one of the most catholic of the arts in its world-wide appeal, and there is nothing sectarian in the best Church Music.[1]

Christ and Orpheus.

It is interesting to recall that the Early Christians at times represented Christ as Orpheus charming

[1] Cf. Professor W. Knight, *The Philosophy of the Beautiful* (London : John Murray, 1893), vol. ii. pp. 125 ff.

the wild beasts by the music of his lyre, a beautiful symbol of Christ's Divine power to cast out the powers of evil from the human heart, and "to subdue all things to Himself."

1 Sam. xvi. 14–23 ; xviii. 10–11 ; xix. 9–10.

In St. John's truly inspired description of the Beatific Vision, he pictures the Redeemed as wearing crowns, and with harps in their hands. These are not to be interpreted with prosaic literalism (which is to be deplored), but as typifying the royal descent of the Saints, and the perfect worship they render unto Him that sits upon the Throne. As discords may contribute to a harmony which takes them up and blends them into a more perfect concord, in like manner the different temperaments and experiences of those redeemed by Christ shall cause to reverberate throughout the Holy City the majestic chorus of the Thrice Holy, and complete the chord of God's eternal Harmony and Service.

The symbolism of the Book of the Revelation.

David, with his music, could soothe the storm-tossed soul of Saul, but only for a time. Twice it is placed on record that he failed, and had to escape for his life. But a greater and more wonderful Musician has come, Who has suffered for those whom He loves. By His Music the evil spirits of sin and despair are driven from us never to return, peace and rest come to our souls.

> " O Saul, it shall be
> A Face like my face that receives thee ;
> A man like to me,
> Thou shalt love and be loved by, for ever :
> A Hand like this hand
> Shall throw open the gates of new life to thee !
> See the Christ stand." (R. Browning.)

XVII

AN OLD STORY RETOLD

Now the Philistines gathered together their armies to battle,
and were gathered together at Shochoh, which *belongeth* to
Judah, and pitched between Shochoh and Azekah, in Ephes-
dammim. And Saul and the men of Israel were gathered
together, and pitched by the valley of Elah, and set the battle
in array against the Philistines. And the Philistines stood
on a mountain on the one side, and Israel stood on a mountain
on the other side : and *there was* a valley between them.

And there went out a champion out of the camp of the
Philistines, named Goliath, of Gath, whose height *was* six cubits
and a span. And *he had* an helmet of brass upon his head, and
he *was* armed with a coat of mail ; and the weight of the coat
was five thousand shekels of brass. And *he had* greaves of
brass upon his legs, and a target of brass between his shoulders.
And the staff of his spear *was* like a weaver's beam ; and his
spear's head *weighed* six hundred shekels of iron : and one
bearing a shield went before him. And he stood and cried unto
the armies of Israel, and said unto them, Why are ye come out
to set *your* battle in array ? *am* not I a Philistine, and ye
servants to Saul ? choose you a man for you, and let him come
down to me. If he be able to fight with me, and to kill me, then
will we be your servants : but if I prevail against him, and kill
him, then shall ye be our servants, and serve us. And the
Philistine said, I defy the armies of Israel this day ; give me a
man, that we may fight together. When Saul and all Israel
heard those words of the Philistine, they were dismayed, and
greatly afraid.

Now David *was* the son of that Ephrathite of Beth-lehem-
judah, whose name *was* Jesse ; and he had eight sons : and
the man went among men *for* an old man in the days of Saul.
And the three eldest sons of Jesse went *and* followed Saul to
the battle : and the names of his three sons that went to the

An Old Story Retold

battle *were* Eliab the firstborn, and next unto him Abinadab, and the third Shammah. And David *was* the youngest : and the three eldest followed Saul. But David went and returned from Saul to feed his father's sheep at Beth-lehem. And the Philistine drew near morning and evening, and presented himself forty days. And Jesse said unto David his son, Take now for thy brethren an ephah of this parched *corn*, and these ten loaves and run to the camp to thy brethren ; And carry these ten cheeses unto the captain of *their* thousand, and look how thy brethren fare, and take their pledge. Now Saul, and they, and all the men of Israel, *were* in the valley of Elah, fighting with the Philistines.

And David rose up early in the morning, and left the sheep with a keeper, and took, and went, as Jesse had commanded him ; and he came to the trench, as the host was going forth to the fight, and shouted for the battle. For Israel and the Philistines had put the battle in array, army against army.

And David left his carriage in the hand of the keeper of the carriage, and ran into the army, and came and saluted his brethren. And as he talked with them, behold, there came up the champion, the Philistine of Gath, Goliath by name, out of the armies of the Philistines, and spake according to the same words : and David heard *them*. And all the men of Israel, when they saw the man, fled from him, and were sore afraid. And the men of Israel said, Have ye seen this man that is come up ? surely to defy Israel is he come up : and it shall be, *that* the man who killeth him, the king will enrich him with great riches, and will give him his daughter, and make his father's house free in Israel. And David spake to the men that stood by him, saying, What shall be done to the man that killeth this Philistine, and taketh away the reproach from Israel ? for who *is* this uncircumcised Philistine that he should defy the armies of the living God ? And the people answered him after this manner, saying, So shall it be done to the man that killeth him.

And Eliab his eldest brother heard when he spake unto the men ; and Eliab's anger was kindled against David, and he said, Why camest thou down hither ? and with whom hast thou left those few sheep in the wilderness ? I know thy pride, and the naughtiness of thine heart ; for thou art come down that thou mightest see the battle. And David said, What have I now done ? *Is there* not a cause ?

And he turned from him toward another, and spake after the same manner : and the people answered him again after the former manner. And when the words were heard which David spake, they rehearsed *them* before Saul: and he sent for him.

And David said to Saul, Let no man's heart fail because of him; thy servant will go and fight with this Philistine. And Saul said to David, Thou art not able to go against this Philistine to fight with him: for thou *art but* a youth, and he a man of war from his youth. And David said unto Saul, Thy servant kept his father's sheep, and there came a lion, and a bear, and took a lamb out of the flock: And I went out after him, and smote him, and delivered *it* out of his mouth: and when he arose against me, I caught *him* by his beard, and smote him, and slew him. Thy servant slew both the lion and the bear: and this uncircumcised Philistine shall be as one of them, seeing he hath defied the armies of the living God. David said moreover, The LORD that delivered me out of the paw of the lion, and out of the paw of the bear, he will deliver me out of the hand of this Philistine. And Saul said unto David, Go, and the LORD be with thee.

And Saul armed David with his armour, and he put an helmet of brass upon his head; also he armed him with a coat of mail. And David girded his sword upon his armour, and he assayed to go; for he had not proved *it*. And David said unto Saul, I cannot go with these; for I have not proved *them*. And David put them off him. And he took his staff in his hand, and chose him five smooth stones out of the brook, and put them in a shepherd's bag which he had, even in a scrip; and his sling *was* in his hand: and he drew near to the Philistine. And the Philistine came on and drew near unto David; and the man that bare the shield *went* before him. And when the Philistine looked about, and saw David, he disdained him: for he was *but* a youth, and ruddy, and of a fair countenance. And the Philistine said unto David, *Am* I a dog, that thou comest to me with staves? And the Philistine cursed David by his gods. And the Philistine said to David, Come to me, and I will give thy flesh unto the fowls of the air, and to the beasts of the field. Then said David to the Philistine, Thou comest to me with a sword, and with a spear, and with a shield: but I come to thee in the name of the LORD of hosts, the God of the armies of Israel, whom thou hast defied. This day will the LORD deliver thee into mine hand; and I will smite thee, and take thine head from thee; and I will give the carcases of the host of the Philistines this day unto the fowls of the air, and to the wild beasts of the earth; that all the earth may know that there is a God in

An Old Story Retold

Israel. And all this assembly shall know that the LORD saveth not with sword and spear : for the battle *is* the LORD'S, and he will give you into our hands. And it came to pass, when the Philistine arose, and came and drew nigh to meet David, that David hasted, and ran toward the army to meet the Philistine. And David put his hand in his bag, and took thence a stone, and slang *it*, and smote the Philistine in his forehead, that the stone sunk into his forehead ; and he fell upon his face to the earth. So David prevailed over the Philistine with a sling and with a stone, and smote the Philistine, and slew him ; but *there was* no sword in the hand of David. Therefore David ran, and stood upon the Philistine, and took his sword, and drew it out of the sheath thereof, and slew him, and cut off his head therewith. And when the Philistines saw their champion was dead, they fled. And the men of Israel and of Judah arose, and shouted, and pursued the Philistines, until thou come to the valley, and to the gates of Ekron. And the wounded of the Philistines fell down by the way to Shaaraim, even unto Gath, and unto Ekron. And the children of Israel returned from chasing after the Philistines, and they spoiled their tents. And David took the head of the Philistine, and brought it to Jerusalem ; but he put his armour in his tent.—1 SAM. XVII. 1–54.

ONE of our earliest recollections of the Bible is that thrilling story of David and Goliath, which so fired our imaginations when first read to us by our elders. I Sam. xvii. 1– 54.

This story, one of our earliest recollections.

The height of Goliath was "*six cubits and a span*" (verse 4), that is from nine to ten feet. He was indeed a veritable giant. His strength matched his height. The coat of mail he wore must have been from one hundred and fifty to two hundred pounds in weight (verse 5), while the iron head of his spear did not weigh less than twenty-five pounds, and these formed only part of his equipment ; besides all this, an armourbearer advanced in front of him with a shield (verse 7).

Its fascination for us.

As he was described to us, we could see him

177   M

1 Sam.
xvii. 1–
54.

going up and down in front of the armies of the
Israelites setting them at defiance, and challenging
them to produce a man who could prove to be his
match, and stand up against him in mortal combat.
Terrible were the terms fixed by the giant in his
certainty of victory, " *If he be able to fight with me,
and kill me, then will we be your servants : but if I
prevail against him, and kill him, then shall ye be our
servants, and serve us* " (verse 9).

Its
romance.

For a few moments we were overawed by Goliath's
insolent bearing and proud boastfulness. And
then there suddenly appears on the scene David,
a mere stripling, come to see his three eldest brothers,
bring them provisions, and carry back word to their
father how they fared (verse 18). Not long after
his arrival, if he does not actually catch sight of
Goliath he hears him breathing words of defiance,
and can see the dismay they produce on those
around him. He questions those who stand by,
and instantly Eliab suspects that his eager young
brother is becoming fired with the desire to challenge
the Philistine himself, and his bitter jealousy is
aroused. For a few moments our thoughts dwelt
with sympathy on the rebuff David receives from
his eldest brother for having left the sheep and
come down to see the battle, but that was soon
forgotten, for the dramatic scene draws rapidly to
a head. David is brought before Saul, and in
answer to the question how he, a mere youth,
without any experience of fighting, could hope to
stand up against such a formidable adversary, he
quietly replies that in looking after his father's

An Old Story Retold

sheep he had had to contend with a lion and a bear, adding simply, "*the Lord delivered me*" (verse 37). Has he not therefore every right to assume that in fighting this enemy of the Lord the same strong, loving Hand would be outstretched to help him ?

1 Sam. xvii. 1— 54.

The Lord delivered me.

Whereupon he advances to fight Goliath, un-armed, save for a sling in his hand, and a wallet or bag, into which he had placed five smooth stones picked up from the brook (verse 40).

Do we not remember at this part of the story how we almost held our breath, and then the relief and delight as we heard how David hurled the stone with his catapult, and struck Goliath on the fore-head, so that he fell on his face to the earth ? Thus did David prove himself his country's deliverer that day, prevailing through his steadfast courage and unfaltering trust in the Lord of hosts.

Our relief and delight.

Since then many years have passed by, and when the story of David and Goliath is mentioned, a smile steals across our faces, and memories of long ago return. But for all of us, no matter what our age may be, it will be well to read through this story from time to time, and we shall discover, what is true of the Bible as a whole, that the deeper we dig into it, the finer the gold we shall be able to extract from its hidden depths. The Divine assist-ance was rendered to David, not only when he slung the stone at Goliath, but also at the time when the best equipment in the army was being placed at his service. He tried to wear Saul's armour, but so far from helping him, it impeded his movements. He therefore discarded it altogether, and declined to

The story never loses its charm.

The Divine help rendered to David in the choice of his armour.

179

1 Sam.
xvii. 1–
54.

David's
common
sense.

wear any armour at all. Herein David showed his common sense. The heavy armour of a full-grown man of war would be entirely unsuited to a youth, and the deadly use of the catapult had been brought to perfection, as we know from the instance of the left-handed men of Benjamin, of whom it is recorded " Among all this people there were seven hundred chosen men left-handed ; every one could sling stones at an hairbreadth, and not miss " (Judg. xx. 16). Doubtless the young shepherd was an adept in its use. Should he fight Goliath with ordinary weapons, there could be but one result, certain defeat and death. On the other hand, should he use the weapon with which he was most familiar, the chances of victory would be very much increased. The mention of common sense might seem to magnify David's share in the great victory, and to

A gift of
God.

belittle that of God. But this is not the case. There is a sanctified common sense. Few of us pass through life without finding ourselves sometimes in most awkward positions. To surmount the difficulty demands swiftness of decision as well as prompt action. But we are not absolved from using our intelligence. To shut our eyes, and do the first thing that suggests itself to our minds, would be to court disaster. The alternatives must be quickly balanced by us, and, provided we are seeking the Divine guidance, we shall be led to say the right word, as was Nehemiah in the presence of Artaxerxes (Neh. ii. 4, 5), and the right reasons for embarking on a certain course of action will be made clear to us.

How
David's

The deliberate manner in which David singled

out the five smooth stones from the others in the
brook, the steady aim he took at his terrible enemy,
betoken his calm and steadfast reliance upon God.
" In quietness and confidence shall be your strength "
might well have been his motto.

While tending his sheep David must often have
aimed at some distant object, to while away the
tedium of the solitary hours. Little did he think
that this practice of his would give him such pro-
ficiency in the use of the catapult, that one day his
own life would be saved, and the fate of his country
decided thereby.

All unknown to him was the tremendous significance also of those daily acts of devotion, wherein
he put himself and his sheep under the protecting
care of God. In the stillness of the country and
isolation of the mountains and valleys amongst
which he wandered with his sheep, he would often
lift up his eyes unto the hills, and his heart unto Him
under Whose wings was " curing and securing."
Thus are habits formed, of the spirit as well as of
the outward man, and in the moment of supreme
need the habit would instinctively assert itself, and
his heart leap up to Him Who had never yet failed
him. The " sure trust " which had been storing
itself, by daily intercourse with his Rock and
Defence, in the reservoir of his soul, was justified
in this crisis of his life. God gave him the courage
and nerve which he needed. The victory was
swift and absolute. It is an inexorable law of
human souls, but in reality the revelation, not of
an austere master but of a gracious Father, " that

[margin notes:] 1 Sam. xvii. 1–54. faith gave him steadiness of aim. His previous experience.

The importance of habit.

The First Book of Samuel

1 Sam. xvii. 1—54.

we prepare ourselves," as George Eliot writes in *Romula,* " for sudden deeds by the reiterated choice of good over evil which gradually determines character."

The value of Christian experience.

David declined to wear Saul's armour, for " *he had not proved it* " (verse 39). Herein is concealed a profound spiritual truth. Sunday after Sunday we may express our adhesion to the foremost verities of the Christian faith, but until they have in some measure come to form part of our religious experience, they will prove a weak reed upon which to lean in the time of stress and storm. Far be it from us to speak slightingly of the great Christian Creeds, for in them are enshrined the experiences of countless souls of all ages and climes. " To borrow an image from Lotze, creeds are like the bones of the body, the outcome of the life-process itself, and also the means by which it gives firmness, stability and definiteness of outline to the animal organism."[1] The Christian religion could not maintain itself without carefully thought-out statement, tested by time and experience, of the principles implied in

Truth must become part of us.

its own life. But for any truth to be of value to the individual, it must be laid hold of by him. No longer, then, outside and independent of him, it enters into his experience and forms part of his life. It will always be beyond him, but it is now within him. Christ was born in Bethlehem, but He must be formed within the heart (cf. Gal. iv. 19). The Cross erected on the green hill outside the city wall,

---

[1] Cf. *The Philosophy of Religion,* by G. Galloway (Edinburgh ; T. & T. Clark, 1914), p. 165.

means nothing to a man unless he has experienced **1 Sam.** its redeeming power and grace, even though he **xvii. 1—** may be able to give a most accurate account of the **54.** various theories, propounded and held, concerning the significance and efficacy of the Atonement. The Resurrection of Christ is a fact which happened at a particular time in the world's history, but we only come to apprehend its value when we are daily dying into sin, and seeking those things which are above (Col. iii. 1), and are in contact with the Ever-living and Ascended Lord.

Past experience had proved to David the value of the sling, therefore he would make trial of it in the face of his enemy. With regard to the armour and helmet with which Saul armed him, the exact reverse was true, no other course was open to him but to discard them. "*I cannot go with these*," and David put them off him. Already he had proved how God had delivered him from the jaws of death, thus David knew that He would not desert His servant in the time of his extreme peril. "O taste **Ps. xxxiv.** and see that the Lord is good." Put Him to the **4 ff.** test, try and see how true to His promises He is in your life, and you will find that He will not fail you, and that He is ever blessing you (Ps. xxxiv. 4 ff.).

Originally we believed on the testimony of others, but now we believe, for we have heard for ourselves and know that Jesus is indeed the Saviour of the **St. John iv.** world (St. John iv. 42). **42.**

This does not imply that each man is at liberty to believe what he likes, and that in his grasp of

The First Book of Samuel

1 Sam.
xvii. 1–
54.

Our grasp of Christian truth not independent of others.

Christian truth he is independent of others. David did not discover for himself the use of the catapult. It was a recognised weapon in his country. In like manner our faith depends on the Witness of the Incarnate Son of God, and of the Holy Spirit which finds its clearest expression in the Holy Scriptures. It also owes much to the testimony of believers throughout the centuries, that is, the Church of God, to the miracles of Grace manifested in changed and consecrated lives. But the ultimate appeal must be to the conscience and reason of the individual man. The Faith must become his faith if he is to wrestle successfully against the principalities, Eph. vi. 12. against the powers, against the world-rulers of this darkness (Eph. vi. 12 f.). Left to ourselves, each one of us would fail, but in Luther's strong and virile words—

> " But for us fights the proper Man,
>   Whom God Himself hath bidden
>   Ask ye, who is this Same ?
>   Christ Jesus is His Name,
>   The Lord Zebaoth's Son ;
>   He, and no other one,
>   Shall conquer in the battle."

Nay, in all things we are more than conquerors through Him Who loved us (Rom. viii. 37).

184

XVIII

THE WITHDRAWAL OF THE SPIRIT OF GOD, AND ITS CONSEQUENCES

But the Spirit of the LORD departed from Saul, and an evil spirit from the LORD troubled him.

And David went out whithersoever Saul sent him, *and* behaved himself wisely : and Saul set him over the men of war, and he was accepted in the sight of all the people, and also in the sight of Saul's servants. And it came to pass as they came, when David was returned from the slaughter of the Philistine, that the women came out of all cities of Israel, singing and dancing, to meet king Saul, with tabrets, with joy, and with instruments of musick. And the women answered *one another* as they played, and said, Saul hath slain his thousands, and David his ten thousands. And Saul was very wroth, and the saying displeased him ; and he said, They have ascribed unto David ten thousands, and to me they have ascribed *but* thousands : and *what* can he have more but the kingdom ? And Saul eyed David from that day and forward.

And it came to pass on the morrow, that the evil spirit from God came upon Saul, and he prophesied in the midst of the house : and David played with his hand, as at other times : and *there was* a javelin in Saul's hand. And Saul cast the javelin ; for he said, I will smite David even to the wall *with it.* And David avoided out of his presence twice.

And Saul was afraid of David, because the LORD was with him, and was departed from Saul. Therefore Saul removed him from him, and made him his captain over a thousand ; and he went out and came in before the people. And David behaved himself wisely in all his ways ; and the LORD *was* with him. Wherefore when Saul saw that he behaved himself very wisely,

The First Book of Samuel

he was afraid of him. But all Israel and Judah loved David, because he went out and came in before them.

And Saul said to David, Behold my elder daughter Merab, her will I give thee to wife : only be thou valiant for me, and fight the LORD's battles. For Saul said, Let not mine hand be upon him, but let the hand of the Philistines be upon him. And David said unto Saul, Who *am* I ? and what *is* my life, *or* my father's family in Israel, that I should be son in law to the king ? But it came to pass at the time when Merab Saul's daughter should have been given to David, that she was given unto Adriel the Meholathite to wife. And Michal Saul's daughter loved David : and they told Saul, and the thing pleased him. And Saul said, I will give him her, that she may be a snare to him, and that the hand of the Philistines may be against him. Wherefore Saul said to David, Thou shalt this day be my son in law in *the one of* the twain.

And Saul commanded his servants, *saying*, Commune with David secretly, and say, Behold, the king hath delight in thee, and all his servants love thee : now therefore be the king's son in law. And Saul's servants spake those words in the ears of David. And David said, Seemeth it to you *a* light *thing* to be a king's son in law, seeing that I *am* a poor man, and lightly esteemed ? And the servants of Saul told him, saying, On thi manner spake David. And Saul said, Thus shall ye say to David, The king desireth not any dowry, but an hundred foreskins of the Philistines, to be avenged of the king's enemies. But Saul thought to make David fall by the hand of the Philistines. And when his servants told David these words, it pleased David well to be the king's son in law : and the days were not expired. Wherefore David arose and went, he and his men, and slew of the Philistines two hundred men ; and David brought their foreskins, and they gave them in full tale to the king, that he might be the king's son in law. And Saul gave him Michal his daughter to wife.

And Saul saw and knew that the LORD *was* with David, and *that* Michal Saul's daughter loved him. And Saul was yet the more afraid of David ; and Saul became David's enemy continually. Then the princes of the Philistines went forth : and it came to pass, after they went forth, *that* David behaved himself more wisely than all the servants of Saul ; so that his name was much set by.

And there was war again : and David went out, and fought

with the Philistines, and slew them with a great slaughter ; and they fled from him. And the evil spirit from the LORD was upon Saul, as he sat in his house with his javelin in his hand : and David played with *his* hand. And Saul sought to smite David even to the wall with the javelin ; but he slipped away out of Saul's presence, and he smote the javelin into the wall : and David fled, and escaped that night. Saul also sent messengers unto David's house, to watch him, and to slay him in the morning : and Michal David's wife told him, saying, If thou save not thy life to night, to morrow thou shalt be slain.

So Michal let David down through a window : and he went, and fled, and escaped. And Michal took an image, and laid *it* in the bed, and put a pillow of goats' *hair* for his bolster, and covered *it* with a cloth. And when Saul sent messengers to take David, she said, He *is* sick. And Saul sent the messengers *again* to see David, saying, Bring him up to me in the bed, that I may slay him. And when the messengers were come in, behold, *there was* an image in the bed, with a pillow of goats' *hair* for his bolster. And Saul said unto Michal, Why hast thou deceived me so, and sent away mine enemy, that he is escaped ? And Michal answered Saul, He said unto me, Let me go ; why should I kill thee ?

So David hid himself in the field : and when the new moon was come, the king sat him down to eat meat. And the king sat upon his seat, as at other times, *even* upon a seat by the wall : and Jonathan arose, and Abner sat by Saul's side, and David's place was empty. Nevertheless Saul spake not any thing that day : for he thought, Something hath befallen him, he *is* not clean ; surely he *is* not clean. And it came to pass on the morrow, *which was* the second *day* of the month, that David's place was empty : and Saul said unto Jonathan his son, Wherefore cometh not the son of Jesse to meat, neither yesterday, nor to day ? And Jonathan answered Saul, David earnestly asked *leave* of me *to go* to Beth-lehem : And he said, Let me go, I pray thee ; for our family hath a sacrifice in the city ; and my brother, he hath commanded me *to be there :* and now, if I have found favour in thine eyes, let me get away, I pray thee, and see my brethren. Therefore he cometh not unto the king's table. Then Saul's anger was kindled against Jonathan, and he said unto him, Thou son of the perverse rebellious *woman,* do not I know that thou hast chosen the son of Jesse to thine own confusion, and unto the confusion of thy mother's nakedness ? For as long as the son of Jesse liveth upon the ground, thou shalt not be established, nor thy kingdom. Wherefore now send and fetch him unto me, for he shall surely die. And Jonathan answered Saul his father, and said unto him, Wherefore shall he be slain ? what hath he done ? And Saul cast a javelin at him to smite him : whereby Jonathan knew that it was determined of his father to slay David. So Jonathan arose from the table in fierce anger, and did eat no meat the second day of the month : for he was grieved for David, because his father had done him shame.—1 SAM. XVI. 14 ; XVIII. 5–30 ; XIX. 8–17 ; XX. 24–34 ; XXII. 5 to end.

1 Sam. xvi. 14 ; xviii. 5–30 ; xix. 8–17 ; xx. 24–34 ; xxii. 5 to end.

An evil spirit troubles Saul.

Its meaning hard to understand.

St. James i. 13.

The Spirit of God, a spirit from God.

JUDGEMENT had already been delivered upon Saul, and we read that the Spirit of the Lord had departed from him. When the grace of God is withdrawn from a man's life, he becomes a prey to evil influences; in Old Testament language, " *an evil spirit from the Lord troubles him* " (1 Sam. xvi. 14).

This last sentence raises difficulties in our minds. We shrink, and quite rightly shrink, from entertaining even the bare thought that evil can be associated with the Being we worship, the God and Father of our Lord Jesus Christ. St. James writes, " Let no man say when he is tempted, I am tempted of God.: for God cannot be tempted with evil, and He Himself tempteth no man " (i. 13). In considering this statement about Saul, it should be observed that there is a distinction between " the Spirit of God," and " a spirit from God." The former applies to God in a way which is peculiarly His own, His Holy Spirit (cf. Ps. li. 11). On the other hand, " a spirit from God " is not part of the Divine Essence, and is outside the Divine Life, except in so far as all created Beings derive their existence from, and are dependent upon, God.

Withdrawal of the Spirit of God

This particular judgement upon Saul will be better I Sam. xvi. 14 ; xviii. 5– 30 ; xix. 8–17; xx. 24– 34 ; xxii. 5 to end. understood if placed side by side with St. Paul's condemnation of the moral failure of the Gentiles, to be found in the latter half of the opening chapter of his letter to the Romans. On account of the idolatry practised by the Gentiles, changing the glory of the incorruptible God into an image made like to corruptible man (Rom. i. 23), three times is it repeated that God gave them up (verses 24, 26 and 28), and it has been pointed out that the meaning of the words " gave them up," not only includes the ideas of God allowing them to have their own way, and the withdrawal of His gracious aid, but is judicial as well. It is the punishment which automatically follows upon those who, when they know God, glorify Him not as God.

God's withdrawal of aid is judicial.

The Semitic mind did not believe in so-called secondary causes. Speaking of the Great European War, a devout Jew, living in Old Testament times, would have said, without any misgivings or searchings of heart, that it had been brought upon mankind by God. He would go on to say that an evil spirit had been sent to stir up the German Government, and, through its agency, had caused the war. To-day we should express ourselves differently.

The Semitic mind. And the Great War.

Returning to Saul, " *He had cast away the fear of God.*" God had been ignored in his life, and therefore he was left to the mercy of his own wayward passions and inclinations. It is a solemn fact that a man may, by his own acts, cut himself off from God. By no arbitrary fate, but by the accumulated acts, the deliberate trend of his life, he has it in his

What had happened to Saul.

189

power to quench the longsuffering, the long-patient Spirit of God (1 Thess. v. 19).   He will never forsake the man of humble and contrite heart, resolutely bent on doing the Will of God at all costs, but will take up His abode with him, and amongst all the difficulties, intellectual, moral and spiritual, which beset his path, will enlighten him " more and more unto the perfect day."   The Holy Spirit can never be sought in vain.   According to the paradox of St. Bernard, " He alone is God Who can never be sought in vain : not even when He cannot be found."

Certain results followed.

The results of the departure of the Spirit of the Lord from Saul, caused by his rejection of God, were speedily manifest.   They involved him in a series of sorrows and disasters.   From that day to the end of his life, the downward course in his career was inevitable and rapid.

Envy.

When David returned from the slaughter of the Philistine, the women came out from all the cities of Israel, with every manifestation of joy and delight, to meet Saul, and the refrain of their song was, " *Saul hath slain his thousands, and David his ten thousands* " (xviii. 7).   Saul's anger flared up, and he was overcome by envy.   " *And Saul eyed David from that day and forward,*" are the Bible's expressive words.   According to Dante, envy is the second of the three sins caused by love for a neighbour's ill.

" There is, who fearing lest he lose his own
Power, grace, fame, honour, by another's rise,
Grows sad, and for the contrary is prone."
(*Purg.* xvii. 118–120.)

In Saul's case, the centre of his life was not God

but self, and when the dethronement of that self **1 Sam.**
from its place of honour and glory was threatened **xvi. 14 ;**
by the successes of another, envy, like some horrible **xviii. 5–**
reptile which noiselessly creeps into a house, found **30 ; xix.**
its way into Saul's heart. The great Italian Poet **8–17 ;**
has placed the envious in the lowest circle of **xx. 24–**
Purgatory, clad in hair cloth, and with their eyes **34 ; xxii.**
sewn up by iron threads. Herein is portrayed a **5 to end.**
sad fact of experience. Even among those who **The sins of**
belong to Christ, many have to guard against **Saints.**
envious and jealous thoughts. We have heard a
sermon preached on the sins of Saints, and the
virtues of Sinners, and alas! to the discredit of
Saints, envy and jealousy must often be placed to
their account. Church work is continually ham-
pered and spoilt by the petty jealousies amongst
otherwise excellent Christian people. To a certain
individual has been assigned an important position
in a society, guild or club, and on account of this,
another worker who considers that he had every
right to fill the post, feels that he has been slighted,
and therefore declines to help, or even goes out of his
way to hinder the work of the one who has been
appointed. Instead of Christ being glorified, and **Their**
His Kingdom advanced, He is dishonoured and **disputes and**
wounded by the disputes and bickerings of those **bickerings.**
who are His friends, and yet are hardly on speaking
terms with one another. They will kneel together
at the Lord's Table, but when they meet each
other in the street, with a stiff bow they pass by.

So hard is it for certain natures to overcome this
particular fault, that it has given occasion for the

The First Book of Samuel

1 Sam.
xvi. 14 ;
xviii. 5–
30 ; xix.
8–17 ;
xx. 24–
34 ; xxii.
5 to end.
remark passed by La Rochefoucauld, " that in the troubles of our good friends there is always something that does not displease us," and for the further comment, " And with still greater justice may we assert that there is always something in the good fortune of our friends that does not entirely please us." What an overmastering effect upon the world Christianity would have had, could it have been said of her, all down the Christian centuries, as of the Early Church, " See how these Christians love one another " !

No quarter allowed to envy.

When the first traces of these jealousies and envyings arise in the breast, and they will arise, they should at once be recognised as utterly alien to the mind of Christ, traitors in the camp, and treated accordingly. No extenuating circumstances pleaded, no quarter given, they must by God's grace, be cast out. If allowed, harboured, nursed, no one knows whither they may lead, as many a one beside Saul has found to his cost.

In pleasing contrast to all this, let the examples of Moses and St. Paul be placed before us. The friends of Moses viewed with anything but favour the prophesying of Eldad and Medad, as calculated to undermine the authority and influence of their leader. But Moses showed the nobility and greatness of his spirit by asking Joshua, " Art thou jealous for my sake ? would God that all the Lord's people were prophets, that the Lord would put His Spirit upon them ! " (Num. xi. 29). St. Paul writes that there were some who preached Christ from envy and a spirit of contention, hoping to vex him. How

Moses and St. Paul without a trace of envy.

192

does he treat them ? This is what he writes to the Philippians : " Some indeed preach Christ even of envy and strife ; and some also of good will : . . . what then ? only that in every way, whether in pretence or in truth, Christ is proclaimed ; and therein I rejoice, yea, and will rejoice " (Phil. i. 15, 18).

1 Sam. xvi. 14 ; xviii. 5–30 ; xix. 8–17 ; xx. 24–34 ; xxii. 5 to end.

He could take up this attitude, for to him life was Christ (Phil. i. 21). He had drunk so deeply of His Spirit, that he had become not only broadminded but broadhearted. As we shall see in the case of Jonathan, whose love for David was self-effacing, so was it in that of St. Paul. His love for his Master was such, that self no longer counted, it was submerged, gone out of sight and hearing. Thus in composing his hymn in praise of Love, with his eyes fastened on his beloved Master, he could say, " Love suffereth long, and is kind ; love envieth not ; . . . seeketh not its own, is not provoked, taketh not account of evil " (1 Cor. xiii. 4, 5).

1 Cor. xiii. 4, 5.

This feeling of envy in Saul soon passed into that of jealousy. Fear (1 Sam. xviii. 12, 15) and hatred displaced any consciousness of inferiority that Saul might have had concerning David. He regarded him as a possible rival to his throne. The very sight of David so enraged him that he lost control of himself altogether.

Envy soon turns into jealousy.

At last a murderous impulse swayed him. Twice when David was playing on the harp before him, Saul brandished his spear (" And Saul cast the spear," xviii. 11), the son of Jesse effecting his escape in time. As the monarch brooded over

Jealousy leads to murder.

1 Sam. xvi. 14 ; xviii. 5– 30 ; xix. 8–17 ; xx. 24– 34 ; xxii. 5 to end. imaginary wrongs, his enmity against David increased. The latter might be out of sight, but he was not out of mind. Under pretence of doing him honour, Saul made David captain over a thousand, and afterwards proposed that he should marry his elder daughter Merab, thereby taking occasion to place him in situations of such danger that humanly speaking he must certainly have lost his life. There was indeed one short interlude when Saul's better nature asserted itself, and David was restored to his presence (xix. 7), but the old jealousy broke out once more. Eventually, another outburst of passion compelled David to fly from his presence. Saved by the quick-witted resourcefulness of his wife Michal from the messengers sent to slay him in his own house, he made his escape to Naioth in Ramah, where he took refuge with Samuel (xix. 19).

Saul turns against his own son. But the worst has not yet been told. Saul turned against his own son, and endeavoured to take his life, reviling him in language of the coarsest description for his friendship with David, when Jonathan sought to account to his father for his **His treatment of the city of Nob.** friend's absence (xx. 30). The climax, however, was reached when, by his command, eighty-five priests were slain at Nob, and the city and its inhabitants destroyed (xxii. 17–19), simply because Ahimelech the priest had on a previous occasion allowed David to partake of the shewbread, and to carry away with him the sword of Goliath.

Saul blinded by passion. Thus was Saul blinded by passion. Soon after David's rise to fame, Saul perceived that the Lord was with him (xviii. 12). That the son of Jesse,

Withdrawal of the Spirit of God

far from plotting against his throne, wished to afford him all the help he was capable of giving against their country's foes, weighed with Saul not at all, and he could not see that in striving to compass David's overthrow he was fighting a losing battle, inasmuch as he was fighting against God.

1 Sam. xvi. 14 ; xviii. 5–30 ; xix. 8–17 ; xx. 24–34 ; xxii. 5 to end.

Sin always produces this effect.

An eye to the main chance.

Sin always exercises a blinding effect upon those who are its servants, in the case of nations and individuals alike. How often do we hear it said of a man that he has an eye to the main chance, implying that where his own private interests are concerned he is quick and astute, able to grasp at any opportunity of making money, or furthering his own advancement ! He often gains his ends with an entire disregard for others, and looks upon pity as weak sentiment, and nothing more. Business is business. He intends to succeed, and succeed he will. If, however, the truth were to be known, that same individual has not an eye to the main chance. Apart from the saying that the shroud has no pockets, what does he gain thereby ? loss of inward happiness and peace. Were he to gain the whole world, it would be at the expense of his higher self. On the other hand, the work of the Spirit of Truth is to open our eyes to the finer issues of life, to enable us to see life steadily and to see it whole, to understand that the supreme purpose of existence is not getting but giving, and that the true riches are not on earth but in the kingdom of our inner selves, and in the kingdom of Heaven, above all to reveal to us Christ and His claim upon

1 Sam.
xvi. 14 ;
xviii. 5–
30 ; xix.
8–17 ;
xx. 24–
34 ; xxii.
5 to end.

Saul's life a
warning.

us. This is the true wisdom in comparison with which worldly wisdom is but folly.

Saul's life is a tragedy, the light within him had become darkness, and his last state was worse than the first, and the pity of it is, that he has many successors. Well may we remember the warnings, " Grieve not the Holy Spirit of God," " Quench not the Spirit."

XIX

A FRAGMENT OF THE GOSPEL

Then came David to Nob to Ahimelech the priest : and Ahimelech was afraid at the meeting of David, and said unto him, Why *art* thou alone, and no man with thee ? And David said unto Ahimelech the priest, The king hath commanded me a business, and hath said unto me, Let no man know any thing of the business whereabout I send thee, and what I have commanded thee : and I have appointed *my* servants to such and such a place. Now therefore what is under thine hand ? give *me* five *loaves of* bread in mine hand, or what there is present. And the priest answered David, and said, *There is* no common bread under mine hand, but there is hallowed bread ; if the young men have kept themselves at least from women. And David answered the priest, and said unto him, Of a truth women *have been* kept from us about these three days, since I came out, and the vessels of the young men are holy, and *the bread is* in a manner common, yea, though it were sanctified this day in the vessel. So the priest gave him hallowed *bread :* for there was no bread there but the shewbread, that was taken from before the LORD, to put hot bread in the day when it was taken away. Now a certain man of the servants of Saul *was* there that day, detained before the LORD ; and his name *was* Doeg, an Edomite, the chiefest of the herdmen that *belonged* to Saul.

And David said unto Ahimelech, And is there not here under thine hand spear or sword ? for I have neither brought my sword nor my weapons with me, because the king's business required haste. And the priest said, The sword of Goliath the Philistine, whom thou slewest in the valley of Elah, behold, it *is here* wrapped in a cloth behind the ephod : if thou wilt take that, take *it :* for *there is* no other save that here. And David said, *There is* none like that ; give it me.

And he said unto them, Have ye never read what David did, when he had need, and was an hungred, he, and they that were with him ? How he went into the house of God in the days of Abiathar the high priest, and did eat the shewbread, which is not lawful to eat but for the priests, and gave also to them which were with him ?—1 SAM. XXI. 1-9 ; ST. MARK II. 25-26.

1 Sam. xxi. 1-9 ; St. Mark ii. 25-26.

Our Lord made use of this story.

THE story of the meeting between David and Ahimelech at Nob is of unusual interest to us on account of our Lord's use of it, in order to justify the action of His disciples, on a particular Sabbath Day. It is mentioned in the first three gospels (St. Matt. xii. 3-4 ; St. Mark. ii. 25-26 ; St. Luke vi. 3-4) to illustrate and enforce one of the most important principles of our Lord's teaching. For this reason, if for no other, this incident will repay our most careful study.

David an outlaw from Saul's court. Goes to Nob.

Alone and unattended.

He lulls Ahimelech's suspicions, and requests him for bread.

David is at last convinced that he is an outlaw, and from this time onwards is a fugitive from King Saul's court. He first makes his way to Nob, a city of the priests (1 Sam. xxii. 19), situated a little to the north of Jerusalem, of which every trace has disappeared. Outside this first book of Samuel it is only mentioned twice (Neh. xi. 32 ; Is. x. 32). David comes to the place for the purpose of seeking counsel and help from God (1 Sam. xxii. 13). He is alone and unattended, though very shortly to be joined by some young men of the court (verses 2 and 5). Ahimelech the High Priest expresses surprise at the sight of David without any of his ordinary retinue, whereupon David invents a story to allay any suspicion that he may have incurred Saul's displeasure. He asserts that he has been sent by the king on an important errand which involves the utmost haste, and the greatest possible

A Fragment of the Gospel

secrecy, and he accounts for the absence of his 1 Sam. xxi. 1–9 ; St. Mark ii. 25–26. servants on the ground that arrangements had already been made for them to meet him at a specified place. He then begs Ahimelech to give him five loaves, or any food that he may happen to have at hand. In answer to this, Ahimelech states that he has nothing but consecrated bread. This he could not part with unless certain ceremonial requirements had been observed by David and his young men. He receives from David an assurance that they have been observed, or if that is not the exact meaning of his reply, we may understand it to be that the circumstances of the case precluded any danger of sacrilege. The scruples of Ahimelech thus overcome, he gives the shewbread, literally "the Bread of the Presence," to David ; and on his further request for a spear or a sword, the sword of Goliath, wrapt in a cloth behind the Ephod, is delivered into his hands (verse 9).

Ahimelech gives him the shew-bread. Also the sword of Goliath.

For us, the point of the narrative is not that David told a lie, and that therefore we may conclude that, in certain circumstances, lying and deception are justifiable. Our Lord passes over this feature of the story in silence, and although the Bible makes no comment upon David's conduct, yet the terrible vengeance executed by Saul on the inhabitants and city of Nob, must have been a source of the keenest pain to David, as we can clearly see from his words of deep regret to Abiathar, the sole survivor of the massacre, " I knew on that day, when Doeg the Edomite was there, that he would surely tell Saul : I have occasioned the death of

David's lie is not the point of the narrative. It was passed over by our Lord in silence.

The First Book of Samuel

1 Sam.
xxi. 1–9 ;
St. Mark
ii. 25–26.

all the persons of thy father's house " (1 Sam. xxii. 22). And we cannot doubt that an additional bitterness would enter into this regret through the consciousness that the help he had received on that occasion had been afforded him on the assumption that he had told the truth, and nothing but the truth.

Why our Lord quoted the story.

Our Lord quotes the instance of the shewbread being given to David by Ahimelech to enforce the superiority of moral claims over ceremonial regulations. The Pharisees had found fault with the disciples, and through them designedly with Christ, for plucking and eating the ears of corn, as they walked through the cornfields on the Sabbath day. To pluck the ears of standing corn was permitted by the Law, provided that no instrument such as a sickle was used (Deut. xxiii. 25). The Pharisees' real objection was, that according to their tradition, the disciples had done this on the Sabbath Day. From the Talmud we gather that if a woman " rolls wheat to remove the husks, it is considered as sifting ; if she rubs the heads of wheat, it is regarded as threshing ; if she cleans off the side-adherences, it is sifting out fruit ; if she bruises the ears, it is grinding ; if she throws them up in her hand, it is winnowing." [1] The Disciples then were guilty of breaking the Sabbath. Therein lay the stone of stumbling and the rock of offence, from the Pharisees' point of view. Our Lord replied by

The disciples, according to the Pharisees, guilty of breaking the Sabbath.

Christ justified their action by what David did at Nob.

[1] Cf. Edersheim, *The Life and Times of Jesus the Messiah* (London : Longmans, Green & Co., 1894), 8th ed. vol. ii. pp. 55, 56.

A Fragment of the Gospel

holding before them the example of David, their 1 Sam. xxi. 1-9 ; great national hero, and also the recognised type of Old Testament piety.

St. Mark ii. 25-26.

In his particular case the law was set on one side and disregarded. Technically, David had no right to eat the shewbread. Legal enactments must be judged in the light of great moral principles. The first are subservient to the second. The basic principle upon which all the Mosaic Legislation concerning the Sabbath was founded, consisted in the truth enunciated by our Lord, that " the Sabbath was made for man, not man for the Sabbath." That must be the criterion by which all violations, so-called or otherwise, of its observance should be judged.

The basic principle of the Sabbath.

David had been dispensed from the observance of the ceremonial law because threatened with starvation, the Disciples from that of the Sabbatic Law on account of hunger. In both cases the course taken had been justified. The letter of the law had been broken, but its spirit had been observed.

The letter of the law broken, its spirit observed.

The average man delights in cut-and-dried rules, provided that there are not too many of them. Vagueness he abhors, definiteness he loves. " Tell me precisely what I may do, what I may not do " is often heard. To such appeal the religion of Christ vouchsafes no answer. Our Lord's teaching and method are quite otherwise. Little stress is laid on the actual keeping of rules ; it is the motive which governs a man's action, the disposition of his heart, the attitude he adopts towards God and the

The average man's delight in definite rules.

But motives and disposition of the heart all-important.

201

The First Book of Samuel

carrying out of His Will, which are all-important. Our Lord then recalls men's minds, not to this or that rule respecting the Sabbath, but to the underlying principle embodied in the command that one day in the week should be marked out from the other six and regarded as holy.

Work on the Sabbath Day.

Work of some kind may have to be done on the Sabbath Day in order that it may be a rest day. " Necessity breaks iron and knows no command " is true in the sense, that any rule, the observance of which runs counter to a man's highest and best interests, must be disregarded. The Sabbath was made for man, so that any rules framed for the observance of that day must take his true well-being into first consideration, and even then, the best thought-out regulations may at times have to be laid on one side.

How the Lord would treat the Sunday question to-day.

To-day this aspect of the Sabbath, or as we prefer to call it, of the Sunday, does not need the emphasis laid upon it which was necessary in our Lord's days. It has been rightly observed that Christ " puts the accent on the side which humanity is tempted to neglect." [1] In modern times the principle that the Sabbath is made for man, not man for the Sabbath, has obtained universal recognition, but not in the spirit in which it was originally uttered by our Lord. Its Godward side is often neglected. The Sabbath was made for man, but what was man made for ? Could it be better expressed than in the words of the Shorter

What is the chief end of man ?

[1] *The Authority of Christ,* by Dr. D. W. Forrest (T. & T. Clark, Edinburgh, 1906), p. 171.

A Fragment of the Gospel

Catechism of the Westminster Assembly of Divines ? **1 Sam.**
"The chief end of man is to glorify God and enjoy **xxi. 1–9 ;**
Him for ever," or as St. Irenæus wrote hundreds of **St. Mark**
years ago, "For as the glory of man is God, so the **ii. 25–26.**
sum of the works of God, and the recipient of all
His Wisdom and Power, is Man." Would not
our Lord remind us that in all our discussions as to
what may be done or not done on the Sunday, the
greatest care must be taken, both for our own sake
and that of others, to guard it as the day in which
man can find rest of body and mind, and, what is of
even greater importance, have the opportunity of
finding God, Who alone can satisfy the heart and
give rest to the soul ? To seek God in His House,
and not to forsake the assembling of ourselves for
the purposes of prayer and worship, is the prime
object for which the Sabbath was made for man.

Our Lord's quotation from David's life also **The need of**
brings before us the need of preserving a due sense **a proper**
of proportion. In fact, it may be said that this **sense of proportion.**
is one of the main lessons derived from our study
of the first book of Samuel. Obedience is better
than sacrifice, the state of the heart more important
than the outward appearance. In our Saviour's
day, men's minds were so taken up with the
observance of minute rules and endless details,
that they forgot the main principles of life. The
true observance of the Sabbath was so smothered
under burdensome enactments, declaring what was
allowed, and what forbidden, with all the pains and
penalties consequent upon their infringement, that
the true end of the Sabbath was often forgotten.

The First Book of Samuel

1 Sam. xxi. 1-9 ; St. Mark ii. 25-26.   This particular instance of the letter contradicting the spirit is dwelt upon here, as it is connected by our Lord with the story of David and Ahimelech. There are, as we know, many others, and of a different kind. How different would have been the history of the Church, and how far more effective her witness to the world, had she thrown all her weight into those truths which were emphasised by her Divine Head, and spent less time on matters which we can now see were often of only secondary importance !

First things first.   The "*firsts*" of Christ's life should be our "*firsts*." It behoves us to be on our guard lest, like the Pharisees, in our extreme anxiety "to strain out the gnat, we swallow the camel." Our perspective and our standard of values should ever be those of our Lord and Master.

204

XX

GOD'S GREAT GIFT OF FRIENDSHIP

And it came to pass, when he had made an end of speaking unto Saul, that the soul of Jonathan was knit with the soul of David, and Jonathan loved him as his own soul. And Saul took him that day, and would let him go no more home to his father's house. Then Jonathan and David made a covenant, because he loved him as his own soul. And Jonathan stripped himself of the robe that *was* upon him, and gave it to David, and his garments, even to his sword, and to his bow, and to his girdle.

I am distressed for thee, my brother Jonathan : very pleasant hast thou been unto me : thy love to me was wonderful, passing the love of women.—1 SAM. XVIII. 1–4 ; 2 SAM. I. 26.

ALLUSION has already been made, and will be made again in the course of our exposition, to Jonathan's love for David, but the study of the first book of Samuel would be very incomplete without a closer view of this great classic of Friendship. "The best that Greece and Rome have to show of friendship," so wrote the late Professor Shairp, "looks pale beside this."

Such a story as that of David and Jonathan, so full of romance and adventure, fires our imagination and warms our hearts whenever it is recited. Something in David drew Jonathan to him on the very

1 Sam. xviii. 1–4 ; 2 Sam. i. 26. Jonathan and David the great classic of friendship.

205

The First Book of Samuel

1 Sam. xviii. 1–4 ; 2 Sam. i. 26.

first occasion of their meeting. After David's formal introduction to Saul, and the conversation which ensued : " *The soul of Jonathan was knit with the soul of David, and Jonathan loved him as his own soul* " (xviii. 1).

Their souls knit to each other.

Had Jonathan tried to explain how he came to be so greatly attracted to the son of Jesse, he might have found it difficult to analyse his own feelings. If pressed for an answer, he would have descanted on David's charm, as well as the bravery exhibited by him when face to face with the champion of the Philistines, and then he might well have flung up his hands with a gesture of despair, and exclaimed, " But after all he *is David.*" Jonathan's experience is not unique. Similar words have risen to the lips of all of us to whom has been accorded the privilege of true friendship. Turn over in our minds as we may the whys and wherefores of the attraction certain people exercise over us, the spell they cast upon us, we can never arrive at an answer satis-

The mystery of friendship.

factory to ourselves. There is always something about the relationship which baffles and mystifies us. On both sides the feeling is uppermost, para-doxical as it may sound, that we did not choose our friends, but that they chose us. No forcing of ourselves, or compulsion on their part, produced the friendship. Judged from our point of view, they came, we saw, they conquered.

Friendship, a gift from God.

But whence originated this attraction ? How did it arise ? who kindled this spark of friendship till it became a bright, red flame ? From one source it came ; as to *how* it came we know not, but the spark has fallen from off the altar of God. The Beloved Disciple writes, not according to the rendering of the Authorised Version, " We love Him because He first loved us," but " We love, because He first loved us." The very fact that we can love at all is to be attributed to God. Further, love is not simply a Divine quality, it is of the essence of God, He IS love. All true love and friendship spring from God. They are His gifts. As Emerson has said, " My friends have come to me unsought. The great God gave them to me."

1 Sam. xviii. 1–4 ; 2 Sam. i. 26.

1 St. John iv. 19.

It is recorded that on one occasion Jonathan went to David into the wood of the wilderness of Ziph and " *strengthened his hand in God* " (xxiii. 16). We may be certain that this was not the only time that Jonathan performed this beautiful act of friendship. And very often must David have been uplifted merely by the presence of his friend. Nay, more, of both it would be true to say that the Divine Companionship became nearer and more intimate after they had communed with each other.

One of the most beautiful offices of friendship.

The roads to God are many and various. It is not for us to limit their number, so long as they lead ultimately to Jesus Christ, Who is the Way, the Road into the very heart of God. Many a man, and many a woman, has considered that the very fact that love and friendship exist at all, bearing as they do the hall-mark of the Divine, gives cause for the belief that He Who dwells in the Light unapproachable is also Love. Not merely Beauty, Truth and Goodness bear the im-

Love and friendship, a revelation of God.

1 Sam.
xviii. 1–
4 ; 2
Sam. i.
26.

press of the Divine, a fourth may be added, Love or Friendship, for

> "The Loving worm within its clod
> Were Diviner than a loveless God
> Amid His worlds, I dare to say."

Greatly daring as are these words of Robert Browning, it is the daring of a true and lofty faith.

When the love of God has been shed abroad in our hearts by the Holy Ghost, friendship is one of the means used by the same Blessed Spirit whereby our apprehension of that Divine Love is deepened and strengthened. From the contemplation of earthly friendship our thoughts turn to the Highest Friendship of all, to Him Who said, "No longer do I call you servants ; for the servant knoweth not what his lord doeth : but I have called you friends ; for all things that I heard from My Father I have made known unto you" (St. John xv. 15).

Earthly friendship suggests the highest of all friendships. St. John xv. 15.

The two friends of the ancient Hebrew story, as they pledged their loyalty to one another (1 Sam. xx. 16, 17, 42 ; xxiii. 18), and realised that the tie which bound them was stronger than any cords or bands of iron, could not fail to have had their thoughts directed to God's unswerving fidelity and steadfastness. Again and again must this truth have broken in upon them, and flooded their souls with light. Delighting in each other's presence, they would feel that if earthly friendship brought with it such gladness and uplift to the soul, what then must the Friendship of God be ? "Whom have I in Heaven but Thee, and there is none upon

God's unswerving fidelity and steadfastness.

earth that I desire beside Thee " (Ps. lxxiii. 25). It is through human relationships that we come to appreciate the highest of all relationships, in this or in any other world.

1 Sam. xviii. 1– 4 ; 2 Sam. i. 26.

How insistent is St. John on the necessity of cultivating love for the brethren (1 St. John ii. 10 ; iii. 10 ff. ; iv. 7, 11–12, 20 ; cf. St. John xiii. 33, 34) ! It is one of the tests which manifest whether a man is born of God or not (1 St. John iii. 10), whether he has passed from death unto life (1 St. John iii. 14). Love is the flower which springs from " the seed of God which abideth " in the Christian (1 St. John iii. 9) ; but it is a flower which must be cultivated and tended. And the Evangelist clinches his argument by saying, " for he that loveth not his brother whom he hath seen, cannot love God Whom he hath not seen " (1 St. John iv. 20). By this he would have us understand that it is by loving our brethren that we come to know what is the love of God. It is an argument in a circle, but the circle is large enough to embrace a great truth.

Ps. lxxiii. 25.

Our Lord also reasoned from the less to the greater, " If ye then, being evil, know how to give good gifts unto your childen, how much more shall your Heavenly Father give the Holy Spirit to them that ask Him " ? (St. Luke xi. 13). As a lady once informed the writer, " I never had any difficulty in believing in the Fatherhood of God ; I had only to think of my own father." In like manner, true unselfish friendship helps us to realise the Friendship of Christ. Suso, a mystic of the Middle Ages, apostrophizes the Eternal, " O tender God, if Thou

St. Luke xi. 13.

How to realise the Friendship of Christ.

1 Sam.
xviii. 1–
4 ; 2
Sam. i.
26.

art so fair and loving in Thy creatures, how fair and
loving must Thou be in Thyself ! "

"Show me, Lord Christ, the Beauty of Thy Face !
  Reveal to me the Love Supreme Thou art !
My spirit longs to look upon that grace,
  So dim my vision, and so cold my heart."

"Reach out to Me through those whose eyes and smile
  Reveal in human love the Love Divine,
Thy mother, lover, child. Thou shalt the while
  In that dear intimacy, taste of Mine.

"That Love, that Beauty, is Myself in them,
  Poured through the Human. Though not thine to see
Yet, but a little span, one star, one gem,
  Veiled, of the radiant circle that shall be."

                                    (A. E. DAWSON.)

The limitations of earthly friendship. The Giver is greater than the gift. Human
friendship has its own limitations which loom all the
larger when placed side by side with the Eternal.
Earthly friendship is a faint reflection of the
" Friend Who sticketh closer than a brother " ; it is
the lesser light in our sky.

Our Lord's startling claim. Our Lord makes a claim which to our Western
ears is of a most startling nature : " If any man
cometh unto Me, and hateth not his own father,
and mother, and wife, and children, and brethren,
and sisters, yea, and his own life also, he cannot
be My disciple " (St. Luke xiv. 26). Not that we
are bidden to hate our own relations any more than
our own lives, either of which would contradict
the spirit and tenour of His teaching, but whenever
a conflict of claims arises, every other claim must

God's Great Gift of Friendship

give way to the claim of Christ. We use the word *claims* advisedly rather than *duties*, for in whatever particular situation a man may find himself, there can be but one line of action for him to pursue, even though he may sometimes find it difficult to know what that line is. We repeat, whenever a conflict of claims arises, such as, for example, country, home, health, all must give way to Christ, when His Will in this matter has been made known, as it assuredly will be, in response to earnest prayer and waiting upon Him.

1 Sam. xviii. 1—4 ; 2 Sam. i. 26.

Every human claim must give way to Christ.

Jonathan must often have felt surely perplexed about his friendship for David, " Am I guilty of disloyalty in this close intimacy with David ? " " Is it really to the interest of my country that I should show such delight in the son of Jesse ? " For himself the question was settled, because he saw that God had chosen his friend to be Saul's successor on the throne. Even then his heart must have been torn in different directions, and perhaps this underlies the expression which occurs in David's lament over them both : " In their death they were not divided " (2 Sam. i. 23).

Jonathan's misgivings.

Hackneyed as are the words : " I could not love thee, dear, so much, loved I not honour more," they reveal both the greatness and the limitations which cling to any earthly friendship, even of the closest and most precious kind. Upon one Friend *alone* in the world, can the human heart be bestowed without any reservations, Jesus Christ, the Will of God Incarnate, or, as a Mohammedan woman once expressed it, the Soul of God.

Jesus Christ, the Absolute Friend.

211

1 Sam. xviii. 1– 4 ; 2 Sam. i. 26.

The solitariness which besets human life.

The human soul wears a veil.

A very sparing use of the word *absolute* should be made, and as regards friendship it can only be applied to spiritual communion with the Father of spirits. All human friendship is relative.

United as two friends may be, there are depths within them which neither can reveal to the other. Each soul has a solitariness of its own. It both lives and dies alone. More than nine-tenths of our inner lives are unknown even to our dearest and our best. And granted that the veil which covers the inner recesses of the heart can be lifted for a kindred soul to look upon and behold, it can be but for a moment. In his poem on the buried life Matthew Arnold wrote :

" I knew the mass of men conceal'd
Their thoughts, for fear that if reveal'd
They would by other men be met
With blank indifference, or with blame reproved ;
I knew they lived and moved
Trick'd in disguises alien to the rest
Of men, and alien to themselves—and yet
The same heart beats in every human breast !

" But we, my love ! doth a like spell benumb
Our hearts, our voices ? must we too be dumb ?
Ah ! well for us, if even we,
Even for a moment, can get free
Our heart, and have our lips unchain'd ;
For that which seals them hath been deep-ordain'd."

Christ alone dwells in the Holy of Holies of the human soul.

The veil may be lifted for a moment into the holy place, but into the innermost sanctuary of the human heart none can enter. But it need not be empty, for in that Holy of Holies may dwell Jesus Christ,

the unchanging Friend. He abides with us for
ever, passing with us through the gates of death,
into the Unknown, and not Eternity itself shall be
able to exhaust either the secrets or the wonders of
that Friendship.

1 Sam.
xviii. 1–
4 ;   2
Sam. i.
26.

XXI

JONATHAN, A NEGLECTED TYPE OF CHRIST

And it came to pass, when he had made an end of speaking unto Saul, that the soul of Jonathan was knit with the soul of David, and Jonathan loved him as his own soul. And Saul took him that day, and would let him go no more home to his father's house. Then Jonathan and David made a covenant, because he loved him as his own soul. And Jonathan stripped himself of the robe that *was* upon him, and gave it to David, and his garments, even to his sword, and to his bow, and to his girdle.

And David fled from Naioth in Ramah, and came and said before Jonathan, What have I done ? what *is* mine iniquity ? and what *is* my sin before thy father, that he seeketh my life ? And he said unto him, God forbid ; thou shalt not die : behold, my father will do nothing either great or small, but that he will shew it me : and why should my father hide this thing from me ? it *is* not *so*. And David sware moreover, and said, Thy father certainly knoweth that I have found grace in thine eyes ; and he saith, Let not Jonathan know this, lest he be grieved : but truly *as* the Lord liveth, and *as* thy soul liveth, *there is* but a step between me and death. Then said Jonathan unto David, Whatsoever thy soul desireth, I will even do *it* for thee. And David said unto Jonathan, Behold, to morrow *is* the new moon, and I should not fail to sit with the king at meat : but let me go, that I may hide myself in the field unto the third *day* at even. If thy father at all miss me, then say, David earnestly asked *leave* of me that he might run to Bethlehem his city : for *there is* a yearly sacrifice there for all the family. If he say thus, *It is* well ; thy servant shall have peace : but if he be very wroth, *then* be sure that evil is determined by him. Therefore thou shalt deal kindly with thy servant; for thou hast brought thy servant into a covenant of the LORD with thee: notwithstanding, if there be in me iniquity, slay me thyself; for why shouldest thou bring me to thy father? And Jonathan said, Far be it from thee: for if I knew certainly that evil were determined by my father to come upon thee, then would not I tell it thee? Then said David to Jonathan, Who shall tell me? or what *if* thy father answer thee roughly?

And Jonathan said unto David, Come, and let us go into the field. And they went out both of them into the field. And Jonathan said unto David, O LORD God of Israel, when I have sounded my father about to morrow any time, *or* the third *day*, and, behold, *if there be* good toward David, and I then send not unto thee, and shew it thee: The LORD do so and much more to Jonathan: but if it please my father *to do* thee evil, then I will shew it thee, and send thee away, that thou mayest go in peace: and the LORD be with thee, as he hath been with my father. And thou shalt not only while yet I live shew me the kindness of the LORD, that I die not: But *also* thou shalt not cut off thy kindness from my house for ever: no, not when the LORD hath cut off the enemies of David every one from the face of the earth. So Jonathan made *a covenant* with the house of David, *saying*, Let the LORD even require *it* at the hand of David's enemies. And Jonathan caused David to swear again, because he loved him: for he loved him as he loved his own soul. Then Jonathan said to David, To morrow *is* the new moon: and thou shalt be missed, because thy seat will be empty. And *when* thou hast stayed three days, *then* thou shalt go down quickly, and come to the place where thou didst hide thyself when the business was *in hand*, and shalt remain by the stone Ezel. And I will shoot three arrows on the side *thereof*, as though I shot at a mark. And, behold, I will send a lad, *saying*, Go, find out the arrows. If I expressly say unto the lad, Behold, the arrows *are* on this side of thee, take them; then come thou: for *there is* peace to thee, and no hurt; *as* the LORD liveth. But if I say thus unto the young man, Behold, the arrows *are* beyond thee; go thy way: for the LORD hath sent thee away. And *as touching* the matter which thou and I have spoken of, behold, the LORD *be* between thee and me for ever.

So David hid himself in the field: and when the new moon was come, the king sat him down to eat meat. And the king sat upon his seat, as at other times, *even* upon a seat by the

wall : and Jonathan arose, and Abner sat by Saul's side, and
David's place was empty. Nevertheless Saul spake not any
thing that day : for he thought, Something hath befallen him,
he *is* not clean ; surely he *is* not clean. And it came to pass
on the morrow, *which was* the second *day* of the month, that
David's place was empty : and Saul said unto Jonathan his son,
Wherefore cometh not the son of Jesse to meat, neither yesterday, nor to day ? And Jonathan answered Saul, David
earnestly asked *leave* of me *to go* to Beth-lehem : And he said,
Let me go, I pray thee ; for our family hath a sacrifice in the
city ; and my brother, he hath commanded me *to be there :* and
now, if I have found favour in thine eyes, let me get away, I
pray thee, and see my brethren. Therefore he cometh not
unto the king's table. Then Saul's anger was kindled against
Jonathan, and he said unto him, Thou son of the perverse
rebellious *woman,* do not I know that thou hast chosen the son
of Jesse to thine own confusion, and unto the confusion of thy
mother's nakedness ? For as long as the son of Jesse liveth
upon the ground, thou shalt not be established, nor thy kingdom.
Wherefore now send and fetch him unto me, for he shall surely
die. And Jonathan answered Saul his father, and said unto
him, Wherefore shall he be slain ? what hath he done ? And
Saul cast a javelin at him to smite him : whereby Jonathan
knew that it was determined of his father to slay David. So
Jonathan arose from the table in fierce anger, and did eat no
meat the second day of the month : for he was grieved for
David, because his father had done him shame.

And it came to pass in the morning, that Jonathan went out
into the field at the time appointed with David, and a little lad
with him. And he said unto his lad, Run, find out now the
arrows which I shoot. *And* as the lad ran, he shot an arrow
beyond him. And when the lad was come to the place of the
arrow which Jonathan had shot, Jonathan cried after the lad,
and said, *Is* not the arrow beyond thee ? And Jonathan cried
after the lad, Make speed, haste, stay not. And Jonathan's
lad gathered up the arrows, and came to his master. But the
lad knew not any thing : only Jonathan and David knew the
matter. And Jonathan gave his artillery unto his lad, and said
unto him, Go, carry *them* to the city.

And as soon as the lad was gone, David arose out of *a place*
toward the south, and fell on his face to the ground, and bowed
himself three times : and they kissed one another, and wept
one with another, until David exceeded. And Jonathan said

Jonathan, a Neglected Type of Christ

to David, Go in peace, forasmuch as we have sworn both of us in the name of the LORD, saying, The LORD be between me and thee, and between my seed and thy seed for ever. And he arose and departed : and Jonathan went into the city.

And Jonathan Saul's son arose, and went to David into the wood, and strengthened his hand in God. And he said unto him, Fear not : for the hand of Saul my father shall not find thee ; and thou shalt be king over Israel, and I shall be next unto thee ; and that also Saul my father knoweth. And they two made a covenant before the LORD : and David abode in the wood, and Jonathan went to his house.—1 SAM. XVIII. 1–4 ; XX. ; XXIII. 16–18.

FROM the earliest days of Christianity men have loved to see in the Old Testament Saints, types of Christ. The writer of the Epistle to the Hebrews, in the course of his argument, refers to Melchizedech, whose rank and office are typical of the eternal Kingship and Priesthood of Jesus, the Son of God.

The early Fathers of the Church quote Jacob and Joshua, the former as an example of Him who went forth conquering and to conquer,[1] the latter as bringing His people into the Heavenly land of Promise.[2] Besides these, Abel, Noah, Abraham, Isaac and Moses are often cited. In early Christian art Jonah is the favourite type, based on St. Matt. xii. 40. This list of names does not profess to be exhaustive, but so far as we know, Jonathan's name is not mentioned anywhere in this connection, and even to-day he is treated with similar neglect in many quarters.

And yet, in numerous respects, he resembles

1 Sam. xiv. ; xviii. 1–4 ; xx. ; xxiii. 16–18.

Old Testament types of Christ.

A favourite subject with the early Fathers.

Jonathan never mentioned.

In many ways he resembles Christ.

[1] Cf. Irenæus, *Adv. Hær.*, iv. xxi. 3.
[2] Justin Martyr, *Dial. cum Trypho*, cxiii.

217

The First Book of Samuel

1 Sam. xiv. ; xviii. 1–4 ; xx. ; xxiii. 16–18.

His first introduction to us.

Christ more closely than any other figure in the Old Testament.

From beginning to end, there are no dark and ugly passages in his life. He is the knight *sans peur, sans reproche*, noble and chivalrous. His first introduction to us is when he and his armour-bearer, by an extraordinary act of daring, surprise the garrison of the Philistines, and put to death twenty of their number, after an expression of his faith and hope in God, "*It may be that the Lord will work for us : for there is no restraint to the Lord to save by many or by few*" (1 Sam. xiv. 6). His sentiments were very similar to those uttered by Judas Maccabæus, centuries afterwards, before the battle of Beth-Horon, when he cheered on his small company of faithful men against the mighty army of Seron, Commander of the Syrian host. "With the God of heaven it is all one to save by many or few ; for victory in battle standeth not in the multitude of a host ; but strength is from heaven" (1 Macc. iii. 16–21). When confronted with the hosts of evil, God's people should recall such words, and be encouraged by them, for as it has been truly said, "One, with God, is always in the majority," and the Saviour Himself declared, on the eve of His Passion, when the hosts of darkness were gathering round Him, "Be of good cheer ; I have overcome the world" (St. John xvi. 33).

His unconcern for his own safety.

One of the characteristics in which Jonathan most resembles our Lord, is his selflessness. We have an instance of this in the story of the honey, his partaking of which brought him unwittingly

218

under the curse pronounced by his father. When
acquainted with the consequences, even sentence of
death, he manifested not the slightest concern for
his own safety (1 Sam. xiv. 43).[1] His one thought
was of the unwisdom of the order itself, and how
hardly it pressed upon his people and country.

1 Sam. xiv. ; xviii. 1–4 ; xx. ; xxiii. 16–18.

This selflessness is also forcibly brought before
us in Jonathan's relations with David, in which
no trace of jealousy is to be found, although he
was well aware that the son of Jesse should occupy
the throne, he himself being debarred in consequence
from succeeding his father as king of Israel. More
than this, when Saul issued orders both to him and
to his servants to slay David, not content with a
merely passive attitude, he took it upon himself
to remonstrate with his father, and " *spake good of
David unto Saul* " (xix. 4–6) so effectually that he
swore by the Lord that he should not be slain.

Selflessness character-istic of the man.

Without a trace of jealousy.

His concern for David.

What he did for David.

Later on when Saul's jealousy broke out afresh,
and David fled to Naioth, David's appeal to
Jonathan did not fall on deaf ears. A covenant
was made between them to be true the one to the
other, Jonathan's one proviso being that David
should show kindness to him during his lifetime
and to his descendants after his death (xx. 14, 15).
The feast of the new moon was at hand ; if David
were present his life would probably be in danger,
and if he absented himself Saul's anger would be

---

[1] Both the A.V. and R.V. render the latter part of verse 43
in chapter xvi. : " and, lo, I must die," but with the majority
of modern scholars we prefer the translation, " *Here I am !
I am ready to die.*"

The First Book of Samuel

1 Sam.
xiv. ;
xviii. 1–
4 ; xx. ;
xxiii. 16–
18.

aroused against him. Jonathan suggested the latter course, promising to discover from his father's behaviour on the occasion, what his intentions towards David were. By means of signs agreed upon between them, intelligible to themselves alone, David was to know what those intentions were, and whether he could safely return to the court or not. The scene which followed between the son and the father, so dramatically described, nearly cost the son his life, but the thought uppermost in Jonathan's mind was, not so much the insult and attempted injury he had suffered at his father's hands, as grief *"for David, because his father had done him shame"* (xx. 34).

On two other occasions do we read of a meeting between Jonathan and David, first when Jonathan acquainted his friend with the result of his interview with his father, secondly in the wilderness of Ziph where he encouraged him in faith towards God.

His last appearance on the scene. The last occasion upon which he comes before us is fighting on Mount Gilboa, where he met his end at the hands of the Philistines, thereby giving his life for his country (xxxi. 2).

Our Lord's character.

He "pleased not Himself." St. Paul sums up the impression he received from studying the life and character of his Lord and Master Jesus Christ thus : He "pleased not Himself" (Rom. xv. 3). Never for one moment did He consider His own personal comfort. St. Mark gives us a specimen example of how twenty-four hours were spent by Christ. It is a Sabbath Day, a rest day ! The Lord is found in the Synagogue, teaching, and healing a man with an unclean spirit. After

220

this He goes to the house of Simon, and heals his
mother-in-law of a fever. At eventide multitudes
throng around Him, and many cures are wrought.
That these were not effected by a mere word of
command, but were exhausting to Himself as mental
and spiritual efforts, we may gather from His own
words, " I perceived that power had gone forth from
Me " (St. Luke viii. 46). And notwithstanding this,
" a great while before day, He rose up and went out,
and departed into a desert place, and there prayed "
(St. Mark i. 25-35). Another time, hungry and
weary, the Master sits by a well, and a woman
comes, a woman with a sinful past, and a conversation arises. His own physical needs are forgotten,
as with loving insight, and strong but tender
sympathy, He draws from her lips a confession of
the sinful life she has been and is still leading, and
at the same time He offers to her the Living Water.
When the disciples on their return from the neigh-
bouring city urge Him to partake of food, He replies,
" I have meat to eat that ye know not. My meat
is to do the will of Him that sent Me, and to accomplish His work " (St. John iv. 32, 34).

1 Sam.
xiv. ;
xviii. 1–
4 ; xx. ;
xxiii. 16–
18.

When He was on the Cross, the taunt was levelled,
" He saved others, Himself He cannot save." Quite
true, He never did spare Himself, and from His
blessed Presence there ever streamed forth healing
for the sick, life for the dying, love for the sinner.

He never
spared
Himself.

One incident above all others in the life of
Jonathan reminds us of Christ. It was when he
encountered David on his return from the slaughter
of the Philistine. The writer says that " *the soul*

Jonathan's
love for
David.

1 Sam.
xiv. ;
xviii. 1–
4 ; xx. ;
xxiii. 16–
18.

of Jonathan was knit with the soul of David, and
Jonathan loved him as his own soul " (xviii. 1, 3).
The love began on Jonathan's side first, and in
David's lament over Saul he says of Jonathan,
" Thy love to me was wonderful, passing the love of
women " (2 Sam. i. 26).   To those who have been
privileged to receive a good woman's love, David's
words, it must be confessed, do strike a jarring note,
but at least they express the wealth of Jonathan's

The Lord's
love for
His own.

love.   Hereby we are reminded of another Father's
Son, who " loved His own unto the uttermost," or
" unto the end " (St. John xiii. 1).   The Eternal
Son of God, having knit Himself into our race
(Heb. ii. 14), has proved the greatness of His love
wherewith He hath loved us.   May we reverently
say, He was greater than His own words (cf. St.
John xv. 13), for He laid down His life for us when
we were at emnity with Him.   His love for us was
in existence long before we were born, and it is the
greatness of His love which is the moving cause of
the love we have towards Him, poor and weak
though it is in comparison with His.   Even human
love at its truest and best, gives but a faint idea of
the love which Jesus has for the souls He died to
save.   Thy love to me, O Christ, is wonderful.   And
we may well ask, Shall we ever be able to apprehend
" with all the saints, what is the breadth and length
and height and depth, and to know the love of
Christ which passeth knowledge " ? (Eph. iii. 18, 19).
It is an interesting coincidence that the word "passing " is used of the love of Jonathan and of that
of the Lord, but Christ's love surpasses all other.

Jonathan, a Neglected Type of Christ

Mark also how Jonathan proved his love for David. He made a covenant with him, he " *stripped himself of the robe that was upon him* " (1 Sam. xviii. 1–4), his royal robe, or at any rate a garment " worn by the well-to-do, and gave it to David, and his accoutrements also, including his sword, his bow, and his girdle. The simple lad is thus fitted to shine at court " (Prof. H. P. Smith). In like manner did the great Messenger of the Covenant (Mal. iii. 1) lay aside His kingly glory. His garments were taken away from Him by the soldiers, but with His own consent, for it was He who gave His life as a ransom for many (St. Mark x. 45) and claimed to lay down His life : " No one taketh it away from Me, but I lay it down of Myself. I have power to lay it down, and I have power to take it again " (St. John x. 18). He could at any moment have summoned to His side twelve legions of angels (St. Matt. xxvi. 33). He Who had not the slightest acquaintance with sin was made sin on our behalf ; He took the sinner's place, and thus clothed us with the robe of His righteousness, and enabled us to tread the courts of heaven. By the laws of heredity we should have expected Jonathan to have a nature in some respects resembling that of his father. Had his character displayed envy and jealousy, it would not have surprised us, but not a trace of these qualities is to be found. It is an interesting point that Saul should have had such a son, and that Samuel should have produced his ! Another proof that these things do not " stand in the following of nature," but of grace. As Dante

1 Sam. xiv. ; xviii. 1–4 ; xx. ; xxiii. 16–18.

Jonathan's covenant with David.

The Saviour's Covenant.

He took the servant's place to make the servant king.

That Saul should have such a son, a matter for surprise.

The First Book of Samuel

1 Sam.
xiv. ;
xviii. 1–
4 ; xx. ;
xxiii. 16–
18.

The second Adam.

says of genius, God will not permit it to follow, by right of natural descent, but creates it as and when He will. Jonathan then was just the very opposite to what we should have expected a son of Saul to be. In him his family took a new turn. The Saviour, born into the human family, gave the race of mankind a new direction, a fresh start, " as in Adam all die, so also in Christ shall all be made alive " (1 Cor. xv. 22). From outside of and beyond mankind, yet entering into the very life of mankind, He is a new creation, thereby He cuts off the entail of sin, and upon those who yield themselves to Him, His redeeming and life-giving grace and power are bestowed. They are born again of water and the Holy Spirit (St. John iii. 5). In Christ they become a new creature.

Jonathan's life points us to Christ.

That Jonathan's life falls short of the life of Christ in many respects, we need hardly say, but that he points us to the Perfect Man, the Ideal Friend, the King Who laid His glory by, will, we think, be recognised by those who have studied attentively the record of his noble and beautiful life.

XXII

"THE VALE OF SOUL-MAKING"

And David went out whithersoever Saul sent him, *and* behaved himself wisely : and Saul set him over the men of war, and he was accepted in the sight of all the people, and also in the sight of Saul's servants.

So David fled, and escaped, and came to Samuel to Ramah, and told him all that Saul had done to him. And he and Samuel went and dwelt in Naioth.

David therefore departed thence, and escaped to the cave Adullam : and when his brethren and all his father's house heard *it*, they went down thither to him. And every one *that was* in distress, and every one that *was* in debt, and every one *that was* discontented, gathered themselves unto him ; and he became a captain over them : and there were with him about four hundred men.

Then they told David, saying, Behold, the Philistines fight against Keilah, and they rob the threshing floors. Therefore David enquired of the Lord, saying, Shall I go and smite these Philistines ? And the Lord said unto David, Go, and smite the Philistines, and save Keilah. And David's men said unto him, Behold, we be afraid here in Judah : how much more then if we come to Keilah against the armies of the Philistines ? Then David enquired of the Lord yet again. And the Lord answered him and said, Arise, go down to Keilah ; for I will deliver the Philistines into thine hand. So David and his men went to Keilah, and fought with the Philistines, and brought away their cattle, and smote them with a great slaughter. So David saved the inhabitants of Keilah. Then said David, O Lord God of Israel, thy servant hath certainly heard that Saul seeketh to come to Keilah, to destroy the city for my sake.

The First Book of Samuel

Will the men of Keilah deliver me up into his hand ? will Saul come down, as thy servant hath heard ? O LORD God of Israel, I beseech thee, tell thy servant. And the LORD said, He will come down. Then said David, Will the men of Keilah deliver me and my men into the hand of Saul ? And the LORD said, They will deliver *thee* up.

Then David and his men, *which were* about six hundred, arose and departed out of Keilah, and went whithersoever they could go. And it was told Saul that David was escaped from Keilah ; and he forbare to go forth. And David abode in the wilderness in strong holds, and remained in a mountain in the wilderness of Ziph. And Saul sought him every day, but God delivered him not into his hand. And David saw that Saul was come out to seek his life : and David *was* in the wilderness of Ziph in a wood.

Then came up the Ziphites to Saul to Gibeah, saying, Doth not David hide himself with us in strong holds in the wood, in the hill of Hachilah, which is on the south of Jeshimon ? Now therefore, O king, come down according to all the desire of thy soul to come down ; and our part *shall be* to deliver him into the king's hand. And Saul said, Blessed *be* ye of the LORD ; for ye have compassion on me. Go, I pray you, prepare yet, and know and see his place where his haunt is, *and* who hath seen him there : for it is told me *that* he dealeth very subtilly. See therefore, and take knowledge of all the lurking places where he hideth himself, and come ye again to me with the certainty, and I will go with you : and it shall come to pass, if he be in the land, that I will search him out throughout all the thousands of Judah. And they arose, and went to Ziph before Saul : but David and his men *were* in the wilderness of Maon, in the plain on the south of Jeshimon. Saul also and his men went to seek *him.* And they told David : wherefore he came down into a rock, and abode in the wilderness of Maon. And when Saul heard *that,* he pursued after David in the wilderness of Maon. And Saul went on this side of the mountain, and David and his men on that side of the mountain : and David made haste to get away for fear of Saul ; for Saul and his men compassed David and his men round about to take them.

But there came a messenger unto Saul, saying, Haste thee, and come ; for the Philistines have invaded the land. Wherefore Saul returned from pursuing after David, and went against the Philistines : therefore they called that place Sela-hammah-lekoth.

"The Vale of Soul-making"

And David went up from thence, and dwelt in strong holds at En-gedi.

And it came to pass, when Saul was returned from following the Philistines, that it was told him, saying, Behold, David is in the wilderness of En-gedi. Then Saul took three thousand chosen men out of all Israel, and went to seek David and his men upon the rocks of the wild goats. And he came to the sheepcotes by the way, where *was* a cave ; and Saul went in to cover his feet : and David and his men remained in the sides of the cave. Bnd the men of David said unto him, Behold the day of which the LORD said unto thee, Behold, I will deliver thine enemy into thine hand, that thou mayest do to him as it shall seem good unto thee. Then David arose, and cut off the skirt of Saul's robe privily. And it came to pass afterward, that David's heart smote him, because he had cut off Saul's skirt. And he said unto his men, The LORD forbid that I should do this thing unto my master, the LORD's anointed, to stretch forth mine hand against him, seeing he *is* the anointed of the LORD. So David stayed his servants with these words, and suffered them not to rise against Saul. But Saul rose up out of the cave, and went on *his* way. David also arose afterward, and went out of the cave, and cried after Saul, saying, My lord the king. And when Saul looked behind him, David stooped with his face to the earth, and bowed himself.

And David said to Saul, Wherefore hearest thou men's words, saying, Behold, David seeketh thy hurt ? Behold, this day thine eyes have seen how that the LORD had delivered thee to day into mine hand in the cave : and *some* bade *me* kill thee : but *mine eye* spared thee ; and I said, I will not put forth mine hand against my lord ; for he *is* the LORD's anointed.—1 SAM. XVIII. 2–5, 12–30 ; XIX. 18 ; XXII. 1, 2 ; XXIII. 1–15, 19–29 ; XXIV. ; XXVI.

I Sam. xviii. 2– 5, 12– 30 ; xix. 18 ; xxii. 1, 2 ; xxiii. 1– 15, 19– 29 ; xxiv. ; xxvi.

WITH dramatic suddenness had the ordinary course of David's life been interrupted, and directed into a most unexpected channel. The shepherd lad, without warning, becomes the anointed king. Very soon, however, came the great encounter with the champion of the Philistines, which brought David

David's sudden leap to fame.

227

The First Book of Samuel

1 Sam.
xviii. 2–
5, 12–
30 ; xix.
18 ; xxii.
1, 2 ;
xxiii. 1–
15, 19–
29; xxiv.;
xxvi.

into public notice, and made him the hero of the national songs. This valiant deed attracted also the king's attention, and introduced him to Jonathan, whose lifelong friendship served him in such good stead. Not of him could it be said that "his name was writ in water." [1] His name was on all lips, and he became the idol of the people.

A hard time in store for him.

But David was soon to learn the bitter truth of Keats' words : "The world is the Vale of Soul-making." Many years were to elapse before he could ascend the throne. A severe and wearisome preparation was in store for him ere he should reign over the house of Judah (2 Sam. ii. 4).

Disappointment and trial would dog his footsteps. He would pass through the furnace of affliction, for the king of God's own choice must have a heart of gold, in comparison with which the kingly crown should weigh not at all. He must experience the rough paths and the deep shadows of the Vale of Soul-making. It is in this connection that we are about to study some of the incidents of his life.

His preparation at court.

His preparation began straightway at court. There he soon found that envious eyes were cast upon him. Intrigue was rife. It did not take him long to discover the importance of using his ears and closing his lips. "To be swift to hear and slow to speak " (St. James i. 19) must be his policy. He could not fail to perceive that the king lived in a world remote from actual life, surrounded as he was by courtiers skilled in the art of flattery, but

[1] Keats directed that the inscription on his grave should be " Here lies one whose name was writ in water."

"The Vale of Soul-making"

possessing "no faithfulness in their mouth" 1 Sam. xviiii. 2–5, 12–30 ; xix. 18 ; xxii. 1, 2 ; xxiii. 1–15, 19–29; xxiv. ; xxvi. (Ps. v. 9). We may be quite sure that David would note down for his future guidance that when king, he must, at all costs, have around him men who would not be afraid to tell him the truth, however unpalatable it might be at the time. This explains the presence of a man like Nathan at David's court (cf. 2 Sam. vii. 4–12 ; xii. 1–14).

The son of Jesse passed through this part of his training with credit, for " *He behaved himself wisely in all his ways ; and the Lord was with him* " (1 Sam. xviii. 14). He had need of God's help, and he also needed to exercise wisdom, inasmuch as Saul's jealousy of him was patent to every one. When, therefore, the king made him captain over a thousand, and still further dissembled with him by suggesting that he should marry his daughter Merab (xviii. 17 ; cf. xvii. 25), David gathered at once what was in Saul's mind. From Saul's words : " *only be thou valiant for me, and fight the Lord's battles,*" and from the knowledge of human nature which he was fast acquiring, he knew that there could be only one explanation of Saul's change of front, that, not willing to slay him with his own hand, he hoped to compass his death at the hand of the Philistines (1 Sam. xviii. 17).

He passes through it with credit.

If any doubt lurked in David's mind as to Saul's intentions, it was dispelled by his bestowal of Merab at the last moment, not upon himself but upon another, Adriel the Meholathite (verse 19).

In the meantime Michal, Saul's younger daughter, had become attached to David, and this pleased

Saul's plots against him frustrated.

Saul well : " *I will give him her*," said he, " *that she may be a snare to him, and that the hand of the Philistines may be against him* " (verse 21). In roundabout ways it was conveyed to David that the king was prepared to favour his suit, and to David's plea that " *he was a poor man and lightly esteemed*," in other words that he had no dowry to offer, Saul immediately responded that he should be more than satisfied with proof that David had slain a hundred Philistines " *to be avenged of the king's enemies. Now Saul thought to make David fall by the hand of the Philistines* " (verse 25). David returned in safety, and not only carried out the enterprise, but slew double the number required.

David's prestige increased thereby.

In this manner were Saul's machinations against him brought to nought, having the reverse effect to that which had been intended. They served to increase David's prestige " *so that his name was much set by* " (verse 30). Step by step was he being marked out as Israel's greatest leader against her foes.

He is compelled to leave the court.

We are left in ignorance as to how long David remained at court, but the time arrived when it was impossible for him to be anywhere near Saul. Both openly and in secret was Saul planning his death, and in the end it was necessary for him to take to flight. But for his wife's devotion, he must, humanly speaking, have fallen into Saul's hands and been put to death.

His stay with Samuel.

When David escaped for his life, he cast in his mind as to where and to whom to turn. One place of refuge lay open to thim. He would go to Samuel

at " *Naioth in Ramah* " (xix. 19), that quarter of
the town where it has been conjectured that there
must have been a college of the prophets. Here
he remained for a time with Samuel, long enough to
receive further training at the hands of the Prophet,
to fit him for the time when he should be king.
Important as it was that he should become versed
in the ways of the world as represented by the
artificial society at court, of far greater importance
was it for him to be versed in the ways of God.
It was necessary that the true aims and ideals of
kingship should be engraved upon his mind. Many
a long and earnest conversation must in consequence have taken place between the aged Prophet
and Israel's future king. Samuel would relate to
him the history of Israel, and impress upon him that
if he desired to lead his country aright, he must
at all times seek to obey the voice of the Lord and
not rebel against His commandments (1 Sam. xii.
15). Obedience to God must be his first endeavour,
and idolatry must be put down with an unflinching
hand. Then also, David's devotional life, which
may have been somewhat neglected of late, owing to
the atmosphere of the court, needed to be renewed
and encouraged. Both by word, and by example,
would the incalculable value of intercessory prayer
be enforced (1 Sam. xii. 23). David would be
reminded that times must come when he could
do little else for his people but that which is the
most effective of all, pray for them, bringing them
and their needs before the throne of God (cf. Exod.
xxxii. 7–14, 30 ff.). May it not also have been due

Marginalia:
1 Sam.
xviii. 2–
5, 12–
30 ; xix.
18 ; xxii.
1, 2 ;
xxiii. 1–
15, 19–
29; xxiv. ;
xxv.

What
Samuel
taught him.

David's
devotional
life.

231

The First Book of Samuel

1 Sam.
xviii. 2–
5, 12–
30 ; xix.
18 ; xxii.
1, 2 ;
xxiii. 1–
15, 19–
29 ; xxiv. ;
xxvi.

He leaves Naioth.

In fear of his life.

An outlaw in the cave of Adullam.

David's followers.

to Samuel, in the first instance, that David became the sweet Psalmist of Israel, led through him to compose those immortal prayers of penitence and thanksgiving, worship and adoration ? This time with Samuel must have been a " season of refreshing from the presence of the Lord " (Acts iii. 19).

Not for long was David suffered to abide on the Mount of God, the day arrived when he could no longer remain in safety at Naioth, and with a heavy heart he would bid a final farewell to his trusty counsellor and friend, and escape for his life from the pursuers of Saul.

For our present purpose, namely his soul-making, his interviews with Jonathan, the visit to Nob, and his stay with Achish, king of Gath, may be passed over. We now come to the most trying period of David's existence, when he was branded as an outlaw, and hunted from place to place in fear of his life (1 Sam. xxiv. 14 ; xxvi. 20).

His first place of refuge was the cave of Adullam. This is identified to-day with a hill called Aid-el-ma, and according to Sir George Adam Smith, its position is, on the whole, suitable to what we know of David's strongholds. It was on the western edge of Judah, very near the " so-called Shephelah, the debatable ground between Israel and the Philistines," less than twelve miles to the south-west of Beth-lehem.

Hither came to David many of the malcontents of Israel, those who were smarting under Saul's tyranny, those who were in debt, as well as those belonging to his own house and kindred, in number

232

four hundred (xxii. 2). To hold and keep together such a motley band of men must have taxed and developed all David's powers of leadership, and proved a most valuable preparation for the main task of his life. Associating as he was forced to do with all these, he would come to the throne with an unrivalled knowledge of the life and character of his subjects. In this school of experience he came to learn at first hand the meaning of poverty and hardship, the dangers attendant on over-taxation, and above all to gain a deep sympathy with the oppressed and downtrodden classes.

1 Sam. xviii. 2–5, 12–30 ; xix. 18 ; xxii. 1, 2 ; xxiii. 1–15, 19–29; xxiv.; xxvi. What he learnt from them.

To settle petty strifes, as well as more serious quarrels, must have formed part of David's ordinary duties. Strict and impartial justice to all and sundry, without let or hindrance, was imperative, if he was to retain his hold upon them. Again, let us note what splendid training this was for his future career. The king of Israel must not only be a leader in war but a judge in times of peace.

The splendid training they gave him.

Having moved into the land of Moab, he is admonished by the prophet Gad, "*Abide not in the hold ; depart and get thee into the land of Judah*" (xxii. 5). From this we may gather that, notwithstanding the risks he ran from Saul's numerous spies and adherents, it was necessary that he should keep himself before the public eye, as any service he might render would consolidate his future position.

He is forbidden to remain in Moab.

Shortly afterwards, he and his men were able to relieve Keilah (Kela), a fortified city about two miles due south of Adullam, which had been raided

The relief of Keilah.

The First Book of Samuel

1 Sam.
xviii. 2–
5, 12–
30 ; xix.
18 ; xxii.
1, 2 ;
xxiii. 1–
15, 19–
29; xxiv.;
xxvi.

Owing to treachery David flees to the wilderness of Ziph.

A Providential deliverance.

Saul's relentless pursuit.

He is surprised by David.

(1) In a cave.

by the Philistines (xxiii. 1–5). The inhabitants repaid him with base ingratitude, for not long after the deliverance of the city from the enemy, David learned that they were planning to hand him over to Saul.

The result was that both he and his band, now increased in number to six hundred men, removed themselves to quite a different part of Judæa, to the wilderness of Ziph, south-east of Hebron towards the Dead Sea (1 Sam. xxiii. 13, 14) ; but even in this part of the country Saul gave him no respite. Emissaries were sent to effect his capture, Saul himself taking part in the search, aided by the Ziphites, who undertook to give him information of all the possible places in which David and his men could hide. So hardly pressed was David in this neighbourhood, and in the district south of Hebron, that he was only saved from falling into his pursuers' hands by a sudden invasion of the land by the Philistines : "*So Saul returned from pursuing after David, and went against the Philistines,*" a providential deliverance for David.

On Saul's return from following the Philistines, the search for David was renewed. During his absence David had betaken himself to the strongholds at Engedi by the Dead Sea—the wisdom of this step is belauded by modern travellers. Both here, and also in the wilderness of Ziph, Saul was surprised by David and his men. On the first occasion Saul had retired into a cave, in entire ignorance that his quarry was in the same place, concealed in its recesses. Such was the control

234

"The Vale of Soul-making"

exercised by David over his men, that in spite of their remonstrances, he restrained them from laying hands upon "the Lord's anointed" (xxiv. 6, 7). He, however, cut off the skirt of Saul's robe, as a proof that the king had been in his power (xxiv. 11), but reproached himself afterwards for having done so : "*David's heart smote him.*"

1 Sam. xviii. 2— 5, 12— 30 ; xix. 18 ; xxii. 1, 2 ; xxiii. 1—

The second time was in the wilderness of Ziph. Saul had pitched his camp on the hill of Hachilah, which is thought to be six miles east of Ziph and nearly halfway to Engedi, facing "the Waste" or Desert (xxvi. 1, 3 ; cf. xxiii. 19). Here Saul was surrounded by a barricade of wagons in the very centre of his army (xxvi. 5, 7). One night David and Abishai stole up to the camp, passed by the sleeping sentries, and arrived at the very place where Saul also was asleep. Once more David restrained himself, and would not suffer Abishai to touch "the Lord's anointed" ; but took away the spear stuck in the ground at his head, symbol of his authority, and also the cruse of water, to prove that he and Abishai had penetrated into his trench.

15, 19— 29 ; xxiv. ; xxvi.

(2) On a hill.

We cannot withhold our admiration from the wonderful restraint manifested by David in that he twice spared Saul's life (contrast this with Jehu, 2 Kings ix. 1–3, 24), when with a single blow he could, once and for ever, have rid himself of his relentless adversary. More eloquently than by any words did David's attitude towards Saul proclaim to his countrymen the sacredness of the king's most excellent Majesty. When the time came for David to reign over Israel, his subjects

David's self-control in sparing Saul's life.

How it benefited David.

235

The First Book of Samuel

1 Sam.
xviii. 2–
5, 12–
30 ; xix.
18 ; xxii.
1, 2 ;
xxiii. 1–
15, 19–
29; xxiv.;
xxvi.

The formation of David's character.

would have learnt, not only to love and revere his person, but to invest the office he held with peculiar awe and reverence. We can see how David's loyal and generous conduct would eventually further his own interests. David was acquiring self-control, that most necessary characteristic, and one, amongst Oriental monarchs, conspicuous by its absence. Absolute power in the hands of any one man invariably lends itself to abuse. David had to learn that it must not be used to gratify his own desires, or whims and fancies, but that this power was entrusted to him by God for the good of his subjects, and the promotion of the Divine glory.

> " A genius forms itself in solitude ;
> A character in struggling with the world."

So wrote Goethe, and these words apply to David, who possessed great religious genius, and also a strong character, the latter having been formed in the struggle with, what the man of the world would call, his hard lot and adverse destiny. One of the greatest thinkers of modern times, Kant, has said that " Nature may be a niggardly stepmother as regards man's immediate happiness, but she is the power that converts him into a moral being, and drives him on to all his higher attainments." If, side by side, with this we place St. Paul's words, " to them that love God all things work together for good " (Rom. viii. 28), we have unfolded to us the main reason for our existence in this world.

The world is the training ground of character.

By temptation, trial and hardship is character formed, so that it becomes " a completely fashioned

will." Struggle is the law of growth. Were there
no suffering, the larger and more blessed part of
sympathy could find no vocation, if it could exist
at all. Could we attain at once the desires of our
hearts, patience and perseverance would be unknown. It is the same with our instincts. These
are not in themselves wrong, they are the raw
material of character. Often, however, they come
into conflict with each other, and often do they
seek unduly to assert themselves, frequently is a
lawful desire carried to an unlawful extent. Lest
the servants become masters, strict control and
guidance is of the first importance with regard to
all human instincts and impulses. God-controlled,
God-guided, they become instruments of His own
great design. David won a greater victory when
he spared Saul's life, than when he slew the champion
of the Philistines, for he conquered himself.

1 Sam.
xviii. 2–
5, 12–
30 ; xix.
18 ; xxii.
1, 2 ;
xxiii. 1–
15, 19–
29; xxiv.;
xxvi.

Struggle is
the law of
growth.

> " Was the trial sore ?
> Temptation sharp ? Thank God a second time.
> Why comes temptation but for man to meet
> And master and make crouch beneath his feet,
> And so be pedestalled in triumph ? "
>
> (R. BROWNING.)

Faith becomes strong and deep when it clings to
God, notwithstanding that He appears to hide His
Face, and that the path He marks out seems strange
and dark.

We may take comfort from David's example
when tempted to rebel against life, and to complain
of the hardness of our lot. David was sorely tried,

David's
example an
inspiration
to us all.

237

The First Book of Samuel

1 Sam.
xviii. 2–
5, 12–
30 ; xix.
18 ; xxii.
1, 2 ;
xxiii. 1–
15, 19–
29; xxiv.;
xxvi.

We must
give God
time.

Christ's
training of
us.

His
apparent
hardness is
love dis-
guised.

the hopes of his heart were dashed to the ground, and at times he must almost have been over-whelmed by the seeming aimlessness of his existence, and futility of the life he was leading; still through it all, God was moulding him, and fitting him to become the greatest king the chosen people ever had. In like manner, if we only give our God and Father time, He will work out His great purpose in us, and when the whole story is known we shall realise that it could not have been, and that we could not have wished it to be, otherwise.

Christ may appear at times to be a hard and exacting taskmaster, but this is only because He loves us too well to be content with anything less than our very best. In our training He has eternity in view, His hardness springs from, and is the result of, that *long* sight. This is the very reverse of that *short*-sighted and weak sentimentalism which, amongst many people to-day, goes by the name of love, but which in reality is only a hidden and disguised form of cruelty. Tempted and tried we must all be, for " this world is the Vale of Soul-making," but tried we shall not be above that which we are able to bear, and the power of Christ will ever prove to be our refuge and sure confidence.

He fights
our battles.

Trusting Him we shall become ever more confident that our souls " are bound in the bundle of life with the Lord our God," and that not only do we fight the battles of the Lord, but that He Himself fights our battles with and for us.

XXIII

COURTESY AND CHURLISH-NESS

And Samuel died; and all the Israelites were gathered together, and lamented him, and buried him in his house at Ramah. And David arose, and went down to the wilderness of Paran. And *there was* a man in Maon, whose possessions *were* in Carmel; and the man *was* very great, and he had three thousand sheep, and a thousand goats: and he was shearing his sheep in Carmel. Now the name of the man *was* Nabal; and the name of his wife Abigail: and *she was* a woman of good understanding, and of a beautiful countenance: but the man *was* churlish and evil in his doings; and he *was* of the house of Caleb.

And David heard in the wilderness that Nabal did shear his sheep. And David sent out ten young men, and David said unto the young men, Get you up to Carmel, and go to Nabal, and greet him in my name: And thus shall ye say to him that liveth *in prosperity*, Peace *be* both to thee, and peace *be* to thine house, and peace *be* unto all that thou hast. And now I have heard that thou hast shearers: now thy shepherds which were with us, we hurt them not, neither was there ought missing unto them, all the while they were in Carmel. Ask thy young men, and they will shew thee. Wherefore let the young men find favour in thine eyes: for we come in a good day: give, I pray thee, whatsoever cometh to thine hand unto thy servants, and to thy son David. And when David's young men came, they spake to Nabal according to all those words in the name of David, and ceased.

And Nabal answered David's servants, and said, Who *is* David? and who *is* the son of Jesse? there be many servants now a days that break away every man from his master. Shall I then take my bread, and my water, and my flesh that I have

239

The First Book of Samuel

killed for my shearers, and give *it* unto men, whom I know not whence they *be?* So David's young men turned their way, and went again, and came and told him all those sayings. And David said unto his men, Gird ye on every man his sword. And they girded on every man his sword; and David also girded on his sword: and there went up after David about four hundred men; and two hundred abode by the stuff.

But one of the young men told Abigail, Nabal's wife, saying, Behold, David sent messengers out of the wilderness to salute our master; and he railed on them. But the men *were* very good unto us, and we were not hurt, neither missed we any thing, as long as we were conversant with them, when we were in the fields: They were a wall unto us both by night and day, all the while we were with them keeping the sheep. Now therefore know and consider what thou wilt do; for evil is determined against our master, and against all his household: for he *is such* a son of Belial, that *a man* cannot speak to him.

Then Abigail made haste, and took two hundred loaves, and two bottles of wine, and five sheep ready dressed, and five measures of parched *corn*, and an hundred clusters of raisins, and two hundred cakes of figs, and laid *them* on asses. And she said unto her servants, Go on before me; behold, I come after you. But she told not her husband Nabal. And it was *so, as* she rode on the ass, that she came down by the covert of the hill, and, behold, David and his men came down against her; and she met them. Now David had said, Surely in vain have I kept all that this *fellow* hath in the wilderness, so that nothing was missed of all that *pertained* unto him: and he hath requited me evil for good. So and more also do God unto the enemies of David, if I leave of all that *pertain* to him by the morning light any that pisseth against the wall. And when Abigail saw David, she hasted, and lighted off the ass, and fell before David on her face, and bowed herself to the ground, And fell at his feet, and said, Upon me, my lord, *upon* me *let this* iniquity *be:* and let thine handmaid, I pray thee, speak in thine audience, and hear the words of thine handmaid. Let not my lord, I pray thee, regard this man of Belial, *even* Nabal: for as his name *is*, so *is* he; Nabal *is* his name, and folly *is* with him: but I thine handmaid saw not the young men of my lord, whom thou didst send. Now therefore, my lord, *as* the LORD liveth, and *as* thy soul liveth, seeing the LORD hath withholden thee from coming to *shed* blood, and from avenging thyself with thine own hand, now let thine enemies, and they that seek evil to my lord, be as Nabal. And now this blessing which thine handmaid hath brought unto my lord, let it even be given unto the young men that follow my lord. I pray thee, forgive the trespass of thine handmaid : for the LORD will certainly make my lord a sure house ; because my lord fighteth the battles of the LORD, and evil hath not been found in thee *all* thy days. Yet a man is risen to pursue thee, and to seek thy soul : but the soul of my lord shall be bound in the bundle of life with the LORD thy God ; and the souls of thine enemies, them shall he sling out, *as out* of the middle of a sling. And it shall come to pass, when the LORD shall have done to my lord according to all the good that he hath spoken concerning thee, and shall have appointed thee ruler over Israel ; That this shall be no grief unto thee, nor offence of heart unto my lord, either that thou hast shed blood causeless, or that my lord hath avenged himself : but when the LORD shall have dealt well with my lord, then remember thine handmaid.

And David said to Abigail, Blessed *be* the LORD God of Israel, which sent thee this day to meet me : And blessed *be* thy advice, and blessed *be* thou, which hast kept me this day from coming to *shed* blood, and from avenging myself with mine own hand. For in very deed, *as* the LORD God of Israel liveth, which hath kept me back from hurting thee, except thou hadst hasted and come to meet me, surely there had not been left unto Nabal by the morning light any male. So David received of her hand *that* which she had brought him, and said unto her, Go up in peace to thine house ; see, I have hearkened to thy voice, and have accepted thy person.

And Abigail came to Nabal ; and, behold, he held a feast in his house, like the feast of a king ; and Nabal's heart *was* merry within him, for he *was* very drunken : wherefore she told him nothing, less or more, until the morning light. But it came to pass in the morning, when the wine was gone out of Nabal, and his wife had told him these things, that his heart died within him, and he became *as* a stone. And it came to pass about ten days *after*, that the LORD smote Nabal, that he died.

And when David heard that Nabal was dead, he said, Blessed *be* the LORD, that hath pleaded the cause of my reproach from the hand of Nabal, and hath kept his servant from evil : for the LORD hath returned the wickedness of Nabal upon his own head. And David sent and communed with Abigail, to take her to him to wife. And when the servants of David were come to Abigail to Carmel, they spake unto her, saying, David sent us unto thee, to take thee to him to wife. And she arose, and bowed herself on *her* face to the earth, and said, Behold, *let* thine handmaid *be* a servant to wash the feet of the servants of my lord. And Abigail hasted, and arose, and rode upon an ass, with five damsels of her's that went after her; and she went after the messengers of David, and became his wife. David also took Ahinoam of Jezreel; and they were also both of them his wives.—1 SAM. XXV.

**1 Sam.
XXV.**

**Samuel's
death.**

**A general
amnesty.**

**David's
distrust of
Saul.**

**David goes
to Paran.**

IT is probable that when Samuel died an amnesty was proclaimed, and that David availed himself of this to attend the Prophet's funeral. The risk, however, which David incurred was too great for him to remain long, either in Saul's presence, or near at hand. Sooner or later the old jealousy and hatred would flare up again, and the life of the son of Jesse be in danger.

For this reason David removed himself from Palestine, and departed to the desert of Paran, rendered famous by the wanderings of the children of Israel on their way to the promised Land.

**How David
kept his
men
in hand.**

Whilst there, he came across Nabal and Abigail, his wife, one of the most attractive women in the Bible. David must often have longed for the days when he was a shepherd lad looking after his flock of sheep, for his following of six hundred men (verse 13) were bound to make great demands upon his nervous strength and energy, as well as upon his power to enforce discipline, and restrain them from acts of lawlessness and brigandage. So well disciplined were they that at the time of sheep-shearing, on a certain farm belonging to this man Nabal, not one of the farm lads had been treated

Courtesy and Churlishness

otherwise than with the greatest kindness and consideration. David, therefore, was fully justified in sending word to Nabal, " *Thy shepherds have now* *been with us, and we did them no hurt, neither was there aught missing unto them, all the while they were in Carmel* " (verse 7). His message might have been couched in even stronger language, for one of the labourers on the farm confided in Abigail that they had protected them from brigands and the predatory tribes of the desert : " *they were a wall unto us both by night and by day, all the while we were with them keeping the sheep* " (verse 16).

The time was also most opportune for David to request of Nabal to make some return for all the kindness he had shown to him, and to his men. To refuse him a share in his sheep-shearing feast would be a breach of religious custom,[1] and even to this day the Sheikhs of the Bedawin count on the generosity of the sheep masters. Unfortunately David had reckoned without his host, for if ever a name fitted a man's character it was so in this case. " Fool," or better still " reckless," was the meaning of his name, and he certainly acted up to it.

The writer of the narrative makes the man live before us. By reputation Nabal was a hard, shrewd man of business, few could drive a better bargain than he, and in course of time he had gotten to himself great wealth, judged by the standard of those days (verse 2). He was the kind of man who would always make out that times were bad, very bad, and that each year he was losing heavily on his

---

[1] Robertson Smith, *Religion of the Semites*, p. 254.

farm, and complain that men did not work as they used to do in his young days. Those who worked under him were treated more like animals than human beings. He would jerk out his orders to them, with never a word of thanks for the work done, were mistakes to be made, those who were so unfortunate as to make them would know what it was to come under the lash of his tongue. In such terror was he held that hardly any of his servants had the courage to speak to him (verse 17; in contrast cf. 2 Kings v. 13). How he managed to live at his farm in safety seems hard to understand, had it not been that he was the fortunate possessor of a wife who by her tact and gentleness of manners endeared herself to all who knew her. In every respect she was his exact opposite. He was rough and boorish in manner, she was courteous to all who came in contact with her, it mattered little what the position they might occupy on the farm. From the youngest lad to the oldest man, all alike had a good word for her, and regarded her as their best friend. They could go to her with their troubles and grievances, certain of receiving her sympathy and help, and they were never disappointed. Time after time she must have turned aside her husband's fury about to be vented upon some unfortunate individual who had incurred his displeasure, and when at times events on the farm began to wear an ugly aspect, she had seemed to sense the atmosphere so accurately as to be able to intervene at the right moment, and thereby prevent a crisis arising. And although he must

Abigail,
Nabal's
wife.

244

often, in his blustering way, have asserted that he was the master of the house, and would brook no interference with his authority, she would observe a discreet silence, never contradicting or retaliating, although well aware that the place was kept together mainly by her own tact and discretion. We can imagine that this "*woman of good understanding*" would many times get her own wise way without her churlish lord suspecting it, and that she was, in reality, the ruler of that household, holding, gently but firmly, the reins of management.

1 Sam. xxv.

"A woman of good understanding."

Her beauty and grace of manner were not her only asset, she was a deeply religious woman as well. It must have been a sore trial to her to be the wife of such a husband, yet she never rebelled against her lot and remained true to the God of her fathers. Her "patient conversation" did not win him to the fear of God and a new life, but we may be sure a blessing descended upon her household in response to her faith, and the excellence of her character.

Her religious spirit.

Here we cannot refrain from making the observation that if the husband is religiously inclined, and the wife is not so, the attitude of the latter, in the majority of cases, leads him away from God. On the other hand, should the positions be reversed, our experience has been that the woman has remained steadfast, and brought up her children in the fear and admonition of the Lord. Many instances have come to our notice in which the Christian wife has won her husband to the Saviour. The Cross is not the only place where women have proved themselves to be the stronger sex. Happy

The value of a good woman's influence.

is the household which has an Abigail for its head, and fortunate is the nation where sons and daughters can be found in plenty to arise up and call their mothers blessed. For the future of such a household and such a nation there need be no fear.

Nabal's insolent reply to David.

When David sent the messengers to Nabal with a request for help, not only were his servants treated with scant civility, but the insolent message they received was calculated to infuriate their leader. Nabal asked, "*Who is David? who is the son of Jesse?*" the implication being that he was a mere nobody. The services which David had rendered to his country were ignored, and the remark "*There be many servants now a days that break away every man from his master*" (verse 10) was an intimation to David that his followers were outlaws, men who refused to work for an honest

Sarcasm.

living. This thinly veiled sarcasm went home, for it must have applied to some of David's men. Sarcasm has its uses, especially when directed against conventional abuses, or expended upon self-satisfied and conceited people. But it is a dangerous weapon, and one that should be sparingly used. The author of *Lorna Doone* says of sarcasm that it is a polite form of bullying. Not seldom does it recoil upon the heads of those who use it. In Nabal's case, had it not been for his wife's good sense and timely intervention, it would have led to disastrous results.

The Son of Jesse's anger, and his resolve.

No sooner had David received Nabal's reply, and his definite refusal to render him any help whatsoever, than he determined to make instant reprisals.

Courtesy and Churlishness

Without delay, he set out to destroy Nabal and his 1 Sam. xxv. household. David's conduct cannot be justified, although it may be urged on his behalf that the provocation was extreme. His right course would have been to refer the message to God, and to await His counsel. Our judgement of David must be tempered by the remembrance that we ourselves are too often prone, with far less excuse, to take hasty and ill-advised action. If we receive a discourteous letter, we are tempted to write a stinging reply at once. We shall be wise to let it remain on the table for twenty-four hours, and then having prayed about it, it is more than probable that the letter in answer will be dignified in tone, and redound to our credit.

Very mercifully for David, he was saved from the consequences of his headstrong action by Nabal's wife. Having learnt the treatment meted out by her husband to the future "ruler over Israel," Abigail took in the perilous situation at a moment's glance. Her first concern was to gain time, and with this end in view she sent on ahead a plentiful supply of provisions, two hundred loaves, two wineskins, five sheep as well as other luxuries (verse 18), with instructions that she was following immediately. As Jacob felt the need of propitiating his brother Esau's just resentment by generous presents sent in advance (Gen. xxxii. 13 ff.), so Abigail believed that she might be able to mollify David's anger by adopting very similar precautions. Abigail hears of her husband's treatment of David.

Abigail's instant action.

Without apprising her husband of what had She goes forth to

247

1 Sam.
xxv.
meet
David.

happened, she set forth to meet David; and not a moment too soon. On the way she met David's cavalcade (verse 20). As soon as she saw him, she hastened to pay him all the outward signs of respect and deference customary in the East. By that time David's anger had probably somewhat cooled, and he would be in a position to listen to reason.

Her conversation with David.

The conversation was opened by Abigail at once informing him of the character that Nabal bore in the district. She gave him to understand that he was not the only aggrieved person in that part of the world, and further that Nabal's treatment of David had occurred without her knowledge.

Her tact.

Very tactfully she proceeded to follow a line of argument which was certain to appeal to David.

Her appeal to his religious side.

She appealed to his religious side, and let him know that she regarded him as her future king. The honour in which he was held, even in that remote part of the country, could not fail to act as balm to his wounded pride. His past and present achievements were not forgotten, "*My lord fighteth the battles of the Lord*" (verse 28). Touching also was the confidence she expressed in God's watchful Providence over his career, and that all Saul's efforts against him would be brought to nought. "*And though a man be risen up to pursue thee, and to seek thy soul, yet the soul of my lord shall be bound in the bundle of life with the Lord thy God*" (verse 29). The subtle allusion to what God had wrought for him in the past, "*And the souls of thine enemies, them shall He sling out, as from a hollow of a sling*" (verse 29), is clever; and finally she assumed that

Her confidence in God's watchful Providence over him.

Courtesy and Churlishness

1 Sam.
xxv.

he would now desist from taking vengeance, and insinuated that he would have reason in the future to be thankful that he had been prevented from shedding blood. Can we be surprised at David being touched by the appeal of such a fair suppliant, and that his wrath was turned away ? David's wrath is averted.

Afterwards Abigail showed her tact and wisdom by saying nothing to her husband of what had happened until the festivities were over, as these were occasions in which he indulged himself freely in excessive drinking and riotous living.

In the morning when he was in a more sober state of mind, she told him what had occurred, and in the expressive words of the Bible, " *his heart died within him, and he became as a stone. And it came to pass about ten days after, that the Lord smote Nabal, that he died* " (verses 37, 38). Nabal's death.

The sequel ended very happily. Abigail did not long remain a widow, David took her to be his wife. It is quite a common practice in the East for a widow to take a second husband soon after her bereavement. There could not be a more beautiful story with a more romantic and satisfactory ending. The sequel.

Rudeness and courtesy are not confined to any one class, nor are they just simply matters of education, for some people seem by nature to be rough and overbearing, others refined and tactful. Be this as it may, the Grace of God can so alter the character as to make it, what it was not before, gracious and considerate. Christianity is from beginning to end a religion of grace. Grace as well as love has a most interesting history attached Rudeness and courtesy. Christianity a religion of grace.

249

to it. In the case of both words their wealth and depth of meaning have been brought to light by our Blessed Lord.   But in our anxiety to emphasise the main conception of Grace in the New Testament

Grace has two meanings.

—God's free and unbounded love and mercy towards us sinners, who through no merit of our own are restored to His favour by the gift of His dear Son, dying for us, and rising again for our justification— care must be taken lest we lose sight of its original meaning in classical Greek, which is charm or winsomeness.

Our Lord both full of grace and gracious.

Christ was full of grace, and He was gracious, it was this latter quality which endeared Him so much to the hearts of His hearers, and attracts us, His followers to-day.

Jairus's daughter an instance of our Lord's graciousness.

When in the room of Jairus's little daughter, before He recalled her to life, He insisted that all the professional mourners should be put outside, so that upon awaking she might not be unduly frightened by the sight of them ; and after He had performed that great miracle, it was He who anticipated the damsel's bodily wants " and commanded that something be given her to eat " (St. Luke viii. 55), which in all probability would have been forgotten in the excitement of the moment.

After the Resurrection.

The Resurrection changed the conditions of the Lord's life and mode of existence, but not His character.

The same courteous Lord God.

He displayed the same courtesy and tenderness towards His disciples in the forty days before His Ascension as in the olden days. Unknown to Cleopas and his friend, He walked with them that

Courtesy and Churlishness

first Easter Day to Emmaus, and when they arrived 1 Sam. xxv.
at their destination " He made as though He would
go further " (St. Luke xxiv. 28). Not willing to
force Himself upon their company, only after they
had pressed Him to come in and stay with them,
for " the day is now far spent," did He consent to
enter and share their meal. Instances might be
multiplied which fully justify the title Lady Julian
so frequently applied to Him, " Our Courteous
Lord God."

" Courtesy " commends the faith of Christ, just Courtesy commends Christianity.
as its absence has often proved to be a hindrance.
Sometimes it is urged in excuse of an honest
straightforward man, whose ways and manners
leave much to be desired, that he is a rough diamond.
Let that be freely admitted, but after all a polished
diamond is better. The individual who boasts of
speaking out his own mind, is the one of all people
who resents others taking a similar liberty with
himself. Dr. Johnson once said, " Sir, a man
has no more right to say an uncivil thing than to act
one—no more right to say a rude thing to another
than to knock him down," though we cannot resist
saying that it would have been well for Dr. Johnson
had he followed a little more closely his own advice.

Tact and courtesy are the daughters of sympathy. Tact and courtesy the daughters of sympathy.
The less we are wrapt up in our own concerns, the
more we share the interests of others and study
their feelings, the less likely shall we be to give
unnecessary and often perhaps unintentional offence.
By these means increasingly will men and women How they win their way.
open the door of their hearts to us, and only so can

any good be effected in this world. As Abigail completely overcame all David's feelings of wrath and revenge, so alone can sympathy and courtesy break down in others all that is contrary to God, and win them to His Kingdom.

" Our Courteous Lord willeth that we should be as homely with Him as heart may think or soul may desire. But beware lest we take recklessly this homeliness so as to leave courtesy. For our Lord is sovereign homeliness, and as homely as He is, so courteous He is " (LADY JULIAN OF NORWICH).

XXIV

AN ECLIPSE OF FAITH, AND HOW IT VANISHED

And David said in his heart, I shall now perish one day by the hand of Saul: *there is* nothing better for me than that I should speedily escape into the land of the Philistines; and Saul shall despair of me, to seek me any more in any coast of Israel: so shall I escape out of his hand. And David arose, and he passed over with the six hundred men that *were* with him unto Achish, the son of Maoch, king of Gath. And David dwelt with Achish at Gath, he and his men, every man with his household, *even* David with his two wives, Ahinoam the Jezreelitess, and Abigail the Carmelitess, Nabal's wife. And it was told Saul that David was fled to Gath: and he sought no more again for him.

And David said unto Achish, If I have now found grace in thine eyes, let them give me a place in some town in the country, that I may dwell there: for why should thy servant dwell in the royal city with thee? Then Achish gave him Ziklag that day: wherefore Ziklag pertaineth unto the kings of Judah unto this day. And the time that David dwelt in the country of the Philistines was a full year and four months.

And David and his men went up, and invaded the Geshurites, and the Gezrites, and the Amalekites: for those *nations were* of old the inhabitants of the land, as thou goest to Shur, even unto the land of Egypt. And David smote the land, and left neither man nor woman alive, and took away the sheep, and the oxen, and the asses, and the camels, and the apparel, and returned, and came to Achish. And Achish said, Whither have ye made a road to day? And David said, Against the south of Judah, and against the south of the Jerahmeelites, and against the south of the Kenites. And David saved neither man nor woman alive, to bring *tidings* to Gath, saying, Lest they should

tell on us, saying, So did David, and so *will be* his manner all
the while he dwelleth in the country of the Philistines. And
Achish believed David, saying, He hath made his people Israel
utterly to abhor him ; therefore he shall be my servant for
ever.

And it came to pass, when David and his men were come to
Ziklag on the third day, that the Amalekites had invaded the
south, and Ziklag, and smitten Ziklag, and burned it with fire ;
And had taken the women captives, that *were* therein : they
slew not any, either great or small, but carried *them* away, and
went on their way.

So David and his men came to the city, and, behold, *it was*
burned with fire ; and their wives, and their sons, and their
daughters, were taken captives. Then David and the people
that *were* with him lifted up their voice and wept, until they
had no more power to weep. And David's two wives were
taken captives, Ahinoam the Jezreelitess, and Abigail the wife
of Nabal the Carmelite. And David was greatly distressed ;
for the people spake of stoning him, because the soul of all the
people was grieved, every man for his sons and for his daughters :
but David encouraged himself in the LORD his God. And
David said to Abiathar the priest, Ahimelech's son, I pray thee,
bring me hither the ephod. And Abiathar brought thither the
ephod to David. And David enquired at the LORD, saying,
Shall I pursue after this troop ? shall I overtake them ? And
he answered him, Pursue : for thou shalt surely overtake
them, and without fail recover *all.*—1 SAM. XXVII. ; XXX. 1–8.

**1 Sam.
xxvii. ;
xxx. 1–8.**

**Saul's
promise to
David.**

WHEN Saul fell into David's hands the second time,
and the latter forbade Abishai, his nephew, "to
stretch forth his hand against the Lord's Anointed,"
Saul made full and ample acknowledgment of the
debt he owed to David for having spared his life,
so far as words could do so. He promised that
the old feud should come to an end, and admitted
that his conduct hitherto towards David had been
both foolish and wrong. After this incident each
went his own respective way.

An Eclipse of Faith

The reconciliation between them both was of short duration. David soon discovered that Saul continued to cherish the same feelings of animosity towards him as of old, and that he was plotting against his life.

1 Sam. xxvii. ; xxx. 1–8.

The reconciliation of short duration.

In their last encounter, David had hinted very plainly at the possibility of being driven to take refuge in another country, and that he would call down Divine vengeance upon those directly responsible for the necessity of such a step (1 Sam. xxvi. 19). At length the time arrived when he was convinced that, were he to remain any longer in his native land, he should one day perish by the hand of Saul. He felt that there was no alternative open to him but to escape in all possible haste to the land of the Philistines, as should he be allowed to remain there unmolested, he would be out of Saul's reach. His surmises proved to be correct, for after the King of Israel had heard that David was at Gath " *he sought no more again for him* " (1 Sam. xxvii. 4).

David leaves his native land.

What befell David during his sojourn in the land of his country's enemies must briefly be told, as our chief concern is with the frame of mind in which David was found when he took this desperate step, in contrast to the very different spirit which he evinced later when even in a more difficult situation.

His sojourn in the land of the Philistines.

In spite of all the promises that God had made to him, and his almost unique experience of God's mercies and deliverances (cf. 1 Sam. xxiii. 26–28), David's faith underwent for the time being an eclipse, " His soul had been disquieted within him,"

A temporary loss of faith.

1 Sam.
xxvii. ;
xxx. 1–8.

but instead of turning to God, and placing himself under His protection, not a word is said of his asking for Divine help. He turned to Achish the son of Maoch, King of Gath, with the request that he would allow both himself and his followers to find a refuge in his country.

Achish perceived the advantage of having such a redoubtable hero as David on his side in his numerous feuds, and received him with gladness.

Ziklag is made over to David.

Shortly after David had come to Gath, Ziklag, which had once belonged to Judah (Josh. xv. 31), was made over to him, here he, his wives and his followers could dwell in security and peace, living their own lives apart from the Philistines. From this city various raids were undertaken by David and his men, in reality these marauding expeditions being against Israel's ancient foes, the Canaanites and Amalekites, but Achish was deceived into believing that they were directed against Judah (1 Sam. xxvii. 10). Any suspicions Achish may have entertained against David were lulled to rest; he "*believed David.*"

Achish's belief in David.

Storm clouds gathering over Israel.

During this time events were moving rapidly in Israel. Once more the Philistines were gathering themselves together against the armies of Saul, which campaign was to end in the fatal battle of Gilboa, wherein the King of Israel met his death. At the outset Achish desired David to accompany him, but the lords of the Philistines still retained vivid recollections of David's deeds against them in the past (xxix. 4, 5), and prevailed upon Achish, much against his will, to dismiss David, with the result that both he and his men returned to Ziklag.

I Sam. xxvii. ; xxx. 1—8.

Meanwhile, during their absence the Amalekites had come up against that city, set it on fire, and taken away captive their womenfolk including David's two wives, Ahinoam and Abigail (xxx. 1–5). Hereupon followed the greatest crisis in the life of the son of Jesse. Signs of mutiny made themselves evident. Loud mutterings were heard on every side, and it was actually suggested that David should be stoned (verse 6).

What happened during David's absence from Ziklag. His extreme peril.

In times of calamity the people will turn against their own popular hero, and make him the target of their blind rage and fury. Popularity may be very shortlived, and little store can be set by it. One year Savonarola was able to wield such power from the pulpit of the Duomo at Florence, that the city was transformed beyond recognition. Bonfires of the " vanities " were made, and the streets echoed with processional hymns and chants of Divine Love. Another year, with two other Dominicans, he was hanged, and their bodies were burnt in the selfsame city which had been the scene of his greatest triumphs.

Popularity, its insecurity.

The Christian, above all others, has reason to view popularity with suspicion. On Palm Sunday his Lord and Master was greeted on all sides by the glad Hosannahs of the multitude, and the road by which He entered Jerusalem was strewn with palm branches, cut down from the trees by the roadside. Five days afterwards, the shouts of joy had given place to the terrible cries of " Crucify Him ! crucify

The Christian's suspicion of the same on account of the treatment meted out to his Lord and Master.

**1 Sam.
xxvii. ;
xxx. 1—8.**

Him ! " and the Messiah of God was hanging on a Cross.

To seek to please people as a whole is a thankless task. The only One whom we should lay ourselves out to please is our Heavenly Father, with Whom there is no variableness nor shadow of turning.

Strange it is to think that David, the darling of the people, idolised by tens of thousands, this same David should have been in danger of being stoned. Thus much for earthly popularity—in the time of his greatest need he was alone, terribly alone, " wounded in the house of his friends."

What causes David's temporary loss of faith.

Let us go back to the occasion when it seemed to David as if God had deserted him, or as we should prefer to say, David had lost his hold upon the Unseen.

The Bible is silent about the causes which brought David to such an unhappy state, beyond the one already mentioned, the hopeless feeling which came over him that Saul's persistent efforts to track him down would prove one day successful. But it is difficult to avoid coming to the conclusion that there were deeper reasons than this for David's temporary loss of faith in God.

Physical and mental strain.

The attempt must now be made to discover what those reasons were, though it should be borne in mind that the conclusions arrived at are at best only probable.

The physical and mental strain of having to keep together, and maintain discipline over, such a crowd of men as were his followers (xxii. 2) was tremendous. It was quite possible then that David

An Eclipse of Faith

was suffering from a nervous breakdown. This is, in part, an explanation of Elijah's case, when he besought the Lord in the wilderness to take away his life (1 Kings xix. 4). The experience Elijah had undergone on Mount Carmel, when, face to face with the four hundred and fifty prophets of Baal backed by the powerful influence of Ahab and his corrupt court, he vindicated, before the vast and silent multitudes of his countrymen, the Sovereignty and Majesty of Jehovah, was bound to tell upon him. After such a gigantic effort, bodily exhaustion was certain to follow. And Almighty God, Who knoweth our frame, and remembereth that we are but dust (Ps. ciii. 14; cf. Isa. lvii. 16), did not chide His servant, but instead, sent an angel to minister to his bodily needs (1 Kings xix. 5–8) and command him to go to Mount Horeb, where rest and relaxation would render him in a fit condition of health, and frame of mind, to receive the further revelation which the Lord God of Hosts had purposed to vouchsafe to him.

1 Sam. xxvii. ; xxx. 1–8. Elijah's depression.

We can quite well imagine that David also needed rest at this time, and to a certain extent he obtained it in the land of the Philistines, relieved as he was from all anxiety of pursuit, his followers also would be less inclined to discontent and murmuring, having a settled abode, and a city they could call their own. Still more would they be drawn together by the fact of living in a heathen land.

Our Lord always had regard for the bodily needs of His disciples, " Come ye yourselves apart into a desert place, and rest awhile. For there were many

Our Lord's care for His disciples.

259

I Sam.
xxvii. ;
xxx. 1–8.
St. Mark vi.
31.

coming and going, and they had no leisure so much as to eat " (St. Mark vi. 31). Christian people often become morbid, and depressed about the actual state of their souls, and their lack of faith. It may be that they need a rest, or, what amounts to the same thing, a change of scene or occupation. When, therefore, they look within, and analyse their feelings, allowance should be made for the state of their bodily health. Feelings are a very uncertain guide to the true condition of our souls, as they depend so much on the individual temperament, the people with whom we come in contact, yes, and even on the state of the weather. Spurgeon's advice is excellent : " For every look you give to yourself, give three to Christ."

Feelings, a poor foundation on which to build the Christian life.

Discord in David's household.

It is quite likely, also, that there may have been a considerable amount of discord in David's household between his wives. In all probability, David transferred his attentions from Ahinoam to Abigail, the new-comer (cf. xxvii. 3) ; this would provoke the first of the two to jealousy, and the tension between them both would be strained almost to breaking point. Even if David were unaware of the bickerings and quarrellings that were taking place, he could hardly find much repose in their society, and, on account of this friction, Abigail would be quite unfit to give him any spiritual help.

The dark night of the soul.

It is also possible that David had to go through " the dark night of the soul," an experience not unknown to many of God's Saints, in order that he should learn to appreciate more the full sunshine of God's Presence.

An Eclipse of Faith

We have noted in a previous chapter how the long and weary years, when David went in constant fear of his life, and became an outlaw, were used of God to train him for the main task of his life, to govern His people Israel. All that time the steps of David were being ordered by the Lord, and He was upholding him with His Hand (Ps. xxxvii. 23, 24). But this did not exclude special help given for special times, and the manner in which Divine assistance was afforded often took the form of some individual sent to help and cheer the son of Jesse. Obliged to absent himself from court, the court came to him in the person of Jonathan the king's son, and his selfless love must often have increased David's hold upon God, preventing him from becoming hard and bitter.

1 Sam. xxvii. ; xxx. 1—8. How God sent different men to help David.

Special help for special times.

Jonathan.

For a short time, it is not known how long, during the earlier part of his training, David was with Samuel: he went to the Prophet, and dwelt at Naioth (1 Sam. xix. 18). So long as he remained with Samuel, he must have felt very conscious of the nearness of God, being, as he was, in close contact with that holy man of God.

The Prophet Samuel.

Later on, when he intended taking up his residence in Moab "*till I know what God will do for me,*" he was not permitted to remain there for any length of time ; Gad the prophet was sent to him, with the command, "Abide not in the hold ; depart, and get thee into the land of Judah" (1 Sam. xxii. 3–5). But it seems that the day was coming when David must rely no longer on human help, he must be cast on his own resources, thrown upon himself,

Gad and Moab.

David must no longer rely upon any human help.

261

The First Book of Samuel

1 Sam.
xxvii. ;
xxx. 1–8.
Abiathar
and the
Ephod.

The lesson
of God
reliance.

which should act as a springboard from which to cast himself into the arms of God, for the conclusion may be drawn, that as Abiathar is not mentioned as fleeing to Gath with David, and that there is no hint of the Ephod being consulted prior to the flight, therefore he was not with David at that time, but joined him later at Ziklag.

If this was so, we may gather that such was the intention of the Divine Mind, in order that David, left without the help of man, might learn the lesson of entire God reliance, and to act upon that alone.

> "This imports solely, man should mount on each
> New height in view; the help whereby he mounts,
> The ladder-rung his foot has left, may fall,
> Since all things suffer change save God the Truth."
>
> (R. Browning.)

His failure,
but subse-
quent
victory.

David
shows
his true
manhood.

His faith
in God
returns.

He
encouraged
himself in

He did not stand the test. As we have seen, he suffered an eclipse of faith, fleeing to the country of Israel's implacable foe, and safe there only so long as he continued deliberately to deceive his host, the King of Gath, and to commit acts of terrible cruelty (1 Sam. xxvii. 11) in order to escape detection. An end must come to this. The crash came, "*David was greatly distressed*" (xxx. 5). The real man awoke within him then, and was brought to light. God had not deserted His anointed. The faith, for the time being shrouded in darkness, shone forth with the brightness of the noonday sun. "*He strengthened himself in the Lord his God*" (verse 6). And we lay stress on the fact that only after he had so done, are we told that he

262

applied to Abiathar, who, if indeed absent when **1 Sam.** David fled to Gath, had by this time, we know, **xxvii.** ; followed him there. David had learnt the lesson **xxx. 1–8.** to stand by himself, relying upon God alone. **the Lord** Before seeking the assistance of Abiathar, he had **God.** recourse to the more spiritual method of communion with God only.

Personal influence is an important factor in every **Personal** man's life, for good or for evil, and when this great **influence,** gift is consecrated to the service of Christ, who can **its blessings and** estimate the blessings which follow in its train ? **dangers.** Yet it is not without its dangers. People may become so dependent upon a particular individual for spiritual help and guidance, as to feel lost and bewildered should he be removed either by death, or by a call to some other sphere of work.

It is by no means an uncommon remark to hear, **Man** "I shall stop going to church now that I cannot **worship.** hear (a particular name is mentioned) any more." This is man worship, not God worship. Even St. John had to be rebuked by the angel, because he fell down to worship before his feet, " See thou **Rev. xxii. 9.** do it not : I am a fellow-servant with thee and with thy brethren the prophets, and with them which keep the words of this book : worship God " (Rev. xxii. 9).

In contrast to this, the divineness of the Lord's method is worthy of our imitation and devotion. After the Saviour had risen from the dead, He **The Risen** revealed Himself to His disciples only at certain **Saviour's** intervals. His absence is as instructive as His **absences** Presence. In this way He was teaching them not to **instructive.**

The First Book of Samuel

1 Sam.
xxvii. ;
xxx. 1–8.

The
disciples
taught to
depend on
His unseen
Presence.

The gift of
the Holy
Spirit.

depend upon His physical Presence, which must as
such be limited to definite times and places, but
upon His unseen spiritual Presence, which could be
enjoyed by His disciples always and everywhere.
And the results are striking. After He had ascended
into Heaven, His disciples became more courageous,
of stronger faith and greater enthusiasm. Through
the Holy Spirit, the great Gift of the Ascended Lord,
they had learnt to " encourage themselves in Christ."
In the Upper Room the Lord had promised to send
to His disciples the Comforter (St. John xiv. 16, 26 ;
xv. 26 ; xvi. 7 ff.). By this He meant, not that
the Holy Spirit should merely console His followers
in times of sorrow, but that He should at all times
be alongside with them, making them strong, and
filling them with courage.

The result.
The
disciples
became
centres of
encourage-
ment.

This came to pass. And not only did the
disciples encourage themselves in Christ, but they
became centres of encouragement in a world filled
with darkness and despair, and went forth to win
mighty victories for Christ and His Kingdom.

Another
interpreta-
tion of
David's loss
of faith.

But it is possible to take a different view of this
event in David's life. It is open to us to believe
that Abiathar had not left David, and indeed,
considering the perils of his situation, it seems highly
probable that he should remain under the protection
of David and his six hundred men. Why then did
not David consult the Ephod before the flight to
Gath ? for if he had taken such a step he would
surely not have formed such a resolution. Was he

Panic at his
desperate
situation.

seized with panic ? causing him for awhile to suffer
an eclipse of faith in God, and thus to take the

264

An Eclipse of Faith

reins into his own hands, Abiathar meanwhile helpless to influence him in any way?

1 Sam. xxvii. ; xxx. 1–8.

At least this seems to be a legitimate conjecture, and it has for us as necessary a lesson as the former interpretation, one which has come up before, and been touched upon, during our study of this book, and upon which we would here place fresh emphasis.

The guidance of God not sought.

Seized by fear, or in wilfulness, do we not in situations of difficulty too often go to God for guidance as a *last resource*, after we have tried every other expedient? Men sometimes resort to dishonesty in their need, with terrible consequences. Had they waited prayerfully upon God, He would have opened a way for their relief along an honourable path, as many a one, sorely tried, can testify. In Psalm xxxvii., David cries from the depth of his own experience, "Commit thy way unto the Lord ; trust also in Him, and He shall bring it to pass. Rest in the Lord, and wait patiently for Him." If we do this, *before* acting, speaking and writing, instead of *after*, we shall be spared many grave mistakes, and have a far greater influence in the spread of the Kingdom of God.

We should seek God's counsel first, not last. Many a grave mistake thus avoided.

EMMAUS OR ENDOR?

Now Samuel was dead, and all Israel had lamented him, and buried him in Ramah, even in his own city. And Saul had put away those that had familiar spirits, and the wizards, out of the land. And the Philistines gathered themselves together, and came and pitched in Shunem : and Saul gathered all Israel together, and they pitched in Gilboa. And when Saul saw the host of the Philistines, he was afraid, and his heart greatly trembled. And when Saul enquired of the LORD, the LORD answered him not, neither by dreams, nor by Urim, nor by prophets.

Then said Saul unto his servants, Seek me a woman that hath a familiar spirit, that I may go to her, and enquire of her. And his servants said to him, Behold, *there is* a woman that hath a familiar spirit at En-dor. And Saul disguised himself, and put on other raiment, and he went, and two men with him, and they came to the woman by night : and he said, I pray thee, divine unto me by the familiar spirit, and bring me *him* up, whom I shall name unto thee. And the woman said unto him, Behold, thou knowest what Saul hath done, how he hath cut off those that have familiar spirits, and the wizards, out of the land : wherefore then layest thou a snare for my life, to cause me to die ? And Saul sware to her by the LORD, saying, *As* the LORD liveth, there shall no punishment happen to thee for this thing. Then said the woman, Whom shall I bring up unto thee ? And he said, Bring me up Samuel. And when the woman saw Samuel, she cried with a loud voice : and the woman spake to Saul, saying, Why hast thou deceived me ? for thou *art* Saul. And the king said unto her, Be not afraid ; for what sawest thou ? And the woman said unto Saul, I saw gods ascending out of the earth. And he said unto her, What form *is* he of ? And she said, An old man cometh up ; and he *is* covered with a mantle. And Saul perceived that it *was* Samuel, and he stooped with *his* face to the ground, and bowed himself.

Emmaus or Endor?

And Samuel said to Saul, Why hast thou disquieted me, to bring me up? And Saul answered, I am sore distressed; for the Philistines make war against me, and God is departed from me, and answereth me no more, neither by prophets, nor by dreams: therefore I have called thee, that thou mayest make known unto me what I shall do. Then said Samuel, Wherefore then dost thou ask of me, seeing the LORD is departed from thee, and is become thine enemy? And the LORD hath done to him, as he spake by me: for the LORD hath rent the kingdom out of thine hand, and given it to thy neighbour, *even* to David: Because thou obeyedst not the voice of the LORD, nor executedst his fierce wrath upon Amalek, therefore hath the LORD done this thing unto thee this day. Moreover the LORD will also deliver Israel with thee into the hand of the Philistines: and to morrow *shalt* thou and thy sons *be* with me: the LORD also shall deliver the host of Israel into the hand of the Philistines. Then Saul fell straightway all along on the earth, and was sore afraid, because of the words of Samuel: and there was no strength in him; for he had eaten no bread all the day, nor all the night.

And the woman came unto Saul, and saw that he was sore troubled, and said unto him, Behold, thine handmaid hath obeyed thy voice, and I have put my life in my hand, and have hearkened unto thy words which thou spakest unto me. Now therefore, I pray thee, hearken thou also unto the voice of thine handmaid, and let me set a morsel of bread before thee; and eat, that thou mayest have strength, when thou goest on thy way. But he refused, and said, I will not eat. But his servants, together with the woman, compelled him; and he hearkened unto their voice. So he arose from the earth, and sat upon the bed. And the woman had a fat calf in the house; and she hasted, and killed it, and took flour, and kneaded *it*, and did bake unleavened bread thereof: And she brought *it* before Saul, and before his servants; and they did eat. Then they rose up, and went away that night.—1 SAM. XXVIII. 3 to end.

THE Philistines had again encamped against the Israelites, and were determined that this time there should be no ordinary skirmish, but that a decisive battle should be fought. When Saul beheld the vast hosts of the enemy massed against him and his army, *"He was afraid, and his heart greatly*

1 Sam. xxviii. 3 to end.

The Philistines determine to crush the Israelites.

267

**1 Sam.
xxviii. 3
to end.**

**Saul's
despair at
the
prospect.**

**His appeal
to the
prophets
and the
Urim,**

**but all to
no purpose.**

trembled " (verse 5). In his distress he "*inquired
of the Lord,*" but no answer was vouchsafed to him.
Now that Samuel was dead, and had left no successor,
Saul appealed to those who belonged to the school of
the prophets, but they could render him no aid.
Once before he had resorted to the Urim and the
Thummin, and had received assistance (xiv. 41).
He had, if not the original Urim and Thummin,
another of a similar kind, but doubtless he would
be at great pains to secure the original before
the slaughter of the priests at Nob. Possibly,
however, Abiathar may have escaped with it
(xxiii. 9). But from this particular Urim and
Thummin Saul could obtain no answer. The
writer of the Chronicles denies that Saul ever
inquired of the Lord at this time (1 Chron. x. 13, 14),
from which we are to understand that, had Saul
approached God in a spirit of real contrition and
abasement, he would have received, or have been
set in the way to receive, the help he needed.

**He resorts
to a
medium.**

Not knowing where to turn, the distracted
monarch had recourse to means sternly forbidden
by God, and which he had himself taken strong
measures to stamp out in the past. By his command, any one convicted of practising witchcraft
was put to death. Notwithstanding this, Saul felt
that to consult a medium was his only hope.

**He goes to
Endor.**

**The
medium.**

Under cover of night, with two trusty servants,
he betook himself to Endor, where there resided
"*a woman that hath a familiar spirit,*" in modern
language a medium. In disguise he entered her
abode, and then discovered that it was needful to

allay her suspicions and fears, for she was in terror **1 Sam.** as to whether a trap were not being laid for her. **xxviii. 3** Not without a touch of unconscious irony, the **to end.** stranger made use of the Divine Name to assure her of her entire safety in his hands, and that she need not hesitate to practise her arts. Her fears having been overcome, she consented to hold a séance, which transports the reader into a forbidden land of dark horror and weird mystery. She was **The** asked to summon Samuel from the realms of the **apparition.** dead, and as soon as she became aware of the presence of the Prophet she discovered that the disguised stranger was the King of Israel (verse 12). The apparition was invisible to Saul (verse 13), but a conversation was carried on between them both through the medium.

The first sentence uttered by the departed spirit **Samuel's** took the form of a question : " *Why hast thou dis-* **question.** *quieted me, to bring me up ?* " (verse 15). Doubtless it was by the Divine permission that the Prophet appeared, but Saul's faithlessness was the moving cause of his coming.

Here it may not be inopportune to ask, Did **Did Samuel** Samuel actually appear himself, or was it a spirit **actually** impersonating the Prophet ? The whole tenour of **appear.** the narrative is against the latter view. In reading the account it is difficult to avoid the conclusion that the medium, being in a trance, believed she saw Samuel. The writer of the narrative plainly **What the** says that " *the woman saw Samuel* " (verse 12), and **medium** does not suggest in the slightest degree that either **saw.** she or Saul were deceived in this respect. This is

The First Book of Samuel

acknowledged by Prof. H. P. Smith, although he states that the " the more sober Protestant commentators see that it is unreasonable to suppose the souls of the departed subject to such calls, and therefore suppose the Devil to assume the form of the one invoked." He might have added that many of the ancient Fathers of the Church, as well as the Venerable Bede, entertained the same view. It is far safer to go by the text than to trust to à *priori* reasoning, and we reply that no spirit sent on God's errand, for it is not suggested that the medium could summon Samuel at will, could experience any personal discomfort; all thought of self would disappear in the consciousness of executing a Divine command. But from another point of view, the spirit that is sent to be the harbinger of doom must experience disquiet, inasmuch as through entering into the sorrow of God, he comes to share God's attitude, love for the man himself, as well as displeasure with his sin.

We may therefore adhere to the view that Samuel himself did come on this occasion. No theories, however, as to the condition of the departed under the Gospel Dispensation can be built on this appearance of the Prophet.

What the Prophet tells Saul.
To return to the scene recorded in this chapter. After the unhappy king had explained how it was that he had felt compelled to summon Samuel, the news he received was of a most staggering nature. The Prophet reiterated what he had already told Saul when he was upon earth, that the kingdom should not descend to his sons, and added that

Emmaus or Endor?

Israel would be defeated; moreover, that both Saul and his sons would meet their deaths on the morrow (verse 19). On hearing this Saul fainted away, partly from lack of food, and also from the strain of overwrought nerves. At this pitiful sight the womanly nature of the medium asserted itself. With intense sympathy for the lot of the stricken king, and fine delicacy of feeling, she begged as a favour that he would partake of her food. The fee she demanded of him for having risked her life, was that he should partake of the best in her house, so that " *Thou mayest have strength, when thou goest on thy way* " (verses 21–22).

Saul faints away on hearing the news.

Uniting her supplications with those of the servants, they at last prevailed upon Saul to eat of the meal which it would not take long to prepare and serve for him.

The restraint and the simplicity of the narrative demand our admiration. It would have been so easy to have painted the Witch of Endor in the blackest of colours, instead of which she is the one ray of light piercing the gloom, the warmth of her sympathy thawed the icy coldness of Saul's heart. Nevertheless, he who described the whole scene had a horror of Spiritualism into which few of us can enter; he regarded it as nothing short of apostasy from God. Rebellion against God is likened unto the sin of witchcraft (1 Sam. xv. 23).

The character of the Witch of Endor.

In the pleasing character thus presented of the Witch of Endor, we are made to see that the fact of attractive and kind-hearted people embracing certain ideas and opinions, does not of itself render

The test of any doctrine and theory.

271

**1 Sam.
xxviii. 3
to end.**

those views any the less dangerous, or more worthy of our acceptance. Any doctrine or theory that claims to be true must be examined on its own merits. Can it be reconciled with the truth already known, and, broadly speaking, does it tend to enhance the value and dignity of the spiritual life revealed to us by Christ ?

**Our
attitude
towards
Spiritism.**

The story of the Witch of Endor raises, in an acute form, the problem as to what is to be our attitude towards Spiritualism, or as we prefer to call it Spiritism, which is so popular in many quarters to-day.

**Can
Spiritism be
scientfically
proved ?**

At the outset, we have to settle, or at least consider, whether the phenomena brought forward by Spiritism can be proved to originate in a world other than our own, or whether they may be " the genuine products of the subliminal, subconscious memory, multiple personality, and other imperfectly understood processes of the human mind, which can simulate spirit-communications to a surprising extent." From a rigidly scientific point of view, the evidence is somewhat ambiguous, and not altogether satisfactory. This is the opinion expressed by Dr. Schiller,[1] a great authority on the subject, and by no means an unsympathetic judge of the question at issue.

**If true,
gives scope
for limit-
less fraud.**

If, however, the reader adopts a more positive attitude, and feels compelled to take the view that Spiritism is true, what then should be his attitude towards it ? It is admitted on all hands that the

---

[1] Cf. Hastings, *Encyclopædia of Religion and Ethics*, vol. xi., art. on " Spiritism," p. 807.

scope for fraud is unlimited. Those who have
recourse to mediums expose themselves to the
possibility of every kind of trickery and knavery
being practised upon them. Once in the clutches
of unscrupulous people, their victim runs the risk
of being ruined, both in body and soul. Granted,
however, that the mediums chosen are of good
report and above reproach, the practice of Spiritism
in itself is dangerous, and is inimical to our highest
interests.

I Sam. xxviii. 3 to end.

Let it be conceded that through a medium we
can have access to those who have passed over to
the other side. The atmosphere of excitement
which must pervade all such communications is
apt to upset the mental balance of those who seek
them, and the subject threatens to become so
absorbing as to expose them to the danger of
neglecting the vital interests of the present life.
Continuous excitement is never healthy, and does
not foster that steady and quiet devotion which
characterises the lives of the true servants of God.

At its best generates an atmosphere of excitement.

Again, it is noticeable that in Saul's case, the
rock on which he foundered was his lack of personal
knowledge of God. When he addressed Samuel
after the battle with the Amalekites honesty compelled him to say, " The Lord thy God " (1 Sam. xv.
15), and even when he acknowledged his own sin,
he implored Samuel to honour him before the elders
of the people, and before Israel, " and turn again
with me, that I may worship the Lord thy God "
(xv. 30). Not his sin against God and his rejection
by Him, but the fear of losing the respect due to

What led Saul to resort to such method.

himself and the office he held, this was his chief concern.

Many of those who uphold Spiritism assert that through its means they have become convinced of the existence of the Hereafter, when all others have failed them. And even this is an understatement. They would affirm that Spiritism, and Spiritism alone, establishes the existence of the Future Life. As Christians we cannot allow these **The true basis of our belief in the Future Life.** statements to remain unchallenged. The belief in a Future Life is a reasonable faith, grounded upon our acceptance of Christ as the Supreme and Perfect Revelation of the Father's Love, and upon His triumph over sin, by His death on the Cross, and His rising again the third day.

The more real our communion with God becomes, the more certain is it that we are lifted up beyond the limits of space and time, and enter into a Fellowship which death cannot destroy.

A Love which will not let us go. As we look up into the Face of Divine Love, which shines forth so pure and strong amidst the oppressive darkness of that first Good Friday, we become more and more convinced that there is a Love which will not let us go, either in this life, or when we pass out into the Life Beyond.

Signs and wonders. Spiritism bases its appeal on signs and wonders. Our Lord says of an " evil and adulterous generation " that it " seeketh after a sign," and the one sign He consents to give is His Resurrection (St. Matt. xii. 39 ; St. Luke xi. 29). A man does not require to be religious to embrace the tenets of Spiritism. In contrast to this, the promise of

Emmaus or Endor ?

Eternal Life by Christ can only become real, in 1 Sam. xxviii. 3 to end. proportion as those who accept it hunger and thirst after righteousness, and are both ready and willing to take up their Cross and follow the Saviour.

The proofs of our glorious Hope are then both Proofs of our glorious Hope both spiritual and moral. spiritual and moral, and if our belief is genuine, it must help us to become better men and women, and live closer to God. That is the reason why St. Paul prays that he may know Christ, and the power of His Resurrection (Phil. iii. 9, 10). We may be bolder even than Tennyson when he wrote :

> "Thou wilt not leave us in the dust :
> Thou madest man, he knows not why,
> He thinks he was not made to die ;
> And Thou hast made him : Thou art just."

For the closer we live to our Saviour, the more certainly shall we *know* and not merely *think* we were not made to die. Towards the close of his life the Apostle can triumphantly say, " I know 2 Tim. i. 12. Him whom I have believed, and I am persuaded that He is able to guard that which I have committed unto Him against that day " (2 Tim. i. 12). What that Future Life has in store for us we do not know, enough for us that Christ is there.

It is significant that at Endor Saul gained no No additional knowledge gained at Endor. additional knowledge of the future, beyond the confirmation of his worst fears. Has Spiritism so far added to our knowledge of the unseen world ? Its messages may be tainted at their source (Jer. xiv. 14 ; xxvii. 9–10), they may come from evil spirits (cf. 1 Tim. iv. 1 ; 1 St. John iv. 1), at their

1 Sam.
xxviii. 3
to end.
best they do but tell us what we know already, and often they reveal so commonplace an existence, that we are drawn to wonder, much as we shrink from the thought of total annihilation, whether such an Eternity is worth enjoying at all, but is not rather to be dreaded.

We cannot outline our future; as the child leaves its toys behind when it enters upon the fuller life and deeper interests of older years, so, doubtless, many of the harmless pleasures mercifully granted to brighten the days of our earthly sojourn, will cease to be needed when we attain " the fulness of Ps. xvii. 15. joy " in the immediate Presence of God. If, here, we delight in Him, knowing Him we shall gladly leave our future to Him, and He will see to it that our hearts are satisfied (Ps. xvii. 15). " Beloved, 1 St. John
iii. 2. now are we children of God, and it is not yet made manifest what we shall be. We know that, if He shall be manifested, we shall be like Him ; for we shall see Him even as He is " (1 St. John iii. 2). Not Endor
but
Emmaus. Not Endor but Emmaus is our goal. Not a medium, but Christ, the One and only Mediator between God and man, shall we seek (1 Tim. ii. 5). As we talk with Him on life's journey, our hearts will not faint with terror at the prospects of the future, but will burn with love, and a steady enthusiasm for the Highest and the Best. No wraith from the unseen world, complaining that we have disquieted him, can help us, but the Loving Friend, in Whose strong and tender keeping we may safely leave both our dear departed and our own souls. He bids us come to Him, Who alone can solve our doubts and allay

our fears, and Who has promised to those who come
never to cast them out (St. John vi. 37).

And at the end there awaits us, not the extinguish-
ing of our Hope and expectation, but a welcome
Home, and from the lips of Him Whom we learned
to know on earth, we shall hear the words, "Behold,
thou hast heard My voice and opened the door :
I will come in to thee, and will sup with thee, and
thou with Me " (cf. Rev. iii. 20). And even
Emmaus fails in one important respect, the Christ
will not vanish from our sight, but will abide with
us for ever.

I Sam.
xxviii. 3
to end.
At the end
of life's
journey.

Even
Emmaus
fails in one
respect.

XXVI

A TRAGIC ENDING

Now the Philistines fought against Israel : and the men of Israel fled from before the Philistines, and fell down slain in mount Gilboa. And the Philistines followed hard upon Saul and upon his sons ; and the Philistines slew Jonathan, and Abinadab, and Melchi-shua, Saul's sons. And the battle went sore against Saul, and the archers hit him ; and he was sore wounded of the archers. Then said Saul unto his armourbearer, Draw thy sword, and thrust me through therewith ; lest these uncircumcised come and thrust me through, and abuse me. But his armourbearer would not ; for he was sore afraid. Therefore Saul took a sword, and fell upon it. And when his armourbearer saw that Saul was dead, he fell likewise upon his sword, and died with him. So Saul died, and his three sons, and his armourbearer, and all his men, that same day together.

And when the men of Israel that *were* on the other side of the valley, and *they* that *were* on the other side Jordan, saw that the men of Israel fled, and that Saul and his sons were dead, they forsook the cities, and fled ; and the Philistines came and dwelt in them. And it came to pass on the morrow, when the Philistines came to strip the slain, that they found Saul and his three sons fallen in mount Gilboa. And they cut off his head, and stripped off his armour, and sent into the land of the Philistines round about, to publish *it in* the house of their idols, and among the people. And they put his armour in the house of Ashtaroth : and they fastened his body to the wall of Beth-shan.

And when the inhabitants of Jabesh-gilead heard of that which the Philistines had done to Saul ; all the valiant men arose, and went all night, and took the body of Saul and the bodies of his sons from the wall of Beth-shan, and came to

278

A Tragic Ending

Jabesh, and burnt them there. And they took their bones, and buried *them* under a tree at Jabesh, and fasted seven days.— 1 Sam. xxxi.

THE deep shadows of coming defeat and doom had already closed around Saul. And now the fatal day had dawned which was to see his last encounter with the Philistines.

1 Sam. xxxi.

Coming defeat.

Twice before in the history of Israel, battles had been fought in or near the plain of Esdraelon (Judg. iv. 11; v. 21; vii.). On each occasion victory had been granted to God's chosen people, but this time their fortunes were to be reversed. A terrible and disastrous defeat was inflicted upon the Israelites. They fled before their foes.

It takes place in the plain of Esdraelon.

Special attention had been directed by the enemy towards Saul, and his three sons. Jonathan, Abinadab and Melchi-shua were slain, and the Philistines were anxious to capture Saul alive. They would take a peculiar pleasure in making sport of their illustrious prisoner, and maltreating him. At last the opportunity had arrived, the unhappy king was overtaken by the archers. Saul, conscious that the fate he most dreaded was close at hand, directed his armourbearer to draw his sword and thrust him through therewith, " *but his armourbearer would not ; for he was sore afraid* " (verse 4). Saul knew that he had not a moment to lose, took his sword, and fell upon it. In the words of the Bible, rendered still more pathetic by reason of their simplicity, " *So Saul died, and his three sons and his armourbearer, and all his men that same day together* " (verse 6). The Israelites, deprived

The death of Saul and his sons.

279

The First Book of Samuel

of their leader, knew that the day was lost, and fled in all directions, with the result that the Philistines took possession of the cities of the Israelites in the Jordan valley (Prof. H. P. Smith).

The treatment of their dead bodies by the enemy.

On the morrow after the battle, the enemy discovered the bodies of Saul and his sons on Mount Gilboa. His head and his armour they took away as trophies. Messengers were sent round the land of the Philistines to acquaint the people and their gods of the victory they had won, the armour of the dead warriors was placed in the house of the Ashtaroth, or the temple of Astarte, probably at Ashkelon. Saul's body was fastened to the wall at Beth-shan, "the key of Western Palestine."

Sir George Adam Smith has devoted several pages of his great work on the *Historical Geography of the Holy Land* to the important part played by Beth-shan (Beisan) in the history of Palestine. "Alone it has stood," he writes, "less often an outpost of Western Palestine than a point of vantage against it. The one event by which this town becomes vivid in the Old Testament—the hanging of the bodies of Saul and Jonathan upon its walls—is but a symbol of the standing menace and insult it proved to Israel, from its proud position across the plain."

The gratitude of the inhabitants of Jabesh-Gilead.

A faint ray of light pierces the darkness which had descended upon Israel's first king, namely the gratitude of the inhabitants of Jabesh-Gilead. They could not forget what Saul had done for them in the past (cf. 1 Sam. xi.). During the night the valiant men amongst them, fired with a mighty

A Tragic Ending

resolve, issued forth and marched to Beth-shan, **1 Sam. xxxi.**
unfastened the bodies of Saul and his sons, and
returned with them to their own city. There Their
they buried them under a tamarisk tree, with rescue of
all the pomp and ceremony customary in those the bodies.
days.

There is no more tragic figure in the Bible, perhaps Saul is the
even in the whole of history, than that of Saul. most tragic
Our eyes may be dry as we read his life, but our figure in the
hearts are grieving for him all the while. We may Bible.
be sorry for Esau, deprived by underhand means Comparison
of his birthright and blessing, but a closer study of between
his character tempers our feeling of compassion. him and
Esau.
The writer of the Epistle to the Hebrews calls
him "a profane person" (Heb. xii. 16), in our
modern speech, a man without religion. Genial
and generous, without vices, he was a man of the
world, his soul possessed no temple. To sell his
birthright on the spur of the moment was both
foolish and wrong, and an indication of a character
deficient in self-control, but he was himself the
sufferer by his ill-advised and hasty action, and it
excites our pity rather than our indignation. What
cannot be pardoned is, that having satisfied his
bodily cravings, we hear of no misgivings and
regrets ; " he rose up and went his way," unconcerned as to the result of his action. Therein
lay his sin. He set no store by his birthright.

Saul was called to play a more important part than Saul's
Esau in the history of his country. By reason of religion
this, his failure was on a larger scale. He was not lacked
depth.

The First Book of Samuel

equal to the demands made upon him. Called by God to a great work, He never rose to a true conception of his vocation. Samuel never succeeded in opening his eyes to it. Unlike Esau, Saul was a religious man, but his religion lacked depth. The Visible was much more real to him than the Invisible, although he recognised the existence, and to a certain degree the claims, of the Invisible. God was beyond him but not within him. The Spirit of God was partially withdrawn from him, but to say that He was entirely withdrawn is to be wise above that which is written, and it is false. He died fighting for his country. He fell by his own hand, but his case cannot be classed with that of an ordinary suicide. We may believe that he felt that for the Lord's anointed to suffer abuse at the hand of the uncircumcised Philistine, was not merely a personal affront, but an outrage upon his religion and country.

His ultimate salvation considered. The older commentators discussed at great length the question as to whether Saul enjoyed, or had forfeited, salvation. Some placed him amongst the lost, our own Matthew Henry has exercised a wiser reserve. " The Scripture makes no mention of the souls of Saul and his sons, what became of them after they were dead (secret things belong not to us), but of their bodies only." But with Dr. Davidson we prefer to say, " He was the first king of God's kingdom ; and we desire to think that, having such a place, he was not cast away. We leave his faults where we leave our own—at the feet of the true King of the Kingdom of God, Who did not

A Tragic Ending

leave the kingdom a ruin, as Saul did, but Who **1 Sam.** established it with judgement and justice from **xxxi.** henceforth even for ever; and Who is the propitiation for our sins; and not for ours only, but for the sins of the whole world." [1]

[1] *The Called of God* (Edinburgh: T. & T. Clark), 1903, p. 161.

PRINTED IN GREAT BRITAIN BY WILLIAM CLOWES AND SONS, LIMITED, LONDON AND BECCLES.

THE
 Devotional Commentary

Edited by the REV. C. H. IRWIN, D.D.

Every volume of this Commentary is primarily and distinctly a
Devotional volume—a book which the Bible reader can take
up day by day and find it aid him in applying the words of
Holy Scripture to the needs of his own personal character and life.

Each 3/6 net.

GENESIS (3 vols.)
By the Rev. W. H. GRIFFITH THOMAS, D.D.

These volumes are very fruitful in those personal lessons
which it is the object of this Commentary more especially to
draw out. In the hands of Dr. Griffith Thomas they never fail
to have a spiritual message; thus, whilst the work abounds in
material full of suggestion for the minister of the Word, it also
appeals directly to the reader whose aim is personal edification.

"This Commentary will prove suggestive to Bible students
as expounding this part of the Scripture in a spirit noticeably
distinct from that in which it is usually approached by modern
theologians of the critical sort."— *The Scotsman*.

EXODUS (2 vols.)
By the Rev. F. B. MEYER, D.D.

"No intelligent person can afford to ignore this Book, which
is only second in importance to that of Genesis in the Old Testament and the Gospel of Matthew in the New. . . . The story
of the Exodus is repeated in every soul that seeks deliverance
from the enmeshing and enervating influence of the world.
From this point of view the Book is human from the first verse
to the last."—*Extract from Dr. Meyer's Foreword*.

RUTH.
By the Rev. SAMUEL COX, D.D.

Much in "Ruth" that is necessarily obscure to the ordinary
reader is here clearly explained; the story stands out in all its
primitive simplicity, and its effect is deepened to a remarkable
degree. And not only is the book instructive as to the manners
and customs of the time of Boaz and Ruth; the innermost meaning of the story is revealed.

ESTHER.
By the Rev. J. ELDER CUMMING, D.D.

Dr. Elder Cumming discusses, in a careful and scholarly
fashion, the various difficulties associated with the Book of
Esther; but the definite spiritual import of the story is his main
theme. The field has been, in this way, so little worked by
others, that preachers should find the volume full of suggestive
matter.

THE
 Devotional Commentary

Edited by the REV. C. H. IRWIN, D.D.

Every volume of this Commentary is primarily and distinctly a Devotional volume—a book which the Bible reader can take up day by day and find it aid him in applying the words of Holy Scripture to the needs of his own personal character and life.

Each **3/6** net.

THE PSALMS (3 vols.)
By the Rev. J. ELDER CUMMING, D.D.

In his treatment Dr. Elder Cumming has sought to avoid repetition, whilst adhering to the plan of providing help for the devotional study of each Psalm. His capacity for penetrating to the spiritual message of Holy Scripture is remarkable. But whilst his insight constantly discovers that which others might have overlooked, his exegesis is never strained or unnatural.

JEREMIAH.
By the Rev. H. ELVET LEWIS, M.A.

Jeremiah was a poet-prophet, with the sensitive, ardent, variable temperament that such a title implies, and it is appropriate that the poet-preacher and Archdruid of Wales should here interpret for modern readers the poet-prophet of Israel. The reader will discover in this work deep and refreshing springs, and it will bring to all who go to its pages that spiritual sustenance which the soul needs in its daily contact with the world.

ST. MARK (4 vols.)
By the Rev. J. D. JONES, M.A., D.D.

In these volumes the Rev. J. D. Jones, of Bournemouth, draws out with characteristic skill the personal lessons to be derived from the Gospel. The message to the individual soul is ever present to his mind, and his searching treatment never fails to suggest thought. Alike on its expository and on its devotional side the work should be helpful to all who seek guidance and stimulus for a life of faith and service.

ST. LUKE (3 vols.)
By the Rev. J. M. E. ROSS, M.A.

Mr. Ross's treatment combines, in a very unusual degree, sound scholarship, deep insight into the spiritual import of facts, and the searching application to the conditions of our times. St. Luke—himself a man of letters and a literary artist—has here found an expositor who writes with literary charm, and illustrates his teaching from the resources of a well-stored mind.

THE R.T.S., 4 BOUVERIE STREET, LONDON, E.C. 4.

THE
 # Devotional Commentary

Edited by the REV. C. H. IRWIN, D.D.

Every volume of this Commentary is primarily and distinctly a Devotional volume—a book which the Bible reader can take up day by day and find it aid him in applying the words of Holy Scripture to the needs of his own personal character and life.

Each **3/6** net.

THE ACTS (2 vols.)
By the Rev. CHARLES BROWN, D.D.

It is the purpose of this Commentary, says Dr. Charles Brown, "to catch the soul or spirit of the narrative, and not merely its dress, or outward form, to discover its spiritual lessons and to apply them." Dr. Brown here gives us much "marrow" of Christian teaching, much vivid personification of Paul, Peter and their companions, and of their opponents.

ROMANS (3 vols.)
By the Rev. W. H. GRIFFITH THOMAS, D.D.

This work exhibits all its author's known skill in the clearness of its exposition and the skilful arrangement of its matter in order to facilitate not only a careful study of the Epistle, but also its use for ordered and consecutive meditation. The fruits of wide reading are everywhere manifest, side by side with the evidence of spiritual insight.

GALATIANS.
By the Rev. Canon R. B. GIRDLESTONE, M.A.

The treatment of St. Paul's Epistle to the Galatians by Canon R. B. Girdlestone is precisely such as the devotional student of the Epistle would desire. The argument of the Epistle is lucidly developed, and the line of the Apostle's reasoning everywhere made plain. The application of St. Paul's words to the personal life of the reader, without being strained, is everywhere direct and forcible.

EPHESIANS.
By the Rev. CHARLES BROWN, D.D.

Dr. Brown's well-known expository gifts are admirably revealed in his treatment of this Epistle. What he has to say by way of exposition and application tends to a profitable study of the Epistle, and imparts a fresh interest and meaning to the Apostolic letter.

The book is well balanced. It is written not from the critical but from the devotional standpoint, and there is abundance of "practical application" in the best sense.

THE R.T.S., 4 BOUVERIE STREET, LONDON, E.C. 4.

THE

Devotional Commentary

Edited by the REV. C. H. IRWIN, D.D.

Every volume of this Commentary is primarily and distinctly a Devotional volume—a book which the Bible reader can take up day by day and find it aid him in applying the words of Holy Scripture to the needs of his own personal character and life.

Each **3/6** net.

II. TIMOTHY.

By the late Right Rev. HANDLEY C. G. MOULE, D.D., Bishop of Durham.

The Bishop of Durham published several volumes of studies on St. Paul's Epistles, but never, we think, one which came so near his heart, or which his readers will find so moving and absorbing as this.

It is well conceived, and written with Dr. Moule's usual care and finish, than whom no man wrote with more insight, with a more thorough appreciation of the conditions of his task, when he deals with devotional subjects.

PHILEMON.

By the Rev. A. H. DRYSDALE, D.D.

St. Paul's perfect little Epistle has scarcely ever had more thorough or acceptable treatment than Dr. Drysdale's exposition, which is thorough and lucid, and eminently adapted for the instruction of the general reader as well as for the thoughtful student of the Apostle's writings.

It may be recommended heartily to those who desire to understand the many exquisite touches in this unique specimen of the private correspondence of St. Paul.

HEBREWS.

By the Right Rev. G. A. CHADWICK, D.D., Bishop of Derry.

As a companion to the Epistle this volume takes high rank. Clear exposition and readiness to welcome well-established critical results, combined with complete loyalty to the spiritual authority of Scripture, make it delightful reading, as stimulating to the mind as it is refreshing to the spirit.

JAMES.

By the Rev. CHARLES BROWN, D.D.

Dr. Brown's practical application of the Apostle's message to the varied phases of everyday life and common experience will enlighten and strengthen, uplift and edify.

The book is well arranged upon a plan calculated to enhance its utility to ministers and teachers, and will be found specially attractive by lovers of simplicity who care less for criticism than for Bible teaching.

THE R.T.S., 4 BOUVERIE STREET, LONDON, E.C. 4.